faithful & fruitful

365 daily devotions written by lawyers for lawyers

faithful & fruitful: 365 daily devotions written by lawyers for lawyers
© The Lawyers' Christian Fellowship 2023

The Lawyers Christian Fellowship has asserted its rights under the Copyright, Designs and Patents Act 1988 to be identified as author of this work.

All rights reserved. Except as may be permitted by the Copyright Act, no part of this publication may be reproduced in any form or by any means without prior permission from the publisher.

First published in Great Britain in 2023 by the Lawyers Christian Fellowship.

ISBN: 978-1-3999-7023-5

Email: admin@lawcf.org
www.lawcf.org

Typesetting and design work by Tiger Finch Creatives Limited
Registered in England and Wales No 08886395.

Where indicated (CEV) Scripture quotations marked (CEV) are from the Contemporary English Version Copyright © 1991, 1992, 1995 by American Bible Society, Used by Permission.

Where indicated (ESV UK) Scripture quotations are from the ESV® Bible (The Holy Bible, English Standard Version®), © 2001 by Crossway, a publishing ministry of Good News Publishers. Used by permission. All rights reserved. The ESV text may not be quoted in any publication made available to the public by a Creative Commons license. The ESV may not be translated in whole or in part into any other language.

Where indicated (KJV) Scripture quotations are taken from the King James Version. Public Domain.

Where indicated (NIV) Scripture quotations are taken from the Holy Bible, New International Version®, NIV® Copyright ©1973, 1978, 1984, 2011 by Biblica, Inc.® Used by permission. All rights reserved worldwide.

Where indicated (NIV 1984) Scripture quotations are taken from the Holy Bible, New International Version®, NIV® Copyright ©1973, 1978, 1984, 2011 by Biblica, Inc.® Used by permission. All rights reserved worldwide.

Where indicated (NIVUK) Scripture quotations are taken from the Holy Bible, New International Version® Anglicized, NIV® Copyright © 1979, 1984, 2011 by Biblica, Inc.®

Where indicated (NKJV) Scripture taken from the New King James Version®. Copyright © 1982 by Thomas Nelson. Used by permission. All rights reserved.

Scripture quotations marked NLT are taken from the Holy Bible, New Living Translation, copyright © 1996, 2004, 2015 by Tyndale House Foundation. Used by permission of Tyndale House Publishers, Inc., Carol Stream, Illinois 60188. All rights reserved.

Where indicated (NRSV) Scripture quotations are taken from New Revised Standard Version Bible, copyright © 1989 National Council of the Churches of Christ in the United States of America. Used by permission. All rights reserved worldwide.

Where indicated (NRSVA) Scripture quotations are taken from New Revised Standard Version Bible: Anglicised Edition, copyright © 1989, 1995 the Division of Christian Education of the National Council of the Churches of Christ in the United States of America. Used by permission. All rights reserved.

Scripture quotations marked (MSG) are taken from THE MESSAGE, copyright © 1993, 2002, 2018 by Eugene H. Peterson. Used by permission of NavPress. All rights reserved. Represented by Tyndale House Publishers, Inc.

Please note that unless otherwise indicated Bible references within each day's Word for the Week contribution are taken from the same version of Scripture as the main Scripture quotation.

The Lawyers Christian Fellowship Company limited by guarantee, registered in England & Wales: No 7422674. Registered Charity: No 1139281

In grateful memory of Jon Hyde (solicitor, Word for the Week editor and LCF Chair of Trustees), whose friendship and faith in Jesus have encouraged and inspired so many in the LCF.

Paul writes in Romans 11 -

[33] *Oh, the depth of the riches and wisdom and knowledge of God! How unsearchable are his judgements and how inscrutable his ways!*

[34] *"For who has known the mind of the Lord, or who has been his counsellor?"*

[35] *"Or who has given a gift to him that he might be repaid?"*

[36] *For from him and through him and to him are all things. To him be glory for ever. Amen.*

Romans 11:33-36 (ESV)

Christian lawyers operate in a sphere of secular judgments and worldly ways. The challenge is to see the work we do as emanating from the Lord, to carry it out in His power, and to offer it for His glory. And to do so every day.

Word for the Week has for many years been helping Christian lawyers to look up on Monday morning, and to set their course for the week with a passage from Scripture and a pointer to prayer. It is brief and to the point. Now this aid to Christian living for busy lawyers has been published in a form that is accessible every day of the year.

The encouragement in these pages is from lawyers to lawyers. Every reflection is there to focus the wisdom and knowledge of God, in Jesus, on living for Him in the work we do. These are riches indeed. They place us in the counsel of the Lord.

To Him be the glory for ever.

Janys Scott KC, LCF Trustee

About the Lawyers' Christian Fellowship

The LCF is a fellowship because we are centred in a person and a purpose far greater than ourselves. For almost two centuries the Lawyers' Christian Fellowship has been connecting, uniting, and equipping Christian lawyers who have a love for God's Word, and who are concerned to live it out in their personal and professional lives.

To find out more about LCF membership, and LCF resources, please visit our website. www.lawcf.org

About this publication

We want Christian lawyers to be faithful and fruitful every day in every way. Connecting our Sundays with our Mondays, the LCF Word for the Week is intended to encourage whole-life witness and worship to Jesus Christ. Written by lawyers especially for lawyers, it is one of our most valued resources.

We love the unique voice of our various Word for the Week contributors, reflecting all ages and stages of the legal profession, and a breadth of Christian traditions. Every contribution was carefully considered by the editorial team prior to its original publication, to check that the thought is driven by the Bible passage, and is practical, encouraging a balanced approach to the Christian life.

A selection of such Word for the Week contributions has been compiled for this daily devotional to help the reader as they journey through the year.

If you're not a lawyer, please don't stop reading at this point – our Word for the Week has broad appeal. Christian lawyers with their involvement as counsellors and advocates in a wide range of human experiences, can offer some well-grounded insights from God's word about the realities of life and living for Jesus.

Reader – we hope that you will be encouraged by using this resource every day, but also prepare to be challenged; God's Word is living and active, sharper than any two-edged sword, piercing to the division of soul and of spirit, of joints and of marrow, and discerning the thoughts and intentions of the heart! Above all, may this publication lead you to love Jesus more, and to live faithfully and fruitfully for him.

About our international work 'CLEAR'

'CLEAR' stands for Christian Legal Education Action and Research, and refers to a network of international partners with whom the LCF is engaged in gospel-shaped justice mission. Some of the devotionals refer to our CLEAR work, and there is more information on our website.

⁵ In your relationships with one another, have the same mindset as Christ Jesus:

⁶ Who, being in very nature God,
  did not consider equality with God
  something to be used
  to his own advantage;
⁷ rather, he made himself nothing
  by taking the very nature of a servant,
  being made in human likeness.
⁸ And being found in appearance as a man,
  he humbled himself
  by becoming obedient to death –
    even death on a cross!
⁹ Therefore God exalted him to the highest place
  and gave him the name that is above every name,
¹⁰ that at the name of Jesus every knee should bow,
  in heaven and on earth and under the earth,
¹¹ and every tongue acknowledge that Jesus Christ is Lord,
  to the glory of God the Father.

Philippians 2:5-11 (NIV)

1 JAN — The Servant Lawyer serving the Servant King

… he made himself nothing by taking the very nature of a servant **Philippians 2:7 (NIV)**

Pressures within. Pressures without. Paul, the servant of Christ Jesus (1:1), writes to these dear Christians in Philippi serving God's grace and peace with practical advice, to address the problems which they are facing in life. How like a good lawyer!

If you get the chance today, read Philippians and read it aloud. Notice what happens when you get to Chapter 2:6-11. Suddenly Paul's letter sings! It's poetic (the NIV captures this well). Why so?

Paul turns poetic as he directs our attention to the Jesus story. It's a stunning story, and it's the gravitational centre of Paul's letter. Be pulled into this story then, as you read about the humiliation of Christ, how he made himself nothing, taking the essential characteristics of a servant (lit. "slave" a person with no legal rights), and then stooped further still for our salvation, by becoming obedient to death, even death on the cross.

Worthy is our servant king, now exalted by God to the highest place (2:9-11), for revealing the divine vocation of service!

Dear lawyer, servant of the servant king. Facing pressures within and without. Seeking to serve God's grace and peace with practical advice, to address the problems your clients face in life. Paul wants you to experience this poem, that you may resonate with and retell the Jesus story in every syllable and sentence of your life!

- *Give thanks to God for His beloved Son who for our sakes and our salvation humbled himself, even to death on the cross!*
- *Take a moment to commit the year ahead to Jesus, and ask that he will give you the grace, wisdom, and strength to retell His story faithfully and fruitfully in the legal world.*

– Mark Bainbridge (2022)

2 JAN Thus far the Lord has helped us

Then Samuel took a stone and set it up between Mizpah and Shen. He named it Ebenezer, saying, "Thus far the Lord has helped us." 1 Samuel 7:12 (NIV)

Samuel's ministry came at an anxious and turbulent time in Israel's history. The people of God were in the Promised Land, but they had not found a land flowing with milk and honey – instead it was full of plague and Philistines. Had the Lord given up on his people?

In Samuel chapter 7 the Lord miraculously delivered his covenant people from Philistine attack. They prevailed not due to their strength, but in their weakness: by fasting, confession of sin, a sacrificial lamb and a cry for help to the Lord. In the aftermath Samuel erected a geological aide memoire of the Lord's faithfulness: a stone called Ebenezer ('stone of help') to remind his covenant people that the Lord is in control and rescues his people when they humble themselves before Him.

As Christian lawyers standing at the crossroads of a new year, are we tempted to look back at last year and ask where God has been? In a year of remote hearings, has our Judge seemed remote? In a year of frustration and force majeure clauses, have we lost our faith in 'acts of God'?

Instead let us come before the Lord in gratitude and humility, fixing our gaze not upon a stone but upon the cross where the Lamb of God was sacrificed for our eternal rescue. Only in the Lord's strength can we stand up for justice in a broken world.

- *"Here I raise my Ebenezer, Here by Thy great help I've come, And I hope by Thy good pleasure, Safely to arrive at home." Robert Robinson 1758*
- *Let us echo these words of the hymn 'Come, Thou Fount of Every Blessing' as we give thanks for the Lord's unfailing goodness and for sustaining us throughout last year, and commit to His care our personal and professional plans for the year ahead.*

– Phil Roberts (2021)

3 JAN Looking forward to the year ahead

...Should you then seek great things for yourself? Do not seek them. For I will bring disaster on all people, declares the LORD, but wherever you go I will let you escape with your life. **Jeremiah 45:5 (NIV)**

How easy to find ourselves seeking greatness in our own sphere! We want to thrive in ways that people will applaud. It is what drives most of the legal profession.

God's message to Baruch brought a different perspective. As Jeremiah's scribe his job was to deliver news of imminent judgment within the elite circles of Jerusalem's civil authorities. His message was that the glory of this age would soon count for nothing – both in Jerusalem itself and then in all the surrounding nations. This is not the textbook way to win friends and influence people. Consequently Baruch's status update was: "I am worn out...and find no rest." (45:3)

God's reply diagnoses the root of Baruch's tiredness – he is trying to obey God at the same time as angling for personal greatness within a world which is passing away. If Jerusalem and every other nation will be destroyed, what makes Baruch think his own life can remain a bed of roses? When we understand that even God's children will experience suffering in this age, it relieves us of the stress and burdens of false expectations, freeing us up to glorify God and persevere in hardship. This week let's continue to respond to our challenges by trusting in God and persevering in doing good (1 Peter 4:16ff).

- *Give glory and thanks to God that whatever your situation He is always trustworthy.*

– Andrew Myers (2017)

4 JAN When words fail me

In the beginning was the Word, and the Word was with God, and the Word was God. He was with God in the beginning. Through him all things were made; without him nothing was made that has been made. **John 1:1-3 (NIV)**

As we enter a New Year, let's declutter and go back to the beginning.

In the beginning was the Word. Words are a passion for most lawyers. We have a rich, evocative language although not so complete that we can avoid raiding other languages when looking for *le mot juste*. Maybe that passion has brought you where you are now, and far from where it all began.

Through him all things were made. As well as your vocabulary, you have your skilful use of it through written precision, persuasive oratory, deft use of silence, smooth soothing of the agitated, protective wit and deflecting humour. Skills that are admired by others, maybe even by ourselves, and which we hope will be credited as showing our "rightness" in all matters.

Such abilities were all made through him, not that I may boast or feel the admiration of others, but for the purpose of glorifying him.

So, Lord, may I find the courage to confront within me the 'eloquent in the room'. May my desire be not to impress but to bring glory to you. May my fears of appearing simple or speechless subside. May I be prepared to let my own words falter and fail in prayer, in praise and as I try to tell of what you have done for me.

Free me from those words I have constructed around me and bring me back to *le mot juste* where it all begins (and ends); the Word John proclaims gives life, light and overcomes darkness (John 1:4-5).

It is one simple, beautiful, word: Jesus.

- *Give thanks for the way the Lord has gifted and equipped you with language skills. Ask for courage to use his name in the opportunities he will give you.*

– Mark Jones (2016)

5 JAN Enlightening the load

In him was life, and that life was the light of all mankind. The light shines in the darkness, and the darkness has not overcome it. **John 1:4-5 (NIV)**

A career in law has certainly meant spending some time being illuminated. It has also involved quite a bit of time exploring the "grey areas" (if not trying to create them!). Being candid, it has also involved times of darkness:

- Being demoralised by the actions of those I looked up to;
- A failure to obtain a just outcome;
- Choosing to spend time in the office rather than go home and engage with the challenges there;
- Abusing freedoms and facilities entrusted to me by those I work for.

We each have our own experiences. Jesus does not promise prosperity and success in all we do. We sin. We fall. We fail. He does not, and that is what we cling to – the darkness has not and will not overcome his light, but nor is it hidden from it.

Jesus is not a courtesy light, welcoming those areas we are happy about or are prepared to share or admit to. He is not a light only for those parts that are "sorted". It is the darkness that needs his light: e.g. those times of hurt when we felt enveloped by night; maybe those areas we have convinced ourselves are just different shades of light or best left in the shadows.

- *May the Lord take our ongoing struggles and past hurts and, in the light that is His life, deal with them.*
- *Be encouraged and thankful, the light shines in the darkness, and the darkness has not overcome it.*

– Mark Jones (2016)

6 JAN — Witness Evidence

There was a man sent from God whose name was John. He came as a witness to testify concerning that light, so that through him all might believe. He himself was not the light; he came only as a witness to the light.
John 1:6-8 (NIV)

John had a purpose. He was specially conceived for the purpose (Luke 1:17). The last Old Testament prophet, his purpose was to point people to the Messiah, to make ready a people prepared for the Lord.

Attracting attention, but not wanting to be a distraction from the Christ, John gave a clear message: he was not the light but a witness to the light, directing us not to his own greatness through feigned humility but to Jesus.

By the time of his execution (a consequence of speaking God's truth to royalty) the work he had been set was done. If his life had been a witness to his own greatness, it was a waste, a tragedy. As a life in witness to Christ it was glorious. His purpose was fulfilled.

Has God blessed you with particular legal/pastoral knowledge, wisdom and insight? Are you approached for advice by clients, colleagues, church family casually sidling up after the service? It feels good to be able to be able to shed light on the problems of others, to feel wise, to receive gratitude, to feel useful, to feel purpose, to feel fulfilled.

But does this truly meet the purpose for which we were specially conceived into Christ's family? Do we yearn to be more fulfilled in purpose as witnesses to the light? Are we ready to be?

- *Thank you Lord for the example of John the baptiser.*
- *As you create opportunities for me to talk with others, help me to be a courageous witness to you.*

– Mark Jones (2017)

7 JAN — Recognition

The true light that gives light to everyone was coming into the world. He was in the world, and though the world was made through him, the world did not recognise him.
John 1:9-10 (NIV)

Last week a couple of colleagues finished a project I gave them. They did a great job. I gave it a bit of a polish and sent it out. Those who saw it were duly impressed and my colleagues were of course thrilled when I received all the credit.

I doubt that this is a unique tale within the legal profession. Colleagues and clients may not know or care how hard you worked. Maybe they want the recognition that belongs to you.

John tells how Jesus, the true light, the one through whom the entire world was made, came into the

> *The true light that gives light to everyone was coming into the world.*
>
> John 1:9 (NIV)

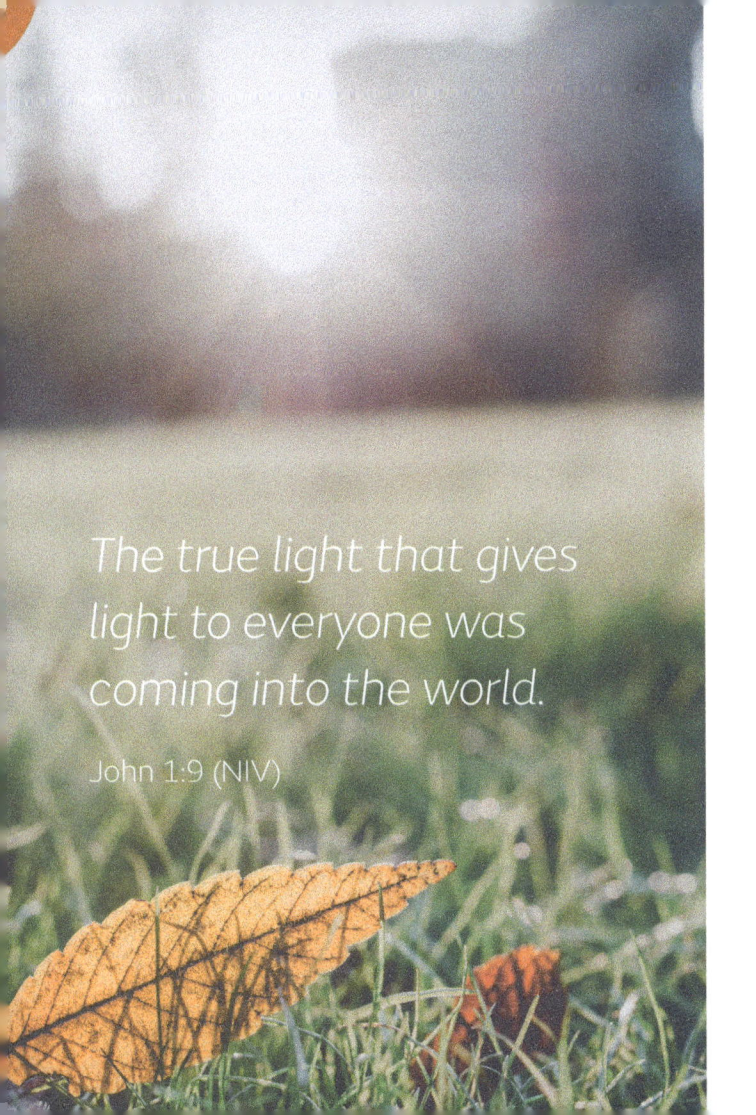

world. The world that owed its existence to him did not recognise him. It still happens, even for those to whom He has revealed himself. Our Lord humbles himself to death on a cross. We, in our sinful nature, cling to crowns rather than give Him the recognition, so any glory might come our way.

In the parable of the bags of gold, the master says 'Well done, good and faithful servant! You have been faithful with a few things; I will put you in charge of many things. Come and share your master's happiness!' (Matthew 25:21)

As a servant, we and others may simply be doing our duty, but we have a God who takes delight and gives us recognition for just fulfilling our job description.

So this week, do we need to learn from His example? Will there be opportunity to show others His example, so they might come to recognise Him?

- *Give thanks that you know Jesus, that He has been revealed to you and you recognise who He is.*
- *Receive His encouragement – "Well, done good and faithful servant... come and share your master's happiness".*
- *Pray for the opportunity to glorify Him through giving due recognition to others.*

– Mark Jones (2017)

8 JAN — Received rather than rejected

He came to that which was his own, but his own did not receive him. Yet to all who did receive him, to those who believed in his name, he gave the right to become children of God – children born not of natural descent, nor of human decision or a husband's will, but born of God.
John 1:11-13 (NIV)

Professionally, the Law can be a privileged, exclusive environment, and a fickle lover. Perhaps I feel comfortable and accepted, or feel/fear being outcast or demeaned. Either way, I have no right that compels her ongoing affection and my welcome within the club.

I similarly cannot compel another person's love. The greater my love, the more agonising its rejection, the deeper those wounds and my reluctance to allow others in. Coldness, arrogance and cynicism aren't just what the public perceive some lawyers to excel in, but are character traits for many who experience or fear rejection – hardened surfaces protecting tender areas.

If anyone had the right not to be rejected, it was Jesus. Our Lord came as bridegroom to his betrothed; and in the greatest act of love he submitted himself to death on a cross for an undeserving and adulterous lover.

John conveys that the right to become children of God is not an entitlement of the self-assured, but a privilege for those who believe in Jesus with hearts open to receive the one who was himself rejected. It is not demanded, earned, deserved or negotiated. It is given. An unmerited act of love that embraces the rejected and our scars, "Welcome to the family, welcome to the inheritance, welcome to the business of God & Sons. Now, let me tend those wounds".

- *For wounds of rejection to be replaced with assurance of our acceptance in Christ.*
- *Eschewing self-assurance for humility, give thanks for the privilege of the right to become a child of God.*

– Mark Jones (2018)

9 JAN — Dwell with me

The Word became flesh and made his dwelling among us. We have seen his glory, the glory of the one and only Son, who came from the Father, full of grace and truth.
John 1:14 (NIV)

Ask someone what they think lawyers are full of and you probably won't get the response "grace and truth". More like "full of greed and aloof". It may be an unfair generalisation, but it is a common perception/representation of lawyers that we are distant and uncaring. That irks, doesn't it?

Many perceive God as distant and uncaring. That is the God they then choose to reject. It is a perception that is false beyond all reasonable doubt and it has grave consequences, now and eternally.

The God of the Bible is not aloof. John says we have seen his glory, the glory of the one and only Son. He came from the Father as the high king of heaven, not ethereal and distant but in flesh as a servant. Our fine words don't successfully fool him that we have no mess – he chooses to make his dwelling among us, in the midst of our mess.

Your path this week may cross with someone believing lies about God. If we have seen his glory, do we care enough to introduce them to the one full of grace and truth who made his dwelling among us and gave his life?

- *In the mess of the week to come, for deeper acceptance of and gratitude for Christ's dwelling among us.*
- *For others to come to see the glory of the one and only Son.*

– Mark Jones (2019)

10 JAN The Test of Testimony

(John testified concerning him. He cried out saying, 'This is the one I spoke about when I said, "He who comes after me has surpassed me because he was before me."')
John 1:15 (NIV)

Lawyers like a good precedent (and love picking apart a bad one).

I am repeatedly told we are living in unprecedented times – that nothing like this has ever happened before. On one level this is true: legal practitioners are advising on the hoof and creating new documents; law students and lecturers are adapting courses and learning methods. However, the one who was there before and after John the Baptiser, who was there in the beginning and who is with us now, has not been taken by surprise. God's Word has not needed the addenda of a Covid-19 statement.

The precedent to follow (for us, our colleagues, clients and neighbours) is to turn to Jesus.

On Thursdays, people are taking the opportunity to stand on doorsteps and lean out of windows testifying their gratitude to those working to provide essential services [this was written in May 2020]. For Jesus, John was unabashed – he testified, he cried out. Although not personally inclined to stand in my doorway banging a saucepan, maybe it's a precedent about testimony from which I could and should learn.

- *Thank God that He remains in command.*
- *Pray that we will grasp opportunities for public testimony about Jesus.*

– Mark Jones (2020)

11 JAN — Amazing Grace

Out of his fullness we have all received grace in place of grace already given. For the law was given through Moses; grace and truth came through Jesus Christ. John 1:16-17 (NIV)

The law sets out boundaries to stay within. It governs our behaviour. Having certainty about its boundaries and borders helps us to help others operate within the law and gives us personal reassurance. This far but no further.

Jesus is full of grace and truth (v14). Full, not just up to the line, but overflowing so that it pours out on all. And out of his fullness we have all received grace. Not a reward available to a 'deserving' few, but already received by all; saturating the undeserving.

Where are my boundaries when it comes to colleagues, clients and third parties I find challenging or graceless? When it comes to generosity, forgiveness, patience, repentance, compassion, love, is my witness one of law – this far but no further? Is it one of grace already received?

On one occasion, anguished by another's transgression of boundaries, God in his mercy showed me a glimpse of his love for that person. It displaced everything else. It overwhelmed. I may find comfort in boundaries, but I've not understood the fullness of his grace if at any time I think it has a constraint. Blessing upon blessing. Gift upon gift. Mercy upon mercy. Grace upon grace.

- Pause to consider the unconstrained fullness of Jesus' grace. Are there resentments I have that I need to stop clinging to?
- Lord Jesus, out of the fullness of your grace and truth, help me radiate to others the grace that you have already given.

– Mark Jones (2022)

12 JAN — Distance learning

No one has ever seen God, but the one and only Son, who is himself God and is in the closest relationship with the Father, has made him known. John 1:18 (NIV)

Post-pandemic, I rarely meet clients (at least three-dimensionally). Remote client meetings tick the more convenient life I crave but interacting in person adds intimacy to the relationship. Barriers can come down on both sides. When a client is at arm's length, I can speak about the law, but can't as easily relate to them or speak to their circumstances and needs.

Jesus "is in the closest relationship with the Father". The trinity is deeply intimate. Relationships require risk and intimacy requires vulnerability, not an aloof, impersonal professional. From His closest relationship, "Jesus has made [the Father] known". In making Him known, we can step out of 'work mode' and be in the closest relationship. Cold objectivity may help within legal practice, but does it make me more prone to keeping Jesus at a distance, like a client? Unless I am intimate with Jesus, how can I know God intimately and properly make Him known?

Will I allow Jesus to go behind the self-penned client care letters and codes of conduct I have in place to govern our relationship? Unreservedly trust Him with the mess; unbind the self-imposed restraints of worship; and, unveiled, laugh, weep and rest intimately in Him?

- *Praise you Father, Son and Holy Spirit that you are a God of intimate relationships.*
- *Thank you Jesus, Son of the Father, for making the Father known to us. I long for a closer relationship with you. Help me to place in your hands my fear of intimacy with you.*

– Mark Jones (2022)

13 JAN I really wanna know "Who are you?"

Now this was John's testimony when the Jewish leaders in Jerusalem sent priests and Levites to ask him who he was. He did not fail to confess, but confessed freely, 'I am not the Messiah.'
They asked him, 'Then who are you? Are you Elijah?'
He said, 'I am not.'
'Are you the Prophet?'
He answered, 'No.'
Finally they said, 'Who are you? Give us an answer to take back to those who sent us. What do you say about yourself?'
John replied in the words of Isaiah the prophet, 'I am the voice of one calling in the wilderness, "Make straight the way for the Lord."'
John 1:19-23 (NIV)

One principle of cross-examination is 'don't ask a question you don't know the answer to'.

The Jewish leaders sent an elite delegation of priests and Levites to seek an audience with John. They wanted to establish whether this possibly significant person and influencer was someone they needed to know. "Who are you?"

We can be interested in who someone is or what they do (and wondering whether who they are can benefit us!). But it's often the wrong question. Knowing John's answers would not satisfy their line managers, and losing control over the witness, they then ask the much more important and interesting question, "What do you say about yourself?"

Resisting temptation to self-aggrandise or display annoyance at this intrusion into his private life, John's answer to their last gasp question revealed what they truly needed to know. Like a good lawyer for their client, he answers that he is a voice for another – the Lord. It is not John they need to know, but the Lord he serves.

At work, or in your studies, rather than asking, "Who are you?" or "What do you do?" what question would you like to ask and to be asked (to help you be a voice of the Lord in the legal wilderness)? Whom could you ask that question of this week?

- Lord, help me to ask and answer personal questions well.
- Grant me opportunities to ask good questions and to give good answers.
- Help me to have the humility of John – seeking honour for you, not myself.
- Help my words, thoughts and actions to proclaim: "Make straight the way for the Lord".

– Mark Jones (2022)

14 JAN Got everything…?

His divine power has given us everything we need for a godly life through our knowledge of him who called us by his own glory and goodness. **2 Peter 1:3 (NIV)**

At the start of a new year it is easy to feel daunted by what lies ahead. We see the coming year with its challenges and opportunities stretching out before us, and we may wonder how we will find the strength to meet them.

Here God's word reassures us that he has given us everything we need in order to live as he wants us to, and to do the things that he has called us to do. Our relationship with him is completely sufficient to equip us for a life of discipleship.

How can we be sure of this? Because in his goodness and power he has already called us to himself and enabled us to start on the journey of faith. As we walk with him, we can be confident that he will continue to sustain us.

- Give thanks to God that he is powerful and good, and is all-sufficient for our needs.
- Pray that you would walk into the coming year in dependence on God, and would desire to know him better and trust him more, rather than relying on our own strength.

– Caroline Eade (2018)

15 JAN Rejoice, really?

Therefore, since we have been justified through faith, we have peace with God through our Lord Jesus Christ, through whom we have gained access by faith into this grace in which we now stand. And we rejoice in the hope of the glory of God. Not only so, but we also rejoice in our sufferings, because we know that suffering produces perseverance; perseverance, character; and character, hope. And hope does not disappoint us, because God has poured out his love into our hearts by the Holy Spirit, whom he has given us. **Romans 5:1-5 (NIV 1984)**

What do we rejoice, or boast in? As lawyers we might be proud of our reputation, our status in society, our families, our homes or our careers.

That leaves us vulnerable to the effects of suffering when we fear, or actually experience, losing any of these things, as some people have in these difficult times.

Paul tells us our suffering can be an opportunity to rejoice. How? Because our hope is not in ourselves and our achievements, but in the glory of God. We are enabled to come into a precious relationship with God where he pours out His love into our hearts by the Holy Spirit, not by our achievements, but through faith in what our Lord Jesus Christ achieved for us on the cross.

And, if we rejoice in the glory of God, we can rejoice that our sufferings are not meaningless, or signs of our failure, but are used by God to develop our character.

So, whatever anxieties and concerns we face at the start of the year, let us rejoice in the glory of God, who is achieving His purposes, and with thanksgiving, receive His peace.

• *Pray that we will rejoice in the glory of God and fix our eyes on Him as He achieves His purposes.*

• *Pray that many will turn to Jesus and put their hope in Him.*

– Debbie Woods (2021)

16 JAN Surrender your plans to the Lord

Trust in the LORD with all your heart,
And lean not on your own understanding;
In all your ways acknowledge Him,
And He shall direct your paths.
Proverbs 3:5-6 (NKJV)

What is the value of surrender when so many of your plans have been forcibly wrenched out of your hands anyway? [This was written during the Covid-19 pandemic.]

Across chambers, firms, law schools and universities, we are all experiencing the challenges of this time in profound ways. The thought of conceding even more to the cruel tide of Covid-19 is almost unbearable. An instinctive response in the face of such drastic change is to replace forfeited plans with new ones.

This popular passage is about maintaining confident trust in God, trust that is evidenced in dependence on God and the submission of our best thoughts on how to proceed to his greater wisdom. Surrender is, of course, never easy, but in the midst of a world of change and in the face of mounting pressures, it can seem a totally reckless response.

Through faith and trust in God, however, we can deny our former natural instincts for new instincts: those of our new life in the Spirit. As we voluntarily bare ourselves before God, even in the already stripped-back circumstances in which we find ourselves, we are assured that He will cloak us in his care, and cause His light to shine on the path before us.

- *Bring before God the most painful disruptions and the deepest disappointments of this season. Ask Him to show you where you are most inclined to strive in your own strength, and seek grace to enable you continually lay these at His feet.*
- *Ask the Lord to direct your steps and give you insight on how best to respond to the challenges that beset you; be they professional, educational, relational or health related.*

– Damilola Makinde (2020)

17 JAN Prayer and praise

I will bless the LORD at all times; his praise shall continually be in my mouth. Psalm 34:1 (ESV)

As the sun has set on one year and rises on another, many of us will take the opportunity to reflect on what has been and make plans for what we hope will be. Whether we're mourning the loss of loved ones, reflecting on difficult personal or professional relationships, taking steps to gain promotion at work, or finally execute that long agonised career move, Psalm 34:1 is a timely reminder that it is right to praise God in all seasons.

God is worthy of our praise at all times and in all circumstances. Just as the Apostle Paul implores us to pray without ceasing (Philippians 4:6), David's vow to praise God continually is an encouragement and a challenge to us.

A posture of continuous prayer and praise helps us to shift our focus from ourselves and the "answers" that the world offers, to God and the ultimate truths: God's graciousness, mercy and steadfast love for us (Psalm 145:8). His goodness and faithfulness (Psalm 100:5). His offer of salvation to all those who repent and put their trust in Jesus Christ.

Prayer and Praise. May they be our spiritual bread and butter today and every day.

- *Thank God for the gift of praise and ask that He would help us to make praising Him a priority – even through challenging times.*
- *Thank God that He is with us through all circumstances and is worthy of our praise.*
- *Praise God for His goodness, His mercy, His steadfast love and His faithfulness.*

– Kiki Alo (2020)

18 JAN — An easy yoke

"Come to me, all you who are weary and burdened, and I will give you rest. Take my yoke upon you and learn from me, for I am gentle and humble in heart and you will find rest for your souls. For my yoke is easy and my burden is light." **Matthew 11:28-30 (NIV)**

If you're anything like me, you are probably feeling quite weary by this point in the year. The fun and joy of Christmas seems a long time ago. It's still dark and cold outside. It's many more weeks before the next holiday. All those well-intentioned New Year resolutions may have already fallen by the wayside or, even if they're still being kept, the first flush of enthusiasm has worn off, and they're starting to become a real chore. And the demands and deadlines of a busy term are piling up.

It is at times like this we need to heed the invitation of Jesus to come to him for rest. Notice that the rest he offers is not simply more leisure or downtime (though that might be a good idea!), nor is it merely physical or mental (important though that is). Jesus offers us a deep rest for our souls.

Rest is a key theme in Scripture. In the beginning, Creation's end-point was rest (Genesis 2:2-3) and God's work of salvation throughout history has been to bring his people into that rest (Hebrews 4:1-3). It is through Jesus that eternal rest is offered to us. And his yoke is easy, because all we have to do is trust him and receive that rest by faith. What a relief in the midst of a busy, cold January, that we can have an eternity of rest secure in Christ!

Let's accept Jesus' invitation and find rest in him this week.

- *Take a moment today to rest in the knowledge that Christ loved you and died for you. Thank God for the rest for our souls we find in him.*
- *Pray for others you know who are weary or burdened, that they might find rest in Christ too.*

– Alasdair Henderson (2019)

19 JAN — That's a very good question

When Jesus came to the region of Caesarea Philippi, he asked his disciples, "Who do people say the Son of Man is?"

They replied, "Some say John the Baptist, others say Elijah; and still others, Jeremiah or one of the prophets." "But what about you?" he asked. "Who do you say I am?" Simon Peter answered, "You are the Christ, the Son of the living God." Jesus replied, "Blessed are you, Simon son of Jonah, for this was not revealed to you by man, but by my Father in heaven."

Matthew 16:13-17 (NIV 1984)

As lawyers we are called upon to answer questions constantly, from clients, students, tutors, assessments, courts, colleagues, the list goes on. The new Solicitors Qualifying Examination involves students answering 360 'Single Best Answer' questions. Our ability to answer questions successfully might depend on our intelligence, diligence, experience or good fortune.

In our passage, Jesus asks his disciples the single most important question any of us will ever be called upon to answer, "Who do you say I am?" Many pick the wrong answer, but Peter answers well, "You are the Christ, the Son of the living God." Jesus makes it clear that Peter knows this, not because of his innate abilities, or his superior faith. After all this same Peter will later three times deny knowing Jesus. No, Peter can recognise Jesus as the Christ, the Messiah whom God would send to save His people from their sins, because the Father in heaven revealed it to him.

As we begin this new year, whatever questions we are called to answer, let us remember that "Who do you say I am?" remains the single best question, and Peter's the single best answer.

- Let us thank God for sending His Son Jesus to save His people and for revealing to us His true identity.
- Let us pray for our colleagues and clients and those we

hold dear, that God, in His grace and mercy, will reveal Himself to them too.

– Debbie Woods (2022)

20 JAN Seeking contentment in work

...You covet and cannot obtain, so you fight and quarrel. You do not have, because you do not ask. James 4:2-3 (ESV)

For all the blessings a career in the law can bring, including financial blessings, it is often easy to survey our contemporaries and to see their lot as better. Whether we perceive others to be earning more, to have a more glamorous practice, or to have a less difficult working life, it can feel that if we were in someone else's position, a feeling of discontentment would disappear.

As with a desire for money (Ecclesiastes 5:10), envy can never lead to contentment and fulfilment. Where we seek out what we need, not from the living God, but by coveting what others have, we will always find ourselves desiring something 'better' than that which God has provided. The attempt to satisfy these desires will lead to us behaving as we should not (James 3:16).

When we find ourselves dissatisfied in some way with our work, which to some extent will for many of us not be an infrequent experience, the biblical advice is to ask. This means seeking from God what we really need, in order that we may serve Him better. When we feel discontented, the best advice is to humble ourselves before the Lord (James 4:10).

- *Pray that this year we see a priority to make our work pleasing to God and that we may find contentment in doing so.*
- *Praise God that it is Jesus – and not our peers – who is the standard of glory. May we grow in humility and recognise that He alone fully satisfies us.*

– James Brightwell (2018)

21 JAN Guilty or not guilty – the highest legal drama

Even as David also describeth the blessedness of the man, unto whom God imputeth righteousness without works, **Romans 4:6 (KJV)**

The moment of highest drama in the Crown Court is when the jury foreman stands to his or her feet and delivers the verdict. A guilty verdict may mean an 18 year prison sentence. A not guilty verdict, instant release.

There will be a day when each of us will appear before the judgment throne of Christ. Unlike a jury trial, each person who stands in the place of judgment deserves but one verdict, guilty, because as Paul writes in Romans 3:23: "all have sinned and fallen short of the glory of God". The consequence of a guilty verdict will be eternal damnation, a prospect too terrible to begin to imagine.

Yet there will be a great multitude, which no man could number (Revelation 7:9), who will be separated and pronounced "not guilty" and who will be admitted to heaven to spend eternity in everlasting bliss. The stakes could not be higher.

The wonderful news is that the "not guilty" verdict is pronounced not only on the Day of Judgment but the moment a sinner repents of their sin and trusts alone in the Lord Jesus for their righteousness for He is "the justifier of him which believeth in Jesus" (Romans 3:26).

May we each be encouraged to pass on this good news so that the highest drama in eternity might be a reality for many of our friends, relations and work colleagues – the pronouncement of a not guilty verdict!

- *Ask that God will this year give you a new sense of urgency and opportunities to speak about the good news of Jesus Christ.*
- *Pray for our judges as they administer justice and deliver verdicts in our respective jurisdictions.*

– Mark Mullins (2017)

22 JAN — Rejoice in the Lord

Rejoice in the Lord always; again I will say, rejoice. Let your reasonableness be known to everyone. The Lord is at hand; do not be anxious about anything, but in everything by prayer and supplication with thanksgiving let your requests be made known to God. And the peace of God, which surpasses all understanding, will guard your hearts and your minds in Christ Jesus. **Philippians 4:4-7 (ESV)**

When caught up with all the worries and concerns thrown up by our busy and challenging practices, it is easy to forget that God is a sovereign living God in whom we can place our trust – even in difficult times. It is also easy to find ourselves drawn into situations where we are tempted to act unreasonably or egocentrically towards others.

In this passage Paul encourages us not to be anxious, but by prayer and supplication to entrust our anxieties and concerns to the hands of a loving heavenly Father, whose peace will guard our hearts and minds in Jesus Christ.

Paul calls upon us, in all that we do, to "Rejoice in the Lord". This ought to govern the way that we conduct our practices and our lives as a whole, and involves us letting our "reasonableness" (or in some translations, our "moderation" or "gentleness"), be manifest; i.e. we should do what is best for others and not just ourselves, and be seen to do so. In this way we can share in the peace of God that passes all understanding.

- Pray that in all that we do in our work as lawyers, and in all other aspects of our lives, we might rejoice in the Lord at all times, and by prayer and supplication entrust our anxieties and concerns to the hands of our loving heavenly Father, and thereby enjoy the peace of God that passes all understanding.
- Pray that our reasonableness might be manifest in all that we do as lawyers, and in all other aspects of our lives, and that all that we do might be in furtherance of God's peace and glory.

– HHJ Mark Cawson KC (2018)

23 JAN — David & Goliath

"You come against me with sword and spear and javelin, but I come against you in the name of the LORD Almighty, the God of the armies of Israel, whom you have defied. ... This very day ... the whole world will know that there is a God in Israel. All those gathered here will know that it is not by sword or spear that the LORD saves: for the battle is the LORD's..." **1 Samuel 17:45-47 (NIV)**

If you had to use one word to sum up Goliath, what would it be? In 1 Samuel 17, the word is "defiant". It appears 6 times by reference to him, in verses 10, 23, 25, 26, 36 and 45. Goliath sets himself up against God and the people of God – with his spear shaft the width of a weaver's beam, its iron point weighing 7kg and with the sword that never left its sheath that day until used by David for decapitation.

As a boy, I used to sing along with others: *Draw your swords, draw your swords, for the battle is the Lord's.* Whilst relying on God's word is, of course, always good, the chorus runs the risk of missing the point. Swords, spears, and human power and resources count for nothing – it is God who determines how the battle will fall out. The battle is the Lord's. The outcome is in His hands.

We are almost certainly usually wrong to compare our own problems and issues with David's situation. There, Goliath was defying the Lord and that could only lead ultimately to one outcome. The Lord will not allow anyone to defy Him for ever and His authority is supreme. Those who stand against the Lord cannot ultimately prevail.

God is not on the side of the big battalions, however formidable they may seem. His purposes cannot be frustrated by human powers, authorities or governments, whether despotic or elected, or even law courts or judges. The battle is the Lord's.

Will we trust in the God who stands with His people? In the God who saves, but not with sword or spear? The battle is His if we stand in His Name.

- *Thank God and take courage from the fact that the battle belongs to the Lord.*
- *Bring to God the things that are problematic today and ask for his peace and guidance.*

– Sir Jeremy Cooke (2015)

24 JAN For whose name's sake?

...He leads me in the paths of righteousness
For His name´s sake.
Psalm 23:3 (NKJV)

I was recently listening to Psalm 23 in the course of my regular Bible reading/listening, and I was tempted to switch off. After all, I knew it by heart! Then I heard verse 3 and I properly heard something for the very first time: '... *for his Name's sake.*'

Why '*for His name's sake*'?

John Piper answers it this way:

> "*God is the beginning and God is the end of all my righteousness. The path of righteousness has His grace as its starting point (for He leads me into it) and it has His glory as its destination (because His leading is for His name's sake).*" *

We Christian lawyers are well-positioned to do much good. But we can easily fall into doing good in such a way that God becomes virtually irrelevant to it all.

Either our earthly good deeds are God-led and God-centred, or we are simply humanists wearing a different label. God is looking to display His glory through us. Will we love Him and live for Him so as to make that a reality in our lives?

*By John Piper. © Desiring God Foundation.
Source: desiringGod.org

Pray:
- *That God would lead us by His Spirit in the paths of His righteousness.*
- *That God would be the head, and His glory the end, of all that we do.*

– Niazi Fetto KC (2019)

25 JAN I AM

Before the mountains were born or you brought forth the whole world, from everlasting to everlasting you are God.
Psalm 90:2 (NIV)

As lawyers, there is no doubt that we carry huge responsibility. We are used to taking the lead, being asked important questions by those who look to us for answers which often carry huge implications for others. The responsibility can weigh heavily, causing us stress, worry, maybe even fear that we make a mistake. We may obtain our sense of identity from it or a misguided sense of self-importance. We may even be in danger of believing that we are, somehow, in control.

However, God's revelation of himself in the Bible directs our attention away from ourselves and to who he is: 'I AM' not 'YOU ARE'. And so we find our security and identity in God as he reveals himself to be:

Jehovah Jireh, our provider (Genesis 22:14)
Jehovah Shalom, our peace (Judges 6:24)
Jehovah Nissi, our banner (Exodus 17:15)
Jehovah Rophe, our healer (Exodus 15:26)
Jehovah Shammah, the Lord who is there (Ezekiel 48:35)
Jehovah Sabaoth, the Lord of Hosts (1 Samuel 17:45)

And so much more, and all that we need besides.

When we call to mind all that He is, we are released from having to be all we think we should be. What relief and peace we find in this.

Pray:
- *That we would know the reality of God as 'I AM' in our daily lives, both personal and professional;*
- *That we would examine our hearts and allow the Holy Spirit to highlight areas of our lives where we are walking in our own strength, rather than in the strength of 'I AM'.*
- *That we would be vulnerable before the Father who*

- *loves us, allowing Him to take the lead in every moment of our day.*
- *That we may always keep our sense of perspective in who we are and who He is and find our rest in Him.*

– Hilary Underwood (2022)

26 JAN Future tense?

I love the LORD because he hears my voice and my prayer for mercy. Because he bends down to listen, I will pray as long as I have breath! **Psalm 116:1-2 (NLT)**

As the detailed minds of lawyers know, the tense in which you write is sometimes important.

Many of the Bible translations put the verses above in the past tense 'he heard my cry for mercy' (NIV). This translation, however, puts it in the present tense and it speaks another truth: that God cares for us deeply right now. He takes the effort to bend down and listen to us, like an adult crouching down to chat at a child's level. Or a lawyer, encouraging a client to speak out, by asking questions and listening intently to every important detail. God encourages us to share with Him our life's detail and problems, to engage with Him and to pray.

With God intently listening, hearing prayers and answering them, the Psalmist makes the bold promise that 'I will pray as long as I have breath' – in the future tense. He has seen God answer prayer; he knows that God cares; and he knows that our response can only be one thing: to engage closely with God for the rest of his life.

As a student, while travelling in Mali's Sahel, a man asked our team to pray for rain. We prayed; it rained. We saw God work in a physical, miraculous way and the memory has stayed with me ever since. I will pray as long as I have breath!

- *Give thanks for the times when God has directly answered our prayers.*
- *Take a moment to recommit: 'I will pray as long as I have breath'.*

– Janet Cole (2021)

27 JAN His way or yours?

Trust in the LORD with all your heart and lean not on your own understanding; in all your ways submit to him and he will make your paths straight. **Proverbs 3:5-6 (NIV)**

As lawyers we are trained to apply our hard-won knowledge in the service of our clients. There is always the temptation to rely on our own ability and resources. These verses remind us that there is One who knows us better than ourselves and that it is to Him we must look for true wisdom and understanding.

> Trust in the LORD with all your heart and lean not on your own understanding; in all your ways submit to him and he will make your paths straight.
>
> Proverbs 3:5-6 (NIV)

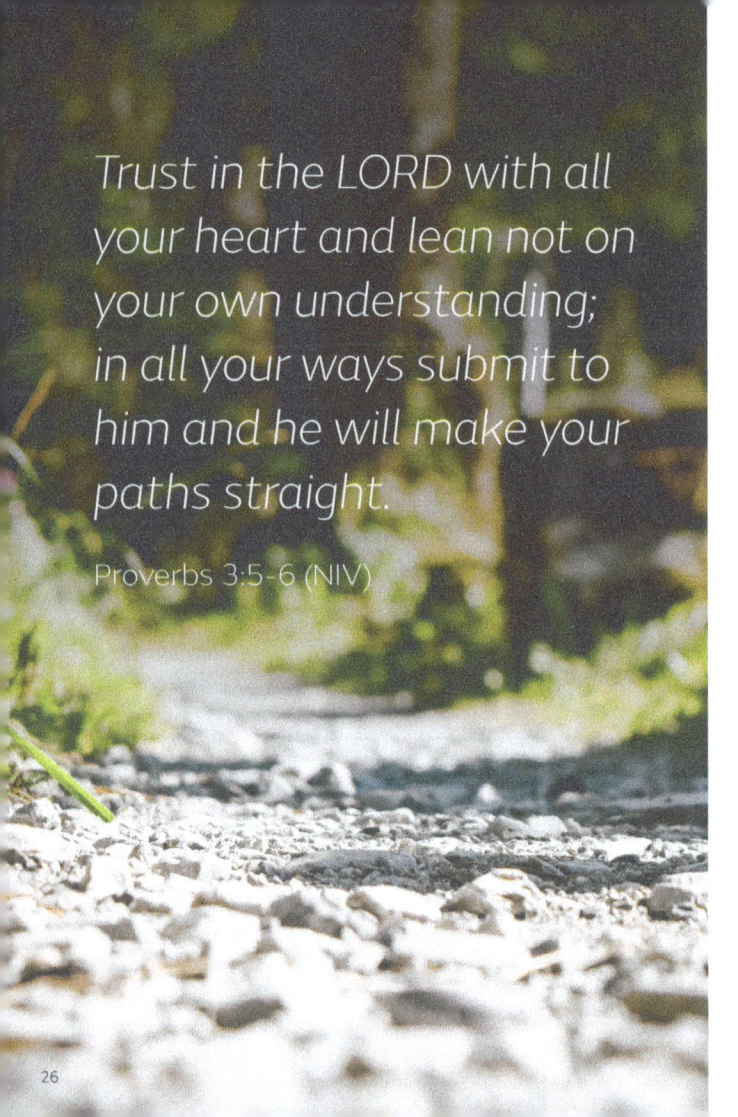

I am sure that in our hearts we know and believe this, but do we actually practise it day by day? Why not make this a prayer before starting your day and look to the Lord to guide you both in work and leisure. Commit to Him those worrying problems you have been given to solve. Let Him show you the path to follow in solving them. May this promise from God take the stress from our busy lives.

- Ask God to enable you to lay before Him the challenges you expect to face today.
- Commit your clients to God both before and after meeting them.
- Endeavour to make these verses true for yourself.
- Ask God to take your intellect and guide you through the tasks of today.

– Michael Hawthorne (2019)

28 JAN Integrated workers

[16] She considers a field and buys it; out of her earnings she plants a vineyard…
[19] In her hand she holds the distaff and grasps the spindle with her fingers…
[20] She opens her arms to the poor and extends her hands to the needy…
[24] She makes linen garments and sells them…
[28] Her children arise and call her blessed; her husband also, and he praises her:

30... a woman who fears the LORD is to be praised.
31 Honour her for all that her hands have done, and let her works bring her praise at the city gate.

Extracted from Proverbs 31 (NIV)

At a recent LCF event on justice in commercial law, we looked at the woman described in Proverbs 31.

A striking thing about her is that her approach to business is so integrated with her Christian faith.

She performs a vast array of different commercial activities – including buying property, manufacturing, selling and more.

And, in an uncommon way in the world of secular commercial law, her skills in commerce are held together with a love for the poor and needy (see, e.g., the parallelism in vs 19-20) and they are also held together with a proper respect for family life (see, e.g., v 28).

But most of all – her work is integrated with her view of the LORD (v 30). Indeed, it is only by keeping our eyes on Him that we can lead an integrated life.

Many of us fail to live properly integrated lives like this. And, in Jesus, there is forgiveness for our failures (Luke 18:9-14). And the more we behold Jesus – the One who gives us such great forgiveness – the more it will make us able to live lives at work that are integrated with our faith in Him.

- *Father, forgive us for when we have done our jobs in a way that is disconnected from our faith in You.*
- *Father, help us to lead lives at work that are integrated with our faith in You.*

– Dominic Hughes (2019)

29 JAN What's the point?

But let justice roll on like a river, righteousness like a never-failing stream! **Amos 5:24 (NIV)**

Monday morning may not infrequently be a time when we ask ourselves what the point is of our work as Christian lawyers. Maybe it's the shock of being back in the office after the weekend, or fatigue from being in the office over the weekend. We may have the same reaction at other times too, be it a difficult opponent or client, or a terrible outcome to a case in which we've invested so much.

Amos reminds us this morning of God's deep desire for justice in this world, and in our cases, however incompletely and imperfectly it can be achieved. We can serve God through our work as Christian lawyers so that more justice might roll on in our cases and in the lives of the people affected by them.

Our workplaces and colleagues might encourage us, subtly or otherwise, to do our work for recognition, career advancement or a pay rise. Whilst those things certainly can be good, if they become our ultimate goal then we will often be disappointed and disillusioned. God offers us a higher and deeper calling to our work, caught up in His heart for justice. So let's commit afresh this week to join with God in His work for justice through our work, asking for His grace and strength to sustain us – and His heart to give us purpose.

Let's pray that in our work this week we are strengthened by God's spirit to work for His justice, and grace.

– Jon Hyde (2015)

30 JAN A joyful lawyer

*Though the fig tree does not bud
and there are no grapes on the vines,
though the olive crop fails
and the fields produce no food,
though there are no sheep in the pen
and no cattle in the stalls,
yet I will rejoice in the LORD,
I will be joyful in God my Saviour.*

Habakkuk 3:17-18 (NIV)

Have you prayed for something – a training contract, a new job or for a loved one to be healed of cancer, depression, or saved only to be met by God's stone-cold silence? Or maybe you've wondered how God can tolerate wrongdoing and watch on as justice is perverted (1:1-4), like I did when standing in a dark, overcrowded and fetid African prison cell?

When in the midst of such faith crises, Habakkuk understands.

He starts his book exasperated, crying out the familiar angry question "How long Lord?" (ch 1) yet finishes it in joy (3:18). How?

As Habakkuk took time out with God and experienced His power and glory (3:2,4), a simple truth stood out: the righteous person will live by his faithfulness (2:4). Trust God. Now standing in awe of God's deeds (3:2) yet facing death, or inevitable famine (3:17), Habakkuk makes a new resolve to rejoice in the Lord, to be joyful in God, His Saviour (3:18).

Though your computer may crash losing vital work, and it rains every day of your holiday, whether you've been rejected by yet another firm, or your client/colleague fails to listen to your advice, or the cancer has spread … are you willing to say: yet I will trust my advocate who is with me, my heart need not be troubled or afraid, I will be joyful in my Lord and my Saviour?

- *Whatever season you or those around you face, pray that you continue to trust and be joyful as you wait to hear from God (2:1).*

- *Whatever comes your way this week, pray to be one who chooses joy in Him, your Saviour, every day. May He give you opportunities to share this joy in Him with those around you.*

– Fiona Mahendran-Gilliland (2017)

31 JAN — Bringing peace to our neighbour

Blessed are the peacemakers, for they will be called children of God. **Matthew 5:9 (NIV)**

If you stopped someone in the street and asked them to describe a lawyer in one word, what odds would you give to them using "peacemaker"? I think we could agree that the prospects of success would be poor!

However, as He opens the Sermon on the Mount with the Beatitudes, Jesus is clear that His disciples should be known as precisely that. In fact, it is evidence that they are children of God. Children reflect their father, and God is the supreme peacemaker. Jesus says that those who emulate God in this way are blessed.

How might we reflect Him as lawyers? One way is by being His instrument as He leads us to make peace between people, particularly in our cases, and also in our workplaces. Moreover, God made peace with us through the cross when we were His enemies and thereby reconciled us to Himself. Accordingly, we can also seek to emulate Him by His Spirit in loving and making peace with our "enemies" insofar as we can, be they opponents in our cases or even colleagues at work. Let us be known and distinctive by reflecting our Heavenly Father in this way.

- *Give thanks to God for making peace possible between Him and us through the cross.*
- *Ask God to show you ways in which you can make peace this week and to empower you by His Spirit to do so.*

– Mark Mullins (2016)

1 FEB — Keeping the main thing the main thing

Let us hold unswervingly to the hope we profess, for he who promised is faithful. And let us consider how we may spur one another on toward love and good deeds, not giving up meeting together, as some are in the habit of doing, but encouraging one another – and all the more as you see the Day approaching … But we do not belong to those who shrink back and are destroyed, but to those who have faith and are saved.' **Hebrews 10:23-25; 39 (NIV)**

One month on, I wonder how many of us are persevering with resolutions made this year. Health, fitness, work-life balance, reading our Bibles and praying more?

Through warnings and exhortations, the writer of Hebrews urges his readers to hold unswervingly to the hope they profess, to spur one another on towards love and good deeds, to encourage one another and to keep meeting together.

In his sacrifice for our sin, Jesus has won the victory for all, and his grace is sufficient. But in that gift of faith we are to persevere. How easy it is for us to let the demands our workplaces on us eclipse all other priorities. To persevere, God knows that we need our brothers and sisters in Christ, and they need us. We need to make every effort to hold on, spur on, meet and encourage, using the same discipline as it takes to meet our client appointments, court dates and assessment deadlines.

We may need to think creatively how we might do this and take advantage of the learning and communication tools available to us; but let us be spurred on, the reward is great.

May we not belong to those who shrink back and are destroyed, but be those who persevere in faith and are saved.

- *Thank God that, in Christ, the victory is won for all who persevere in faith in Him and that he who has promised is faithful.*
- *Pray that, amidst all the pressures of our work commitments, we would prioritise the deepening of our understanding of God's word and our fellowship with and encouragement of our brothers and sisters in Christ.*

– Debbie Woods (2017)

2 FEB The assessment we've all failed

...as it is written:
"None is righteous, no, not one;
  no one understands;
  no one seeks for God.
All have turned aside;
  together they have become worthless;
no one does good,
  not even one."
"Their throat is an open grave;
  they use their tongues to deceive."
"The venom of asps is under their lips."
  "Their mouth is full of curses and bitterness."
"Their feet are swift to shed blood; ...

Romans 3:10-15 (ESV)

Periodically, a list of new King's Counsel is released, identifying advocates who have met a standard of excellence. At the other end of the career ladder, the Pupillage Gateway has hundreds of prospective advocates hoping that they too will be identified as excellent. At any stage in their profession, a lawyer's identity can so often rely on others' assessments.

Well, in this passage, the Apostle Paul pulls no punches in his assessment of us. He quotes from various passages in the Old Testament, weaving vivid and frightening imagery together to deliver a damning verdict. Our identity: sinners. Our CVs may seem impressive to recruiters, but we have certainly not met God's standards. So why then is it one of my favourite passages in the Bible?

Quite simply: it helps me to fully grasp the depth of my sin, and so, to fully grasp the depth of God's grace. However good our drafting skills are, none of us can make the case that we are worthy of God's forgiveness as we are. Instead, we rely completely on God's righteousness, on His divine forbearance, on His grace as a gift (3:24-25). We only escape Paul's verdict by trusting in the blood of Christ Jesus.

Our accomplishments may be impressive, but our most important status has not been earned.

- *Praise God for the depths of His grace!*
- *Pray for those in your workplace who do not yet trust in Jesus to accept this gift.*

– Jen McKelvin (2020)

3 FEB God's big story

In the beginning God created the heavens and the earth.
Genesis 1:1 (NIV 1984)

The grace of the Lord Jesus be with God's people. Amen.
Revelation 22:21 (NIV 1984)

The Bible tells a big story, from God's initiative in creation to the completion of His work of redemption. Yet even that is not the whole of God's story – He existed from eternity before His creation of the heavens and the earth and will continue eternally after they are superseded by a new heaven and a new earth.

We tend to have a view only of our own lifespan. Research suggests that more than half of the UK adult population have not made a Will. Drafting a 999 year lease can seem unreal. Who cares what the ground rent or the landlord's registration fee will be hundreds of years from now?

What makes the difference for us as Christians is in the final words of the story. If we are God's people, the grace of the Lord Jesus is with us. The pivotal event of the Big Story is God's intervention in world history through the birth, life, death and resurrection of His Son, offering the undeserved the gift of eternal life to all who put their trust in Him. If we have received that gift, we will care about the future, and what we do now will matter in the age to come. Are we all living and working with that eternal perspective in view?

- *Pray that we will rest securely in God's grace and not be striving to win His approval through what we do or how well we do it.*

- *Pray that we will remember the eternal significance of the lives we lead and the work we do by His power now at work in us.*
- *Pray that our changed lives will draw others towards Christ and the gift of eternal life He offers.*

– Graham Whitworth (2016)

4 FEB — Testing the quality of what we do

***And let us consider how we may spur one another on towards love and good deeds, not giving up meeting together, as some are in the habit of doing, but encouraging one another – and all the more as you see the Day approaching.* Hebrews 10:24-25 (NIV)**

Love and good deeds are evidence of saving faith. We know that we have passed from death to life, because we love each other (1 John 3:14). Faith without works is dead (James 2:26). God, who saves us entirely by grace, has prepared good works for us to do (Ephesians 2:10).

Such evidence becomes more apparent as believers meet together and encourage one another to manifest it.

Why should we do this? The writer to the Hebrews reminds us that there is a Day approaching on which our deeds, particularly our treatment of other Christians, will be how Jesus as God's appointed Judge explains His decision about our eternal destiny (Matthew 25:34-40). Despite that, our salvation does not depend on anything we do, and is therefore assured. Yet, even if we are saved, the quality of our work will be tested (1 Corinthians 3:13) to determine whether we will receive a reward in the life to come or be saved "as one escaping through the flames" (v 15).

How can we do it? Opportunities for mutual encouragement as Christian lawyers include LCF local practitioners' and student groups, and regional and national events. More generally, belonging to a Bible-based local church enables each of us to be "spurred on" by other believers.

Make the most of every such opportunity. It's not just about your own Christian life – you get to encourage others to be fruitful as well!

- *Pray for wisdom that you might know how best to make the most of every opportunity to encourage your fellow Christian lawyers to be fruitful.*
- *Pray for a willingness to be accountable to other Christians, so that they have your permission to encourage you and spur you on towards love and good deeds.*

– Graham Whitworth (2016)

5 FEB — The serpent crusher

"And I will put enmity between you and the woman, and between your offspring and hers; he will crush your head, and you will strike his heel." Genesis 3: 15 (NIV)

How amazing is God's salvation plan! Sin has just entered the world through Adam and Eve's disobedience. But God even at this stage has a plan – one of Eve's offspring would eventually give birth to a serpent crusher! A key part of Jesus' mission was to defeat Satan.

We know that the devil may prowl around, tempting us to fall into sin, since we are his enemies. But we know that Jesus has ultimately disarmed him (Col 2:15).

So when we are tempted to fall into sin or feel that the devil is leading us astray, we can remember Jesus has already crushed Satan's head! He has no power over us. When we are tempted to live to please our colleagues or put clients' interests above God's glory, we can look back to Jesus as the serpent crusher and remember that these things have no power over us. Jesus has won the victory!

- *Praise God that Jesus disarmed Satan when he died on the cross for us.*
- *Pray that we remind ourselves of this victory in the battle against sin.*

– Peter Thompson (2018)

6 FEB — Pass it on!

This is the book of the generations of Adam. When God created man, he made him in the likeness of God. Male and female he created them, and he blessed them and named them Man when they were created. When Adam had lived for 130 years, he fathered a son in his own likeness, after his image, and named him Seth.
Genesis 5:1-3 (ESV)

Creation in the image of God distinguishes men and women from other creatures and this status is passed on from generation to generation by natural birth.

God's new creation, inaugurated by Jesus' resurrection, includes all those "born again, not of perishable seed but of imperishable, through the living and abiding word of God" (1 Peter 1:23) – children of God, distinguished from the rest of mankind. As we proclaim the Gospel, and others trust in Christ, that status is passed on. But what about passing on our own likeness? Paul wrote to the Corinthians, "I urge you, then, be imitators of me. That is why I sent you Timothy, my beloved and faithful child in the Lord, to remind you of my ways in Christ." (1 Corinthians 4:16-17)

Serving students and junior lawyers is an important role of the LCF. If you are one, why not get to know a more senior member who can help you practise law God's way?

Those of us who are more senior must be ready to help and advise Christians just starting their legal careers. Having made that our priority (Galatians 6:10), if we can do the same for non-Christians in a similar position, we will not only act as salt and light, but also create a context in which the Gospel can quite naturally be communicated.

- *Pray for LCF staff and other members who spend time with students and junior lawyers and for students to join LCF groups in the various postgraduate law schools.*
- *Pray for opportunities to spend time with a more senior Christian lawyer and/or someone at an earlier stage in his or her legal career, for giving and receiving practical help and godly wisdom.*

– Graham Whitworth (2015)

7 FEB A Walk with God

Enoch walked faithfully with God; then he was no more, because God took him away. Genesis 5:24 (NIV)

Many of our Old Testament heroes have been said to be two-way mirrors: showing God's people themselves (as an example to follow – or avoid) and showing them their Saviour (as foreshadows). Often that mirror is broken and flawed, like Samson or David. In Enoch's case, it is incomplete, like a spy hole, showing us one tiny detail: Enoch walked faithfully with God and then he was no more.

To the follower of God reading this short passage, Enoch shows that there is hope. He comes in the midst of a chorus of "then he died" following the fall. For those who walk with God, however, we see that death does not win. For those of us lawyers surrounded by death, violence and exploitation – whether individual or systemic – we know that God provides ultimate rescue.

In reality, Enoch was himself not sinless. Yet, in this peephole, we are shown no sin. A young Jesus, reading this in the synagogue, would have been able to expect, by rights, to have been painlessly removed from this world for his perfectly faithful walk. Nevertheless, he took on the punishment we earned for our faithless walk and freely gave himself over to death. In a performance driven culture, we know that the performance has been completed for us and so are freed from fear: Jesus has no billing targets.

- *Pray for colleagues to see the rescue that Jesus freely offers and for our courage to proclaim it.*
- *Rejoice in our Saviour's faithful walk that frees us from death.*

– Robin Younghusband (2019)

8 FEB — The urgency of praying for colleagues

"Will not the Judge of all the earth do right??"
Genesis 18:25 (NIV 1984)

When He [the Holy Spirit] comes, He will convict the world of guilt in regard to sin and righteousness and judgment? **John 16:8 (NIV 1984)**

Abraham pleads with the Lord for Sodom and his nephew Lot. We pray for our cities and our fellow lawyers.

The depravity of Sodom is plain from its description in Genesis – but Ezekiel also describes a less known aspect of her wrongdoing in chapter 16: "She and her daughters were arrogant, overfed and unconcerned; they did not help the poor and needy. They were haughty and did detestable things before me." He then compares Jerusalem unfavourably.

Lawyers are often seen as arrogant, overfed and unconcerned – fat cats. We are as a breed lacking in compassion for others less fortunate than ourselves, whether or not we indulge in detestable practices.

The Lord sees it all and will judge – that is clear from Jesus' many parables about judgment. Don't we need a greater sense of urgency in praying for our colleagues – for conviction by the Holy Spirit of the justice of God and the need for His mercy? Will you pray for them wholeheartedly this week?

Will not the Judge of all the earth do right?

- *Praise God that He is righteous, just and merciful.*
- *Pray that He would work in our hearts to give us compassion for our colleagues and motivation continually, specifically and wholeheartedly to pray for them.*

– Sir Jeremy Cooke (2018)

9 FEB — The Lord is in this place

When Jacob awoke from his sleep, he thought, 'Surely the LORD is in this place, and I was not aware of it.'
Genesis 28:16 (NIV)

Fleeing a potentially deadly threat from his brother Esau, Jacob dreamed about a stairway, representing Jesus, the mediator who gives access to God (John 1:51, 1 Timothy 2:5). God spoke about Jacob's future, renewing promises made to his grandfather Abraham. Then Jacob awoke.

It was a place he would rather not be in, out of his comfort zone. He had to improvise, using a stone for a pillow. Yet he called it God's house, and there he committed his life to Yahweh (vs 19-22).

Where are you today? Working from home? Uncertain about your future? Worried about money? Grappling with unfamiliar IT? Frustrated by Court delays? Under pressure from anxious clients?

God wants you to know, like Jacob, that He is in this place, even if you were not aware of it. Surely none of the above circumstances can be as bad as the furnace Daniel's three friends were thrown into, but the heathen King Nebuchadnezzar saw "four men walking around in the fire, unbound and unharmed, and the fourth … like a son of the gods" (Daniel 3:25).

Jesus was there! For Jacob this was an awesome place, and it can be for us. We too can hear from God, and even unbelievers may recognise that Jesus is with us.

- *Ask God to speak to you now through His Word, whatever place you may find yourself in this day.*
- *Claim any promises God has made to you in the past about your life, and any promises in the Bible that the Holy Spirit brings to your mind now.*
- *Receive from God a supernatural peace that will be noticed by non-Christians and create the opportunity "to give the reason for the hope that you have" (1 Peter 3:15).*

– Graham Whitworth (2020)

10 FEB Yes, you!

And Joseph took both of them, Ephraim on his right towards Israel's left hand and Manasseh on his left towards Israel's right hand, and brought them close to him. But Israel reached out his right hand and put it on Ephraim's head, though he was the younger, and crossing his arms, he put his left hand on Manasseh's head, even though Manasseh was the firstborn.
Genesis 48:13-14 (NIV)

Do you ever wonder whether God really called you to be Christian lawyer, when there are so many "better" candidates than you? Careful with that thought!

In the passage above, before his incredulous son Joseph, the old man Jacob (now called Israel: see Genesis 32:28) crosses his arms to give his first blessing to Joseph's second son. Why? Jacob knew something of the ways of the God with whom he had wrestled.

Jacob himself was the younger son, who had obtained his brother's inheritance by deception. The "great" men who came after him included Moses, a fugitive murderer, Gideon from the weakest clan in his tribe, David an overlooked shepherd boy, and the apostle Paul, an enemy of the church.

God loves picking lesser candidates, even 'hopeless' cases. If that's you, rejoice and beware! He has much for you to do.

- Pray for God's inspiration and leading into the good works He has set before us (Ephesians 2:10).
- Ask for grace, wisdom and the Holy Spirit's help to get them done.

– Niazi Fetto KC (2022)

11 FEB At his command

But I have raised you up for this very purpose, that I might show you my power and that my name might be proclaimed in all the earth. **Exodus 9:16 (NIV)**

As an Israelite living under Pharaoh's rule, it must have been hard to believe that God was in control. Oppressed by slave labour, forced to produce the same output with fewer resources, and now facing some horrific "natural" disasters – how many of them, I wonder, believed that even the mighty Pharaoh was in God's hand?

I doubt any of us are facing circumstances quite as difficult as that of the Israelites in Egypt. But for many of us, it can be difficult to believe that God has appointed those who are in authority over us, precisely in order to achieve his purposes and display his glory. We may face overwhelming demands, or unreasonable behaviour – and even with the best of bosses, simply a pressure to succeed on their terms.

Let's remember that no-one is out of God's scope, that whoever is senior to you is there at his command, and that he is at work to demonstrate his power – perhaps even through your faithful witness and patient trust. And let's remember too that we owe those above us honour, but not ultimate allegiance; we live as free people, not as slaves, as we await our coming King.

- Pray for those who are more senior to you, and for those who are ultimately responsible for your workplace – that they would not harden their hearts, as Pharaoh did, and would come to acknowledge the God to whom they are accountable.
- Pray for faithfulness for us all in LCF – that we would remember God's sovereignty and goodness, even when working life is difficult, and would be eager to testify about him to others, whatever their position in our workplace.
- Pray for those who are oppressed by unjust authorities, particularly around the world, that they would put their trust in the one who will one day deliver us from all evil.

– Caroline Eade (2015)

12 FEB You do not know what tomorrow will bring

Come now, you who say, "Today or tomorrow we will go into such and such a town and spend a year there and trade and make a profit" – yet you do not know what tomorrow will bring. What is your life? For you are a mist that appears for a little time and then vanishes. Instead, you ought to say, "If the Lord wills, we will live and do this or that." **James 4:13-15 (ESV)**

When the Covid-19 crisis broke, the plans we made had to be changed or were thrown into doubt. Whether we had planned to attend vacation schemes or mini-pupillages, earn a pay rise or go on holiday, our plans were disrupted. The uncertainty of the pandemic showed us that we do not know what tomorrow will bring.

In this passage, James reminds us that it is God who is in control of the world and our lives, not us. Everything takes place according to God's will.

James draws out how we are different to God. He highlights how we are mortal: our lives are "a mist that appears for a little time and then vanishes". Our lack of control and knowledge of what tomorrow will bring reflect our limited lifespan. In contrast, God is eternal and is completely in control.

Our thoughts and speech often fail to acknowledge the fact that God is in control. As lawyers, we often rely on our own intelligence or hard work, rather than trusting in the plans God has for us. This passage shows us that relying on ourselves is misguided, since we do not even know what tomorrow will bring. The knowledge that God is in control should give us great assurance, especially during times of uncertainty.

- *Thank God that He is in control.*
- *Pray that we will acknowledge God as being in control of all aspects of our lives, and that this will be reflected in our thoughts and speech.*

– Owen Vanstone-Hallam (2020)

13 FEB Law for God's glory

When you reap the harvest of your land, do not reap to the very edges of your field or gather the gleanings of your harvest. Do not go over your vineyard a second time or pick up the grapes that have fallen. Leave them for the poor and the alien. I am the LORD your God. Do not steal. Do not lie. Do not deceive one another. Do not swear falsely by my name and so profane the name of your God. I am the LORD. Do not defraud your neighbour or rob him. Do not hold back the wages of a hired man overnight. Do not curse the deaf or put a stumbling-block in front of the blind, but fear your God. I am the LORD. Do not pervert justice; do not show partiality to the poor or favouritism to the great, but judge your neighbour fairly. **Leviticus 19:9-15 NIV (1984)**

In my practice area (charity law), The Charitable Uses Act of 1601 is sometimes mentioned as laying some of the foundations of modern charity law. Perhaps in your practice area, there are roots going further back than that, or maybe your work is very 'cutting edge'.

In this passage we can trace a deeper source to some modern laws – God himself. It was God who gave the law in Leviticus 19, and in these seven verses we have charity/welfare law, law against theft, fraud and robbery, employment law, anti-discrimination/equality law, laws on oaths and against perverting justice, and an implicit property law.

God has a particular concern for the most vulnerable which is seen in the special provision he makes for poor people, immigrants/international visitors and disabled people in this passage. We can catch a glimpse of God's heart in providing the gift of law: he is concerned for his glory, and wants his people to be marked by justice, mercy and love.

- *Pray for good law and good leaders who will make wise decisions which lead to human flourishing.*
- *Pray for our law-makers and policy-makers to be concerned about the most vulnerable in our society and across the world.*
- *Pray for each of us to catch a glimpse of God's heart for our practice area and what that means for our work that we would be people who bring glory to God.*

– Nat Johnson (2022)

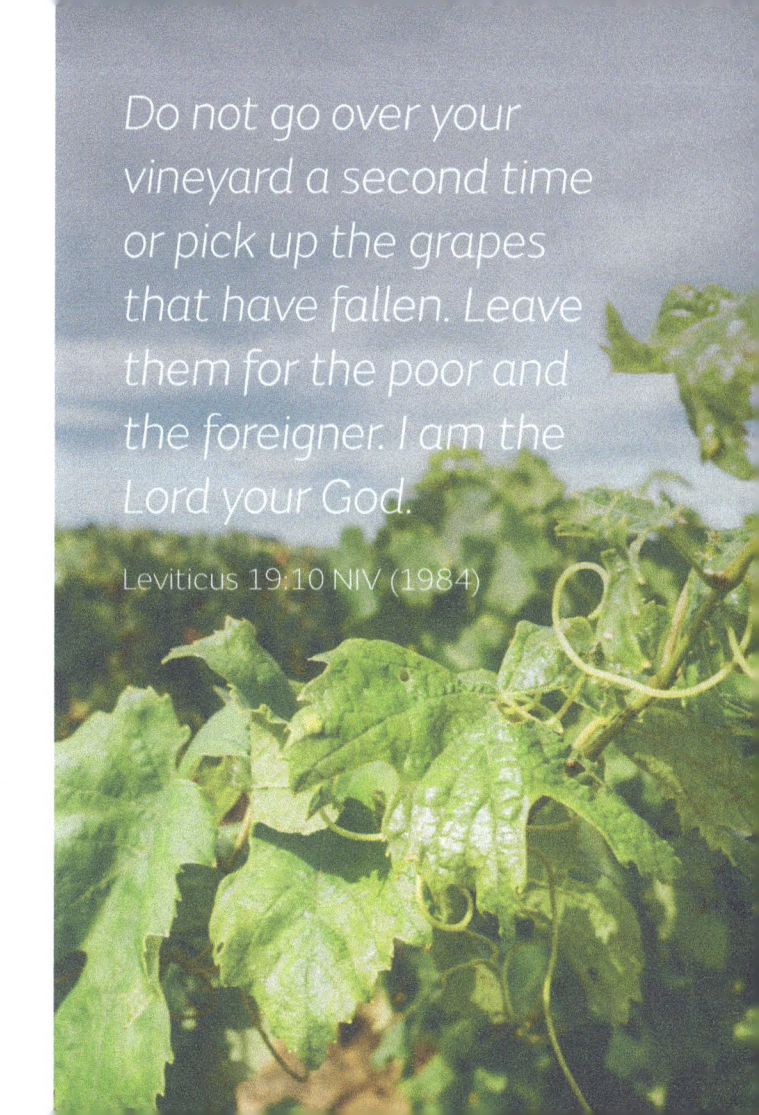

Do not go over your vineyard a second time or pick up the grapes that have fallen. Leave them for the poor and the foreigner. I am the Lord your God.

Leviticus 19:10 NIV (1984)

14 FEB — Gentle lawyer, meek and mild?

Now the man Moses was very meek, more than all people who were on the face of the earth. Numbers 12:3 (ESV)

Effective lawyers have always known the importance of 'soft skills'.

In 2021 the South Eastern Circuit held an event in Middle Temple entitled 'Kindness – an interactive session', to show how 'we can encourage kindness in our workplaces, within the court system, whilst still maintaining excellence with our adversarial skills'.

Tell that to the assertiveness trainers and the tenancy committee!

The Bible got there long ago! How strangely reassuring to read that the greatest lawyer and leader, the finest judge of the Old Testament era, was the most meek.

Meekness in the Bible is linked especially to two people – Moses and Jesus.

History has never seen a lawyer of more strength of character than Moses.

The world has never seen more dynamic and attractive power than throbbed in the personality of Jesus.

Meekness is about power under control. It is the opposite of self-assertion and self-will.

The meek lawyer has a realistic view of themselves, a true grasp of the dignity and worth of others and a submissive awareness that they are dependent on God's grace for everything.

No attribute is more precious, none more consistent with the character of Jesus.

Meek lawyers may not always be noticeable, but they transform everything. They may not be conspicuously successful, but they will inherit the earth.

- *Pray that, by God's Spirit, we may be meek lawyers and judges – making visible and believable the invisible but living reality of God.*
- *Pray that in the office or chambers or university and on the bench, we may be Christ-centred, Christ-shaped and Christ-like.*

– HHJ David Turner KC (2021)

15 FEB — Our unchanging God

God is not a man, that He should lie,
Nor a son of man, that He should repent.
Has He said, and will He not do?
Or has He spoken, and will He not make it good?
Numbers 23:19 (NKJV)

In a period of retreat from busy working lives, it may be a good time to reflect upon God's promises to us in the past and for the future. Is there something that God has laid on your heart that somehow you have never got to grips with, or that you have left off too early? It may be a new task you felt you were being called to, but which has not worked out as you had hoped. Or perhaps it is a client for whom you should have been praying. Or it may be a challenging situation in your workplace which you brought to God in prayer, but which you have ceased to hope can be resolved.

We cannot expect God to answer our prayers in the way we want or expect, and we can be mistaken about what He wants of us. But now that we have a little more time, we can reflect on His mercies to us in the past and, relying upon His unchanging nature, pray that He will guide us in the use of the time given to us on this earth.

- *Looking back, thank God for His faithfulness to us, despite our failings.*
- *We are sorry that, when prompted, we have not always followed His call to action.*
- *Looking ahead, ask that He will help us to know the work He has for us, and pray for His enabling to do it.*

– John Scriven (2020)

16 FEB Prayerful courage

Moses brought their case before the LORD. And the LORD said to Moses, "The daughters of Zelophehad are right. You shall give them possession of an inheritance among their father's brothers and transfer the inheritance of their father to them. And you shall speak to the people of Israel, saying, 'If a man dies and has no son, then you shall transfer his inheritance to his daughter'" … And it shall be for the people of Israel a statute and rule, as the LORD commanded Moses.
Numbers 27:5-8, 11b (ESV)

Zelophehad's daughters approached Moses to request their deceased father's inheritance in the Promised Land. Their family risked being forgotten, dependent upon the whim of extended relatives for provision and care, simply because there was no male heir.

Their petition demonstrates that they knew God's word and His character. God himself had instructed Moses to register families by male heads, upon which the land would be distributed (Numbers 26); yet they also knew God as a God of justice and compassion, who has special regard for the widow and orphan.

The daughters showed prayerful courage in approaching Moses, having clearly considered their request, and its timing (before the land was allocated).

In response, despite being surrounded by advisers, Moses went straight to God. And God answered – clarifying the law, not only for Zelophehad's daughters but also for all future cases.

How do we respond to our workload? Do we know God's word and, through it, recognise His character? Are we making time for Him in our daily lives, and seeking His counsel for our caseloads and clients? Do we have prayerful courage to step out for those who are most in need of our skills, or where the law may need to be clarified?

May I encourage you today to take your cases and your studies to the Lord, for His wisdom, direction and timing – and to have prayerful courage.

- May we remember to lift our cases, workloads and clients up to the Lord, asking for His wisdom, direction and timing in how we engage with them, and for prayerful courage.
- For the LCF's CLEAR partners in Africa who are seeking to speak up for those dispossessed of their inheritance and those who are marginalised and particularly vulnerable: that they would know God's guidance and have prayerful courage for when He calls them to step out.

– Mhairi Hamilton (2016)

17 FEB What is written first at the top of your to do list?

Listen, O Israel! The LORD is our God, the LORD alone. And you must love the LORD your God with all your heart, all your soul, and all your strength. And you must commit yourselves wholeheartedly to these commands that I am giving you today. Repeat them again and again to your children. Talk about them when you are at home and when you are on the road, when you are going to bed and when you are getting up. Tie them to your hands and wear them on your forehead as reminders. Write them on the doorposts of your house and on your gates.
Deuteronomy 6:4-9 (NLT)

The most important of all Jewish prayers, this passage – the Shema Israel – is recited daily. Moses tells the people of God to listen and attend to the law constantly – because in so doing, the law also attends to us. We are meant to be continually renewing, self-reflecting people: asking "Are we the people that we are meant to be?" and remembering "Who is our God?" For those two things together keep us in tune with our God: He who flung stars into space, Master of time, the Creator and redeemer of all things, the Alpha and the Omega – the LORD is our God, and we are to love him with everything we have.

I don't know where you start this week – excited, challenged, stressed, content or confused – maybe all of those things, and more besides. Our lives in the study, practice and application of the law are a high calling – but they can pull us away from the law that endures, and the God who gave it to us.

- Let the Lord encourage you this morning by praying through the Shema Israel.
- Pray over the words of Deuteronomy 6, verses 4 and 5, and entrust yourself to the hands of the Lord again this morning.

– Claire Wilkinson (2017)

18 FEB Responding to our redemption

But it was because the LORD loved you and kept the oath he swore to your forefathers that he brought you out with a mighty hand and redeemed you from the land of slavery, from the power of Pharaoh king of Egypt.
Deuteronomy 7:8 (NIV 1984)

Inside a pawn-broker's shop, the poor obtain short term loans by pledging their family jewellery and other possessions as security. In order to get their goods back, the borrower (or someone on their behalf) has to pay the price of the loan. To do so is to redeem the goods that were at risk of being lost.

The idea of redemption is one of the key descriptions of God's work of salvation. In the Old Testament, God, acting as Israel's kinsman, redeemed them from their slavery in Egypt. In the New Testament, Jesus, acting as humanity's representative, redeems us from our slavery to sin and death.

In the Old Testament, the redemption God won was supposed to transform the social relations in Israel. Leviticus 25 contains a detailed law-code designed to ensure that no Israelite would ever be enslaved permanently. In the same way, the redemption Jesus has won for us ought to inspire us to rescue others.

Christian lawyers have the gifts to help those who are oppressed physically, materially and spiritually. We can spend our time or our money rescuing those who are victimised, we can advocate on behalf of those who are persecuted or neglected, and we can use our way with words to share faithfully the marvellous reality of the redemption from sin and death which we ourselves have experienced.

- *Thank God that He has redeemed us from sin and death.*
- *Pray for those in legal professions and in law enforcement agencies who work to rescue those who are enslaved. Thank God that He has redeemed us from sin and death.*
- *Pray that the knowledge of our redemption would inspire*

us to fight against violence, exploitation and oppression, and to share the good news that Jesus Christ is the one who has saved us from our greatest enemies, sin and death.

– Dr David McIlroy (2021)

19 FEB The rule of law

You shall appoint judges and officers in all your towns that the Lord your God is giving you, according to your tribes, and they shall judge the people with righteous judgment. You shall not pervert justice. You shall not show partiality, and you shall not accept a bribe, for a bribe blinds the eyes of the wise and subverts the cause of the righteous. Justice, and only justice, you shall follow, that you may live and inherit the land that the LORD your God is giving you. **Deuteronomy 16:18-20 (ESV)**

As part of his farewell address to the people as they prepare for their entrance into Canaan, Moses gave these instructions for the appointment of judges in order to judge the people with righteous justice and fairness.

These few verses are particularly prescient in the context of Russia's invasion of Ukraine, and our security in Europe being placed at risk by the actions of the president of an autocratic state in which opponents of the regime are routinely imprisoned by corrupt judges on trumped up charges, and in which there is no legal fetter on the abuse of executive power.

The passage emphasises the importance of the rule of law, and its maintenance through the appointment of judges who will judge people righteously and impartially, and without corruption. This is important, not just because it allows for a fair and ordered society, but more significantly because it represents God's will and what is required by our sovereign and loving God in order that we might share in His Kingdom.

- *We give thanks and praise that we live in a society that respects the rule of law, and in which judges strive to act righteously and impartially, and in which there is no history of judicial or other corruption in our legal system;*
- *We pray that the rule of law may come to prevail in autocratic states throughout the world through the appointment of judges appointed to judge with righteous judgment, free of partiality or other corruption;*
- *We pray for lawyers working in judicial systems that pay little regard to the rule of law or where the rule of law is under threat, that they might strive for justice and righteousness.*

– HHJ Mark Cawson KC (2022)

20 FEB Don't take grace for granted!

Moreover all these curses shall come upon you and pursue and overtake you, until you are destroyed, because you did not obey the voice of the LORD your God, to keep His commandments and His statutes which He commanded you …

Because you did not serve the LORD your God with joy and gladness of heart, for the abundance of everything, therefore you shall serve your enemies, whom the LORD will send against you, in hunger, in thirst, in nakedness, and in need of everything; and He will put a yoke of iron on your neck until He has destroyed you…You shall eat the fruit of your own body.

Deuteronomy 28:45-53 (NKJV)

When I read these words recently, I felt like I had been punched in the face. The wrath of God toward those who disobey Him and are ungrateful is powerful. Deuteronomy 28, as befits the book of the law, contains an exhaustive list of both blessings and curses for God's people, depending on whether they trusted and obeyed His word or went their own way. It's perhaps less familiar to us than other parts of the Old Testament.

As lawyers we know more material blessing than most. As New Testament Christians, we often take comfort in the fact that we are "not under law but under grace" (Rom 6:14). And rightly so. But we also become complacent and forgetful of the blessings God has poured upon us; we serve ourselves and our practices rather than God; we fail to take drastic action with sin in our lives; we forget that our sin nailed Christ to the cross.

Let us resolve to revel in the grace of God, glorifying Him in our daily service, and proclaiming His saving grace to those around us.

- *Praise God that we are under His saving grace. Pray that we may have opportunities this week to proclaim God's grace to those around us.*
- *Pray that we would resolve to glorify God in our daily service, with joy and gladness of heart.*

– Esther Harrison (2018)

21 FEB Is God on your side?

Now when Joshua was near Jericho, he looked up and saw a man standing in front of him with a drawn sword in his hand. Joshua went up to him and asked, 'Are you for us or for our enemies?'

'Neither', he replied, 'but as the commander of the army of the LORD I have now come.' Then Joshua fell face down to the ground in reverence, and asked him, 'What message does my Lord have for his servant?'

The commander of the LORD'S army replied, 'Take off your sandals, for the place where you are standing is holy.' And Joshua did so.

Joshua 5:13-15 (NIV)

It's a surprising answer to read is it not? The Lord says, through His commander (probably the pre-incarnate Son), that He is not on Israel's side any more than He is on the side of the Canaanites whom the land is about to vomit out, at God's instigation, because of their outrageously perverted and distorted way of life.

It is good to remind ourselves that God is not there for us to utilise for our benefit, as we often try to do when we pray for Him to do what we want and to bring our plans to successful fruition. The Lord has His purposes, which He will fulfil. Joshua's response is to ask what the Lord wants of Him, the exact opposite of many of our prayers.

Jesus (the same name as Joshua in Anglicised Greek), if He is the Commander here, tells him that he is not just to listen to Him, but primarily to respond in reverence – and awe – at His 'otherness' (holiness), when in His presence.

Then we can hear his instructions for whatever 'Jericho' lies ahead for us (see Ch 6:1-5).

How close is this to our rushed and squeezed daily devotions?

- *Take time to worship God this morning, giving him the honour and praise that is due to his name.*
- *Ask the Lord to show you what he wants you to do for him today.*

– Sir Jeremy Cooke (2015)

22 FEB No compromise

Israel has sinned; they have violated my covenant, which I commanded them to keep. They have taken some of the devoted things; they have stolen, they have lied, they have put them with their own possessions. That is why the Israelites cannot stand against their enemies; … I will not be with you anymore unless you destroy whatever among you is devoted to destruction. **Joshua 7:11-12 (NIV)**

Joshua 7 is shocking on many levels. It starts with the defeat of an Israelite army by the men of Ai and ends with the stoning of a man called Achan and his children.

It seems that Joshua had failed to ask for God's guidance in deciding whether to attack Ai and the miserable defeat that followed startled him into recognising that God's honour was at stake and drastic action needed.

Achan secretly defied God's command by stashing Canaanite goods from Jericho – by coveting what was forbidden. It's the oldest sin in the book. And in another echo of Adam, Achan's sin affected others.

In our professional lives, it is often seen as a virtue to compromise on the little things so as to secure the main chance. How easily it creeps in; prayerlessness, prizing what the world values like Achan. But it stains the purity of God's bride, his church, and rightly provokes his jealous anger for our undivided hearts.

The chapter is a warning and reminder of our need for continual repentance. However, the stoning of Achan in the Valley of Achor also points forward to the much more drastic action of the one man, Jesus. He stood where we would otherwise stand, facing God's wrath but, as Hosea prophesied, because of this we can have hope. As we turn back to God and away from sin, we are received with open arms.

- Ask the Lord for conviction of sin and repentance – for ourselves, in our churches, and amongst our colleagues – and the courage not to compromise with sin in those areas where it is most difficult for us.
- Praise God that his drastic action in taking our place at the cross means hope for us, if we trust in Christ. Pray for opportunities to tell others about the hope of the gospel, perhaps as a direct result of our counter-cultural lives.

– Caroline Eade (2016)

23 FEB A Christian lawyer's practical motto

March on, my soul; be strong! **Judges 5:21 (NIV)**

Preparation for a European young lawyer and law student programme unearthed the question, "What would speak into their daily challenges; would it be about bribery, corruption, and Islamic fundamentalism, or that evangelical Christians represent only 1% (or less) of people in their countries?".

We too know about daily challenges, like our European partners, and live in times of uncertainty and discouragement, but how do we all progress?

Deborah provides inspiration. Renowned prophetess, honoured judge and (ideal) role model called to lead others, she made it clear who reigned as commander in chief: "The Lord, the God of Israel, commands you" (Judges 4:6). Unlike Jezebel, who sought no-one's counsel, level-headed Deborah obeyed the Lord and insisted his will – not hers – be done. As Christian lawyers, are we seeking God's counsel as we proceed?

Deborah's greatest gift was inspiring people to accomplish more than imaginably possible. Israel had been under enemy occupation, its national infrastructure was crumbling and morale was so low that no-one had the will to fight. Enter Deborah who raised an army, defeated the enemy, and brought peace for forty years. "March on, my soul; be strong!"

Regardless of what frustrating, discouraging and uncertain challenges lie ahead of us this week, we can learn from Deborah. Like her, we can seek God's counsel and, through this, lead and inspire others to turn to Christ and help them grow in faith.

- *Give thanks that God has placed us purposefully, to do His work.*
- *That despite frustrations, discouragement and uncertainty, we can lean on Him and boldly share His love with others today and this week.*

– Fiona Mahendran-Gilliland (2016)

24 FEB Go in the strength you have

The LORD turned to him and said, "Go in the strength you have and save Israel out of Midian´s hand. Am I not sending you?" Judges 6:14 (NIV)

What is your biggest fear? Failing an exam; not getting the 'Newly Qualified' role of choice; delivering unjust news to a client; telling your colleague the urgent truth that they need Jesus? Or perhaps it's your own inadequacy. Despite firmly believing in God's promises, and His ability to help you in life's challenges, is it the nagging sense of failure to summon up enough faith to grasp His assistance that you dread?

Gideon feared his own inadequacy: born to an undistinguished family, and weak in the face of enemy oppression, who was he to save Israel (v 15)? As the Midianites swept down at harvest-time to steal crops and livestock, leaving severe famine in their wake, Gideon stayed away threshing wheat (v 11). Yet to the Lord he was a 'mighty warrior'!

The command to 'Go in the strength you have and save Israel' most likely horrified Gideon because he knew he had no strength at all; but what did the Lord remind him? It was the Lord's strength he had (vs 12, 16), so he must use it!

Gideon proved his faithfulness to God, and his obedience required him to stand against his father and tribe. Although Gideon feared his own people and needed assurance of God's calling, it is evident he feared God much more.

This week, will we fear God and trust in His strength more?

- *Give thanks that the Lord is with us too!*
- *Ask for His help to stop you concentrating on fears, failures and lack of faith, but instead to focus on His faithfulness, and to trust more in His working in and through you for His glory.*

– Fiona Mahendran-Gilliland (2019)

25 FEB Gleaning wisdom for a godly workplace

So Boaz said to Ruth, 'My daughter, listen to me. Don't go and glean in another field and don't go away from here.

Stay here with the women who work for me. Watch the field where the men are harvesting, and follow along after the women. I have told the men not to lay a hand on you. And whenever you are thirsty, go and get a drink from the water jars the men have filled.'

At this, she bowed down with her face to the ground. She asked him, 'Why have I found such favour in your eyes that you notice me – a foreigner?'

Boaz replied, 'I've been told all about what you have done for your mother-in-law since the death of your husband – how you left your father and mother and your homeland and came to live with a people you did not know before. May the LORD repay you for what you have done. May you be richly rewarded by the LORD, the God of Israel, under whose wings you have come to take refuge.'

Ruth 2:8-12 NIV

In Bethlehem in the time of the Judges there were no burnished credentials for inclusive workplaces – no 'Best Agricultural Landowners to Work For' awards – instead "everyone did what was right in his own eyes" (Judges 17:6). Boaz is thus a remarkable example of a godly employer. As a wealthy, male, Israelite landowner of good social standing he needn't have had anything to do with Ruth – a foreign widow, a vulnerable lone woman with no obvious male protector in a patriarchal society, an economic migrant living below the poverty line.

Boaz is risking his reputation even approaching Ruth, but he does not let their disparity in status get in the way of reassuring Ruth that she is very welcome in his workplace. Boaz doesn't simply stop at observing the Levitical obligations concerning gleaning; he goes the extra mile in commending Ruth, socially including her, protecting her, providing for her and maintaining her dignity – all at the expense of his own profits. In Boaz's workplace human beings have dignity and can flourish.

We too can shape the culture of our workplace: this week, whether we are the Head of Chambers or the new paralegal, in all our dealings let us model the grace of our servant King who laid aside his majesty to give dignity and status to ignoble outsiders.

- *Pray that we would each be salt and light in our place of work or study, treating everyone with dignity regardless of hierarchy.*
- *Pray for Christian lawyers in positions of seniority, for humility and servant-heartedness towards more junior colleagues.*
- *Pray for the counter-cultural awareness that our value comes from our status as God's adopted children and not from any earthly titles.*

– Phil Roberts KC (2021)

26 FEB
How to waive a right of pre-emption over land

Then Boaz said, 'On the day you buy the land from Naomi, you also acquire Ruth the Moabite, the dead man's widow, in order to maintain the name of the dead with his property.' At this, the guardian-redeemer said, 'Then I cannot redeem it because I might endanger my own estate. You redeem it yourself. I cannot do it.' (Now in earlier times in Israel, for the redemption and transfer of property to become final, one party took off his sandal and gave it to the other. This was the method of legalising transactions in Israel.) So the guardian-redeemer said to Boaz, Buy it yourself. And he removed his sandal. Ruth 4:5-8 (NIV)

The unnamed "guardian-redeemer" (referred to in the Hebrew as "so-and-so"!) must have had, as closest surviving male relative, the right to redeem land probably sold by Naomi's husband (but over which she retained the right of usufruct). This seemed an attractive option until Boaz presented him with his family responsibility to marry Ruth.

The "guardian redeemer" did not want to take the risk that having a son with Ruth might affect the succession to his estate, because that son, who would bear the name of Elimilech (Naomi's late husband), would inherit it.

So he waived his right of pre-emption in the way you did in those days, by taking off your sandal at the town gate and handing it to your counterparty. So much easier than filling in all those Land Registry forms!

Boaz, the next closest relative, was prepared to sacrifice his own property in that way. As a result, he ended up not just with the land, but with a kind, loyal and brave wife. By making that sacrifice he also became great-grandfather to King David, and, eventually, ancestor of Jesus Christ. Boaz demonstrated commitment, love and personal sacrifice. Unlike the unnamed man whose unwillingness to put his property at risk meant that he failed to step up to the plate when opportunity arose.

If God calls us to do so, how much are we prepared to sacrifice for the sake of Boaz's Descendant? Praise be to God that Jesus lovingly made the supreme sacrifice to save each one of us.

- *Pray that we would be willing to make sacrifices for the glory of our Lord.*
- *Pray that in the run-up to Easter, we would be speaking boldly of the supreme sacrifice Jesus made.*

– Andrew M (2018)

27 FEB — Asking and giving

For this child I prayed, and the Lord has granted me my petition that I made to him. Therefore I have lent him to the Lord. As long as he lives, he is lent to the Lord.
1 Samuel 1:27-28 (ESV)

Hannah was "deeply distressed" (v 17). She longed for a child and, weeping bitterly, out of "great anxiety and vexation" (v 17), pleaded with God to provide one. Eventually God answered Hannah's prayer by giving her a son. Here is Hannah's response more literally: "For this child I prayed, and the Lord gave me the asking that I asked of him".

Hannah asked, and the Lord gave. He doesn't always give us exactly what we ask for, but he does respond to our prayers in love, wisdom and power. But how often we do not ask. We think we can rely on ourselves, or we think we cannot rely on God. Hannah's example teaches us to ask.

But notice (v 28) how Hannah immediately dedicates the very thing she craved, the precious answer to her prayer – her only son – to the Lord. She gave back to God the gift that she had received from Him. As Christian lawyers our careers, skills and money are all gifts from Him. And like all gifts we can choose to grab them, gloat over them and guard them. We can use what we have been given in just the way that we like – and probably ruin them. Or we can lay them down before the giver. Hannah's example also teaches us that the path to contentment is to offer the gift back.

Is there anything you do not ask for in prayer because, deep down, you think the Lord cannot or will not give it? How does Hannah's example challenge you?

What could you give to God even this week? What will that look like?

- Is there anything you do not ask for in prayer because, deep down, you think the Lord cannot or will not give it? How does Hannah's example challenge you?
- What could you give to God even this week? What will that look like?

– Jonathan Storey (2020)

28 FEB — Appearance versus reality

When they came, he looked on Eliab and thought, 'Surely the LORD'S anointed is before him.' But the LORD said to Samuel, 'Do not look on his appearance or on the height of his stature, because I have rejected him. For the LORD sees not as man sees: man looks on the outward appearance, but the LORD looks on the heart.'
1 Samuel 16:6-7 (ESV)

In 1 Samuel 16, the prophet Samuel was told by God to visit Jesse the Bethlehemite and anoint one of his sons to be the successor to Saul as Israel's new king. Naturally enough, Samuel imagined that God had chosen someone tall and impressive looking – someone who would be automatically respected.

Instead, God chose Jesse's youngest son, David, who was so unimportant that he was away "keeping the sheep". This was because "the LORD sees not as man sees: man looks on the outward appearance, but the LORD looks on the heart" (v 7b). God knew that David was a man who sincerely loved God and so, despite David's lowly stature, the Lord chose him to become king and leader of His people.

As lawyers, it is easy for us to fall into the trap of making judgments and decisions based on outward appearances. We can be tempted to work harder on the cases of our wealthier clients or devote more of our time to influential people who we think will be useful to us.

Perhaps more seriously, we can become so concerned with our own image and 'personal brand' within our chambers, firm or university that we forget about what really matters: the state of our hearts. This passage acts as a reminder to us that our God is a God who looks deeply into our hearts and calls us to dedicate them wholeheartedly to Him afresh.

- Thank God for the gift of new hearts in Christ and pray that our hearts would be ever conformed to the will of God.
- Pray for those in authority that they will be given godly wisdom as they lead the country.

– Adam McRae-Taylor (2015)

29 FEB Be a David, not a Don Quixote

David said to the Philistine, "You come against me with sword and spear and javelin, but I come against you in the name of the LORD Almighty, the God of the armies of Israel, whom you have defied." 1 Samuel 17:45 (NIV)

The world is full of idealists who stand up and fight for good causes. Many who do so fight for personal glory and put their trust in their own power. Often this makes them ineffective and earns them ridicule like Don Quixote – an impractical idealist bent on righting incorrigible wrongs.

In the eyes of the world, we Christians are often likened to Don Quixote as our battles against injustice do not make sense to a world characterized by pragmatism and materialism. Battles against injustice are often considered worthless and lost causes. For Christian lawyers fighting against injustice, this can cause a deep sense of discouragement and pessimism. It can seem like we are merely tilting at windmills. *

However, whenever I find myself discouraged, I remind myself that I am not fighting with my power and for my glory but with the power of God and for the glory of God, just as David fought with Goliath.

If we as Christians forget that we are fighting these battles with God and for God, we risk becoming like "Don Quixote". Be like David, not like Don Quixote.

*'Tilting at windmills' is an idiom which means 'attacking imagined enemies' and alludes to the hero of Miguel de Cervantes' Don Quixote, who rides with his lance at full tilt (poised to strike) against a row of windmills, which he mistakes for evil giants.

- *Let us pray for one another today that we would approach our work as lawyers like David, with our hearts, mind and focus on God, and in His strength.*
- *Let us continually lift up our brothers and sisters labouring abroad for justice within very unjust and corrupt countries.*

– Adenil Pjetri (2022)

1 MAR God's kindness

And you shall not only show me the kindness of the LORD while I still live, that I may not die; but you shall not cut off your kindness from my house forever, no, not when the LORD has cut off every one of the enemies of David from the face of the earth. **1 Samuel 20:14-15 (NKJV)**

One of the characteristics of God is His kindness. Find time to do a word search for "kindness" in the Bible and you will be amazed by the depth and the breadth of God's kindness. God not only demonstrates His kindness to us, God wants us to show kindness to others. Kindness is part of the fruit of the Spirit (Galatians 5:22). We see this link between the kindness that God shows to us and the kindness that God expects us to show to others in Jonathan's interaction with David in 1 Samuel 20. Jonathan knows that both David and he have been shown "the kindness of the LORD". He asks David to promise that, despite the conflict between Jonathan's father, Saul, and David, David will show kindness to Jonathan's family forever. David remembered that promise and, years later once he had become king, showed kindness to Jonathan's disabled son, Mephibosheth (2 Samuel 9).

Legal practice or any other demanding work can be extremely stressful at times. You can probably recall moments when the kindness of others made it more bearable. Rejoice in the kindness which God has shown you and look for opportunities to show kindness to others.

- *Thank God for His kindness towards us in Christ and ask Him for forgiveness for those times when you have not treated others with kindness.*
- *Thank God for those who have shown you kindness in your working life and pray for opportunities to show kindness to others.*

– Dr David McIlroy (2018)

2 MAR — Saved from the bloodshed

David said to Abigail, "Praise be to the LORD, the God of Israel, who has sent you today to meet me. May you be blessed for your good judgment and for keeping me from bloodshed this day and from avenging myself with my own hands." 1 Samuel 25:32-33 (NIV)

Poor David, all his personal life is placed on display in the Bible. His story provides endless lessons, especially for lawyers. David was thrust in the middle of some awful situations, albeit one or two of them were of his own making! The text above is taken from the account of David coming into contact with Nabal, a man about whom it would be hard to say something positive. David could probably justify (at least to himself) the vengeance he was about to dish out on Nabal, but in the Lord's providence he sent Abigail to David and she helped him see sense.

Often as lawyers we end up in the Abigail role and our counsel, or even just our presence, can be used to let clients see the folly of their intended course. At other times we can be in some awful situations and our judgement can be clouded, just like David. When an Abigail appears on the scene, listen to the good judgment and act upon it. Of course, we don't need an Abigail in all situations; in John 14:26 Jesus says these words: "But the Advocate, the Holy Spirit, whom the Father will send in my name, will teach you all things and will remind you of everything I have said to you." It's a simple statement worthy of much application – and pause for prayer.

- Ask God, through the Holy Spirit, to remind you of the things in His word that will keep you walking in the ways of the Lord this week.
- Give thanks for the wonderful gift of wisdom and good judgment, and for those who this week God will bring across your path to help you.

– Brent Haywood (2015)

3 MAR — Wilderness years

David was thirty years old when he became King, and he reigned for forty years. 2 Samuel 5:4 (NIV)

This may seem like an unremarkable statement of fact. David, God's mighty King, a man after God's own heart, from whose descendants God brought the Saviour Jesus Christ, was thirty years old when he became King and he reigned for forty years.

However, back in 1 Samuel 16 we see David, Jesse's youngest teenage son, anointed God's chosen King.

So, what happened over those intervening 15 years?

We see David in the wilderness on the run from Saul, living on the margins, with no home, facing prejudice and betrayal, in constant fear for his life.

In that time God provides for his needs, repeatedly intervenes to save his life, sends true friends and wise counsel to keep him from many temptations to sin. Quite a training programme for kingship!

Perhaps you feel you are in the wilderness at work, university, home or church. Remember, you are not alone. David's greater son Jesus Christ is on the throne. God is establishing His kingdom through Jesus, our suffering servant. He will lead home to glory all who trust in Him.

- *Thank God that He understands our trials and temptations and that He gives us encouragement through His Word, strength through His Spirit and salvation through His Son.*
- *Pray that He will use our wilderness times to refine us and to teach us to trust Him in our work, our studies and our relationships.*

– Debbie Woods (2017)

4 MAR Ruling as children

I will establish the throne of his kingdom forever. I will be his Father, and he shall be My son. 2 Samuel 7:13-14 (NKJV)

Often, we are told that a 'Christian lawyer' is an oxymoron. But sometimes we ourselves still struggle to see how our 'working life' in the office relates to our 'spiritual life'.

Another entry point for this conversation is suggested in our text. Here God's promise to David – pointing to Solomon and then to Christ, and us in him – highlights two themes which are connected throughout the Bible: kingship and sonship. Whether it is Adam or Israel, Christ or God's people today, the Bible says we have these two interconnected roles: to exercise godly dominion in God's world, reflecting his rule; and to do it in relationship with God as his children expecting a gracious inheritance.

For David himself in Psalm 27 he knew that during the pressure of kingly responsibilities, surrounded by enemies, he could also take comfort in his sonship: "in the time of trouble he will hide me … when my father and my mother forsake me, then the LORD will take care of me." Psalm. 27:5, 10 (NKJV).

Let's resist a culture of self-sufficiency in the legal world. As Christians, we can work hard in the justice system within the security of a relationship of dependence and protection from a heavenly Father. Will we run to this Father in our times of trouble at work this week? Each of us can then defeat another oxymoron too, and be a 'peaceful lawyer'.

> I will establish the throne of his kingdom forever. I will be his Father, and he shall be My son.
>
> 2 Samuel 7:13-14 (NKJV)

- Pray that in our pressured work as lawyers this week we work with the comfort, peace and security which befits being children of God, as we rest in his protection.
- Pray that colleagues will see that our work flows out from our inner spiritual confidence and identity that we are secure and loved as God's children, expecting an inheritance which doesn't depend on our own effort – so that they too come to know that King Jesus is the Son of God.

– Tim Laurence (2018)

5 MAR — A God of surprises (although not for Him!)

So he departed from there and found Elisha the son of Shaphat, who was ploughing with twelve yoke of oxen in front of him, and he was with the twelfth. Elijah passed by him and cast his cloak upon him... Then he arose and went after Elijah and assisted him. **1 Kings 19:19, 21b (ESV)**

What sort of week are you anticipating? You might have returned from your weekend or a holiday to find a pile of work, some of which you have been dreading. Maybe you have been working all weekend with still a whole load of work or study to do. Or does it just look like another normal week ahead, similar to all the others?

In this passage we find Elisha going about his farming business. Despite his probable wealth (twelve pairs was not an inconsiderable number of beasts to own) he had his hand to the plough, in what was no doubt hard and dusty work. In what was a usual day's work, it is unlikely that he was expecting God, through the prophet Elijah, to show up and call him to a new task, work that God had prepared for him to do in advance (v 16).

Your work as a lawyer is important and stewarding what the Lord has entrusted into your care is a privilege. But are you willing to be open to the unexpected surprise or opportunity that God might have prepared for you this week if you are willing to hear his voice?

It may not mean taking action as radical as shredding your law books to move on – the equivalent of Elisha burning his yoke (v 20) – although it could be. But would you be open to the prompting of the Holy Spirit to pray with a client whose situation looks bleak, or share your faith with an unlikely colleague, or invite a friend who never seems bothered with your faith to an evangelistic event?

Elisha was willing to risk everything to assist Elijah and serve God. Are you willing to do the same this week to serve the King of Kings however surprising that opportunity might be?

- *Ask God if there is anything that He is calling you to do this week, as a witness for Him as you serve in your workplace*

– Mark Barrell (2016)

6 MAR Standing firm

So Ahab spoke to Naboth, saying, "Give me your vineyard, that I may have it for a vegetable garden, because it is near, next to my house; and for it I will give you a vineyard better than it. Or, if it seems good to you, I will give you its worth in money."

But Naboth said to Ahab, "The LORD forbid that I should give the inheritance of my fathers to you!"

1 Kings 21:2-3 (NKJV)

The Old Testament emphasis on the land as God's faithful provision for his covenant people underlies this memorable example of steadfastness and courage in the face of an enticing bargain, which offered a choice of favourable terms many would have accepted without resistance. However, for Naboth, the terms on offer entailed more than just the disposal of fruitful terrain. They called for what would have been the abandonment of an inheritance which was spiritual, as well as physical, signifying God's covenantal relationship with his redeemed people across the generations.

Throughout our lives as Christians, we are regularly tempted to concede ground or compromise, whether on matters of revealed truth, or moral conduct and sometimes for personal advantage. History is rich with examples of those who have stood firm, rejecting worldly gain rather than relinquishing the covenant blessings which belong to God's people and derive from Him alone. For some, standing firm has meant facing persistent challenges, or even persecution. For Naboth, his forthright, openly declared allegiance to the divinely ordained land inheritance cost him his life.

While this week is unlikely to present dilemmas where death is a possible consequence of standing firm as a Christian, the lesser challenges of daily legal practice often embody the risk of sinful compromise. Our frailty is such that, like Naboth, we should be ever mindful of our dependence on God's provision and of the great spiritual inheritance guaranteed by God's everlasting faithfulness to His people.

- *Pray that we would be invigorated by Naboth's example to stand firm, with courage, when confronted by spiritual and moral challenges.*
- *Ask the Lord to use our obedience in the face of such challenges to achieve His purposes (whether or not they are made clear to us).*
- *Pray that, when standing firm, we will have the courage to tell others where we stand and why.*

– James Crabtree (2019)

7 MAR My way or God's way?

"... Now I know that there is no God in all the world except in Israel ..." Extract from 2 Kings 5:15(b) (NIV)

Naaman had it all worked out! He knew how the prophet Elisha was going to heal him. But when Elisha did not even bother to go to the door of his house but simply sent a terse message telling Naaman what he must do, then the sparks flew!

Naaman turned away in anger and was only, with difficulty, persuaded by his servants to follow the simple instructions he had been given – "Wash seven times in the Jordan". Once healed of his leprosy, Naaman declared his commitment to the God of Israel as the only God.

Is there a danger that we too fall into the same trap of wanting to do things in our way, following our plan? If we seek to be kept in God's will, following the path he has planned for us, this will keep us from much heartache and anguish.

In office or chambers, in Court or tribunal, let God guide you by His Holy Spirit. He will not only lead into all truth, He will guide through the uncertain ways where the route cannot be clearly seen.

The world would have us declare "I did it my way!". Our Heavenly Father bids us take His Way.

- *Pray each day to be kept in God's will and follow His path.*
- *Pray that those we work with and for may also be led by the Holy Spirit.*

- *Pray that those who need healing physically, mentally, or spiritually may find the guidance and help that they need.*

– Michael Hawthorne (2021)

8 MAR In times of crisis

And Hezekiah received the letter from the hand of the messengers, and read it; and Hezekiah went up to the house of the LORD, and spread it before the LORD.
2 Kings 19:14 (NKJV)

Particularly in these troubled times, there may be hard circumstances that are seemingly impervious to human intervention. We or our clients may have made mistakes or through no fault may be looking at a potential disaster.

Hezekiah was facing the imminent destruction of Jerusalem, and all he could do – and it was everything – was to lay it before the Lord and ask for His will to be done. Saint Paul reminds us: "… in everything by prayer and supplication, with thanksgiving, let your requests be made known to God". (Philippians 4:6, NKJV)

In the words of the old hymn:

"Can we find a friend so faithful,
Who will all our sorrows share?
Jesus knows our every weakness,
Take it to the Lord in prayer.

"Are we weak or heavy-laden,
Cumbered with a load of care,
Precious Saviour, still our refuge:
Take it to the Lord in prayer."*

*The hymn was written in 1855 by Joseph Scriven. Interestingly, he was our author, John Scriven's great, great uncle.

We can pray
- For our clients going through difficult times, and that (as appropriate) we can let them know that we are doing so.
- For ourselves, knowing that we have a God who cares for us in matters great (however intractable) and small, that we are unafraid to bring these to Him in prayer; and that we do not forget to acknowledge the answers to our prayers.

– John Scriven (2021)

9 MAR We owe our thanks and praise to the Lord

Therefore David blessed the LORD in the presence of all the assembly. And David said: "Blessed are you, O LORD, the God of Israel our father, for ever and ever. Yours, O LORD, is the greatness and the power and the glory and the victory and the majesty, for all that is in the heavens and in the earth is yours. Yours is the kingdom, O LORD,

and you are exalted as head above all. Both riches and honour come from you, and you rule over all. In your hand are power and might, and in your hand it is to make great and to give strength to all. And now we thank you, our God, and praise your glorious name.
1 Chronicles 29: 10-13 (ESV)

During the Covid-19 pandemic we were thankful to, amongst others, the scientists who developed vaccines, and the doctors, nurses and other healthcare workers who looked after the sick. As lawyers, we also owe thanks to those behind the technology that has helped us through the crises, including the technology that has enabled us involved in civil litigation at least to continue to conduct hearings through various video platforms, thereby allowing our work to continue more or less as normal, albeit remotely.

However, as David reminds us in this prayer, everything comes from God. It is from his kingdom that the innovation and wisdom seeing us through this crisis has ultimately come. In his hands are power and might. As our sovereign LORD, it is in his hand to make great and give strength to all, and nobody else's.

David further reminds us that God is our Father for ever and ever, and that his is the greatness and the power and the glory and the victory and the majesty. We can therefore know and rest assured that whatever this world might throw at us, the ultimate victory has been won through Jesus' death on the Cross, and that by placing our trust in God, we have a Saviour in him.

- *We give thanks for the scientists, medics and others who have helped us through the Covid-19 pandemic, but above all we give thanks and praise to God for enabling and empowering them to do so.*
- *We give thanks and praise that the ultimate victory has been won through Jesus' death on the Cross, and that by placing our trust in God, we have an eternal Saviour in him.*
- *We pray that the pandemic and its aftermath might provide an opportune moment for friends, family and work colleagues who have yet to place their trust in Jesus to reflect upon the priorities in their lives, and turn to him as Saviour.*

– HHJ Mark Cawson KC (2021)

10 MAR The battle is not yours, but God's

For we have no power against this great multitude that is coming against us; nor do we know what to do, but our eyes are upon You. 2 Chronicles 20:12 (NKJV)

Some years ago, Rev. Dick Lucas (formerly Rector of St Helen's Bishopsgate), speaking at an LCF conference, said that we need to ask God for both wisdom and courage in addressing the challenges of secularism in our world. Since that time, hostility to Christianity has become more strident and frequently affects us both in and outside the workplace.

We can feel overwhelmed by the challenges involved and can be frozen in the headlights. Faced with seemingly insuperable odds, Jehoshaphat called out to God: "nor do we know what to do, but our eyes are upon You". So we need to ask God for His resources – both for the wisdom to know what to do, and for the courage to do it, remembering Jahaziel's word from the Lord to the people of Judah: "the battle is not yours, but God's" (v 15, NKJV).

- *Pray for those of us facing difficult situations in our professions as a result of our Christian faith: may we rely on God for His guidance and strength.*
- *When talking about our faith with those who have different beliefs to our own, ask that God will give us both wisdom and courage.*

– John Scriven (2018)

11 MAR Are you sitting comfortably?

Then rose up the heads of the fathers' houses of Judah and Benjamin, and the priests and the Levites, everyone whose spirit God had stirred to go up to rebuild the house of the LORD that is in Jerusalem. **Ezra 1:5 ESV**

Trusting God in his sovereign purposes is not always, if ever, easy. In a world where 'now' is king and answers demanded instantly, one lesson, in amongst many, that we have learnt from a global pandemic is the need to develop more patient and trusting hearts.

Maybe, though, we have become too used to working from home. The desire to go back to our workplaces, student digs or courtrooms has worn off and we have become more comfortable with our new life on screen.

The book of Ezra starts when many of God's people had, for seventy years, lived locked down in a foreign place under very different rules. If they felt abandoned and had settled down for the new normal, you may feel some empathy! But this was precisely the time that God called his people to be obedient to his call, promises and purpose, and it is God who stirs their hearts to rebuild the temple.

In Christ Jesus each of us, temples of the Holy Spirit (1 Corinthians 6:19), are built as living stones of His spiritual house, the church (1 Peter 2:5). This week, is God, through the Holy Spirit, stirring you into action, to step out in faith and be fully committed in your witness to your love for and faith in Christ? Are you willing to totally trust Him?

- *Give thanks that you are never alone, and have the Helper, the Holy Spirit, whom the Father has sent in the name of Christ.*

- *Pray that you would be willing this week to trust God and step out in faith in whatever way he stirs your heart and to do so as a witness to and worshipper of the Lord Jesus Christ.*

– Mark Barrell (2021)

12 MAR Rest and recuperation

"So we arrived in Jerusalem, where we rested three days." **Ezra 8:32 (NIV)**

Do you pride yourself on your stamina or are you exhausted? Do you find it difficult to relax? Do you feel under constant pressure to check your phone? Ezra the priest had a big and important job: the proclamation of God's law to God's people. So, the first thing he did when he arrived in Jerusalem was to rest. Instead of making an early start, Ezra took the time to recover properly from the long journey he had undertaken.

God knows that we need rest. One of the most gifted nineteenth century preachers, Robert Murray McCheyne, wrote this, whilst he was dying aged just 29: "God gave me a message to deliver and a horse to ride. Alas, I have killed the horse and now I cannot deliver the message."

If we are to serve God, our churches, our families, and our clients well, we need to recognise that we are not made to work constantly: as the Sabbath principle teaches us, there are times when what we need to concentrate on is resting.

When was the last time you rested for three days? What would it mean for you to rest properly on the next Bank Holiday Weekend? What do you need to do to refresh your body and soul?

- *Take some time to rest in God, and seek from the Lord the refreshment that only He and His word can give to both your body and soul.*
- *Pray for those who you know are anxious or weary, and ask that they may know the peace that passes all understanding.*

– Dr David McIlroy (2021)

13 MAR Pray and press on

They all plotted together to come and fight against Jerusalem and stir up trouble against it. But we prayed to our God and posted a guard day and night to meet this threat. **Nehemiah 4:8-10 (NIV)**

Nehemiah has left his job as cupbearer to the King at Susa to rebuild the walls of Jerusalem, so that God's name would be honoured, His people gathered again and able to worship God at the Temple. He has witnessed God's sovereign power as King Artaxerxes grants him permission to leave, well-resourced for the job, with safe passage to Jerusalem.

Building gets underway and 52 days later it is completed, the wall built. What a triumph! And yet, as is often the case, Nehemiah's service for God met trial and opposition from all sides. The sovereign God did not remove the opposition. Nehemiah did not wake up one morning to find the wall miraculously built. Instead he found God's people compromising with the culture, disobeying God's word, his enemies threatening violence, deriding his efforts, mocking his team and trying to distract him.

So what does Nehemiah, the man of God do? He "prayed to our God and posted a guard day and night" – a model response!

So, whether you have exams to prepare for, difficult cases or clients to face, let us pray to our sovereign God to enable us to use the gifts and opportunities He has given us to make Christ and His Kingdom known.

- Let us bring before the Lord in prayer anything we see as obstacles to our Kingdom activities and allow Him to use the gifts He has given to us and to others to press on.

– Debbie Woods (2019)

14 MAR Meaningful conversations

***They read from the Book of the Law of God, making it clear and giving the meaning so that the people understood what was being read.* Nehemiah 8:8 (NIV)**

I regularly pray for my clients and for wisdom with their cases. Surprisingly often, my experience is that they react with comprehension, and thanks, when I can explain to them the law, even if they didn't get the answer they were hoping for.

An essential task for us as legal scholars and lawyers is to explain the law to those seeking advice, so that they can understand. This applies all the more when it comes to the instruction of God's law, because "the person who obeys them will live by them" (Nehemiah 9:29b).

In Luke 24, we find the risen Lord Jesus also teaching his disciples from the Scriptures. The Old Testament Scripture – the books of the law (Moses), the Prophets and the Psalms (Luke 24:27, 44) – points to Jesus, and through it, He opens the disciples' hearts and minds to understand more fully (Luke 24:32, 45).

But Jesus also explained the meaning and purpose of the law both to his opponents and, in greater detail afterwards, to his disciples (e.g. Mark 10:2-12 concerning divorce).

As lawyers, we naturally seek to provide clear, understandable, and accurate advice on the law. As Christians, do we seek to understand the Scriptures with the same commitment? Are we looking for opportunities to point to Christ in our conversations and conduct as we engage with clients, colleagues and even opponents?

- Let us pray for this gift of explanation and the necessary wisdom for it, as well as an open ear amongst those we serve. And as James 1:5 reminds us, "If any of you lacks wisdom, you should ask God, who gives generously to all without finding fault, and it will be given to you."
- Pray for opportunities to explain to others the reason for our hope in Jesus.

– Martin Franke (2021)

15 MAR — Much to do? Only one thing is needed

As Jesus and his disciples were on their way, he came to a village where a woman named Martha opened her home to him. She had a sister called Mary, who sat at the Lord's feet listening to what he said. But Martha was distracted by all the preparations that had to be made …

"Martha, Martha", the Lord answered, "you are worried and upset about many things, but only one thing is needed. Mary has chosen what is better, and it will not be taken away from her."

Luke 10:38-42 (NIV)

There is always much to be done in the law: clients to see, experts to chase, opponents to deal with, briefs to read, papers to draft. Even when work is quiet, we busy ourselves catching up on admin and drumming up more business. And that is before we turn our attention to matters of family, church, and other out-of-work commitments.

How many of us live lives punctuated by worry and fret? All too easily, like Martha, we can become entirely absorbed and distracted by all that has to be done, such that we fail to take time first to sit at the feet of our Lord and listen to Him.

For Mary and Martha, meals did need to be prepared. For us, cases do need to be progressed (and meals made too!). Let us first, however, put things of first importance first. Let us make sure we have taken the time to sit with our Lord, to hear his priorities, to draw on his strength, to remind ourselves for whom it is we labour. This is the better way; such time will not be taken from us.

- *Spend time meditating on the Lord's priorities for you.*
- *Ask for his wisdom, provision and joy as you labour for Him today.*

– Rob Horner (2020)

16 MAR — When lawyers desire to justify themselves

Then the wrath of Elihu, the son of Barachel the Buzite, of the family of Ram, was aroused against Job; his wrath was aroused because he justified himself rather than God. **Job 32:2 (NKJV)**

If we reflect honestly on how we spend our days, we are likely to conclude that much time is committed to some form of self-justification.

In the world of litigation, beneath the legal and evidential issues which courts and tribunals resolve, there is, in many cases, likely to be a deeper layer of controversy, reflecting the litigating parties' compulsion to self-justify: "I was in the right and can prove this!"

Within our hearts and minds, we carry around the invisible baggage and burdens of self-justification. Our silent thoughts often tell us: "I do my best, despite daily stresses. My motives are good, even if at times I falter."

Beneath self-justification pride often lurks: that implicit, ever-present affirmation of my own worth and merit.

Job 32:2 provides a rude awakening. Job, ever conscious of his perceived integrity, is charged by Elihu with justifying himself rather than God. By focussing on himself, Job has neglected God's character and elevated his own. Job has exalted himself at God's expense.

After Elihu, Job is confronted by God Himself whose questioning reveals Job's true standing before Him. Job lacks wisdom and knowledge ("Who is this who darkens counsel by words without knowledge?" 38:2). He is dwarfed by God's eternal power and greatness ("Where were you when I laid the foundations of the earth?" 38:4).

Self-justification reveals an enlarged view of ourselves and an all too small view of the God who alone justifies.

- *Ask the Holy Spirit to show you where pride has led you to self-justify (like the lawyer in Luke 10:29), and seek forgiveness.*
- *Give thanks that we have a God who truly justifies us through the Lord Jesus Christ (Romans 8:32-24).*

– James Crabtree (2016)

17 MAR Confidence in God's plans

I know that you can do all things; no plan of yours can be thwarted. **Job 42:2 (NIV 1984)**

So often, we may have doubts about whether we are serving God as He would want, either in life generally or in our present work. This can be for many reasons. Our work may seem humdrum, we may find ourselves working for individuals who are hostile to the gospel, or even acting against Christians for whom we have sympathy.

For many of us, these doubts will be more present in these uncertain times, as we have may have less immediate support from fellow Christians.

As Job ultimately realised, however, our God who can defeat the leviathan (Job 41) is in control and will prevail, although many things will happen in our working lives where His plans may not be obvious to us. We should of course pray that those plans be known and that we may delight in being part of them.

In all things, God works for the good of those who have been called according to His purpose (Romans 8:28), and that includes in our work. Whether He is refining us in the midst of dealing with a difficult case or a difficult client, or opening up the possibility of other areas of service whether through our work or elsewhere, we should be sure God is with us in any present doubts and difficulties, and that His plans extend beyond them.

- *Pray that our work may be satisfying to us, and that we may know God's plans for us in it, and that others may do so too through the way approach our work and through our witness.*
- *Pray that we may know how God is ever-present during changes, and be trusting in God's plans for each one of them.*

– James Brightwell (2020)

18 MAR All a bit much?

LORD, how many are my foes! How many rise up against me! Many are saying of me, "God will not deliver him."… I lie down and sleep; I wake again, because the LORD sustains me. Psalm 3:1-2, 5 (NIV)

We may not feel as if we have enemies, exactly, but we may well feel overwhelmed by various things – or even people – that are oppressive to us. Demands from clients or colleagues, court deadlines, family responsibilities, exams, worries about money or housing … It is all too easy to start believing that God doesn't hear or doesn't care, and won't help.

The psalmist reminds us that God does hear and will answer. He sustains us for each day – it is only because of him that we wake each morning. Jesus himself described death as no more than 'sleep' – if we can trust him for our resurrection life, how much more for the strength we need each day.

Let's remind ourselves that we do not and cannot sustain ourselves and that we are already dependent on him in everything. Whatever may overwhelm us, none of it is beyond the Lord's power or love for us.

- *Pray for Christian lawyers we know who are facing significant challenges in their lives – that their trust in God's love and power would be deepened.*
- *Pray for all of us, that as we learn to live in greater dependence on the Lord, those around us would be prompted to ask about the peace and hope they see in us – and that we would be bold to answer.*

– Caroline Eade (2019)

19 MAR — When you suffer false accusations what do you do?

O LORD my God, I take refuge in you; save and deliver me from all who pursue me …
O LORD my God, if I have done this and there is guilt on my hands, if I have done evil to him who is at peace with me … then let my enemy pursue and overtake me … and make me sleep in the dust …
O righteous God, who searches minds and hearts, bring to an end the violence of the wicked and make the righteous secure …
My shield is God Most High, who saves the upright in heart. God is a righteous Judge …

Psalm 7:1-11 (NIV 1984)

Have you ever been bad-mouthed? Criticised unfairly, accused unjustly or been the subject of malicious falsehood? David here had apparently been wrongly accused of treachery to Saul. What does he do?

He takes refuge in God. He reminds himself that God is righteous and searches minds and hearts and cannot be deceived. He knows all the ins and outs and so David examines himself to see if there is any guilt. And he prays. That must be the starting point as even unfair attacks/criticism often have an element of truth. We need to repent of all that is wrong, whether there is some justice in the accusation or merely wounded pride because of what others may think of us, when what matters is what the Lord thinks.

Perceiving the injustice to Him leads David to pray for God to deal with wrongdoing and to preserve the righteous. When we feel the world is treating us badly, is our reaction to pray for our suffering fellow Christians? Will we look beyond ourselves to see the wider world and purposes of God?

Because God is a righteous Judge, our shield is God Most High. David knows that He will save the upright in heart in due course. If not now, then at the end of the age. Maranatha. May your kingdom come.

- *Examine yourself and take the opportunity to repent for those areas in your life where you know you need God's forgiveness.*
- *Pray for your fellow brothers and sisters who are suffering persecutions and false accusation for their faith in the Lord Jesus Christ.*

– Sir Jeremy Cooke (2017)

20 MAR — The assurance of divine justice

Behold, the wicked brings forth iniquity;
Yes, he conceives trouble and brings forth falsehood.

He made a pit and dug it out,
And has fallen into the ditch which he made.
His trouble shall return upon his own head,
And his violent dealing shall come down on his own crown.
I will praise the LORD according to His righteousness,
And will sing praise to the name of the LORD Most High.

Psalm 7:14-17 (NKJV)

In this fallen world, we are surrounded by much that is sinful and unjust, and the Bible consistently shocks us with the truth that the wickedness of mankind produces iniquity, trouble and falsehood, as Psalm 7 declares. However, the fertility of evil is not accompanied by its ultimate supremacy. As the Psalm explains, evil is, in the final analysis, characterised by its futility. The 'pit' or 'ditch' that they have prepared for others becomes the self-prepared and self-defeating snare to which the wicked eventually succumb. The trouble conceived by the wicked and unleashed by them in this life inexorably returns to its creators and renders them subject to God's judgment.

While the daily practice of law might not cause us to rub shoulders with wickedness in one of its many extreme forms, we are nonetheless practising law in a fallen world, where the desires, intentions, words and actions of mankind are revealed in their wickedness when judged against the perfect righteousness of God and His laws. Like the Psalmist, we can praise the Lord Most High for ensuring that there is no wickedness which escapes His attention and goes unjudged. The righteousness of the Lord ultimately prevails over the wickedness of sinful mankind. Of course, for the Christian believer, that righteousness is demonstrated in the gospel itself, which provides assurance that the righteous punishment of sin has been borne by Christ and that His righteousness is credited to the account of every forgiven sinner.

- *Make space to reflect on the Lord's righteousness and what it means for us as Christian lawyers and for mankind in general.*
- *Pray that we might turn daily to the Lord in humble dependence upon Him to avoid falling into the ways of the wicked and to give thanks for the greatness of our salvation from sin through God's gracious provision of the Lord Jesus Christ as saviour.*
- *Pray that an enriched understanding of God's righteousness and just judgments will inform our working lives as lawyers, enabling us to prioritise justice as the Lord's disciples.*

– James Crabtree (2020)

21 MAR Do I or my work matter this week?

When I look at your heavens, the work of your fingers, the moon and the stars, which you have set in place, what is man that you are mindful of him, and the son of man that you care for him? **Psalm 8:3-4 (ESV)**

A Monday (or Tuesday!) morning is a time we might consider some big questions: 'What am I doing here?', or 'Does my work matter?', or even 'Do I matter?' Perhaps you are (professionally) riding the crest of a wave, or perhaps you are concerned that you career has stalled, or worse, is in decline.

Life does not make sense if you simply try and understand it in relation to your career, your possessions, or even your family or friends. Life only makes sense when understood in relation to God.

Having created man to know Him, God is interested in man. On a specific level, He's interested in people. Just think: Jesus was interested in a fraudster called Zacchaeus, in two sisters who had lost their brother, and a man whose had lost his daughter. He was even interested in the hunger of thousands of people on a hillside who had come to hear him.

Note that in the psalm David uses the word "mindful" to underline that God isn't just aware of or vaguely interested in man. He cares for us.

Dear friend, He cares for you.

That's bigger than whatever else might be going on. And it means that you matter, and so (for that matter) does your work.

Now be encouraged, give thanks to God in prayer and get back to work!

- *Give thanks to God, the Creator of the universe, for his love and care for you.*

– Gavin Callaghan (2017)

22 MAR Praying for justice

Arise, Lord! Lift up your hand, O God.
Do not forget the helpless.
Why does the wicked man revile God?

Why does he say to himself,
'He won't call me to account'?
But you, God, see the trouble of the afflicted;
you consider their grief and take it in hand.
The victims commit themselves to you;
you are the helper of the fatherless.
Break the arm of the wicked man;
call the evildoer to account for his wickedness
that would not otherwise be found out.
The Lord is King for ever and ever;
the nations will perish from his land.
You, Lord, hear the desire of the afflicted;
you encourage them, and you listen to their cry,
defending the fatherless and the oppressed,
so that mere earthly mortals will never again strike terror.

Psalm 10:12-18 (NIV)

On 23 June 2016 Willie Kimani, a lawyer from the Kenya office of International Justice Mission, an organisation which works with The Lawyers' Christian Fellowship CLEAR partners, was abducted in Nairobi along with his client Josephat Mwenda and their taxi driver Joseph Muiruri. They were on their way home from a court hearing. Willie had been representing Josephat as he sought to challenge false charges brought against him by a police officer in April 2015.

On 1 July the appalling news came through that the bodies of all three men had been found. There was some evidence that they may have been detained in a police compound, tortured and executed.

This world is full of violence as a result of human sin. At times it can seem overwhelming and, like the Psalmist, we can feel as if God is absent and that those who commit terrible acts of violence do so with impunity.

But also like the Psalmist, we can have confidence that God does see, does consider and will punish wickedness and violence. The brave men and women of International Justice Mission and CLEAR know this and work tirelessly in the name of Christ to achieve justice for those who have been the subject of police abuse and other forms of violent oppression in Kenya and elsewhere around the world. And we have a sure hope in a future day when the Lord Jesus will return as King to right every wrong and end all violence.

- *Cry out to the Lord about the violence in our world and ask Him to intervene. Pray that the guilty would be brought to justice.*
- *Continue to pray for the families of the men murdered in Kenya.*
- *Praise God that He is sovereign and that one day soon King Jesus will return and there will be no more violence or injustice ever again.*

– Alasdair Henderson (2016)

23 MAR — What do we do when things are falling apart?

"... if the foundations are destroyed, what can the righteous do?"
The LORD is in his holy temple; the LORD's throne is in heaven; his eyes see, his eyelids test the children of man.
Psalm 11:3-4 (ESV)

It seems like much of our politics and news is very fearful at the moment. Fear of a no deal Brexit. Fear that democracy is being undermined. Fear of climate change. Fear of increasing polarisation and anger in our public debate. Many people are worried that the very foundations of our society are crumbling.

And even if we are not affected by such news ourselves, as lawyers we often have to help our clients at a time when everything seems to have fallen apart for them because of an injury, dispute, family breakdown or criminal charge.

Psalm 11 describes King David's response to this kind of situation. It is not clear what exactly has happened, but it is bad enough that those around him feel 'the foundations are destroyed' (v 3). Yet in such a situation David says, 'in the LORD I take refuge' (v 1) and rebukes those who counsel him to give up and run away.

How can David have such confidence? Because (v 4), 'the LORD is in his holy temple'. David knows that whatever is going on around him, God remains in control and will one day ensure that justice is fully and completely done. Let us follow his example. As Christian lawyers we should never despair but can always have hope in a holy God, and we can persist in doing good to our clients and colleagues no matter how hard the circumstances seem.

- *Ask God to help you remember this week that God sees everything and will judge all; and pray that this would give you hope and perseverance to keep doing good this week.*
- *Pray that Christians would be distinctively full of hope in a society full of fear, and that we would have the opportunity to explain why to those around us.*

– Alasdair Henderson (2019)

24 MAR Are you a happy lawyer?

You make known to me the path of life;
in your presence there is fullness of joy;
at your right hand are pleasures forevermore.
Psalm 16:11 (ESV)

So often I think one of the significant weaknesses in my Christian life is that I don't often enough stop and intentionally gaze upon the beauty of Christ. And I don't grasp the wonder of that promise that through my union with Christ, I will be in God's presence forever – and that is a place of joy.

That should impact on how I work, how I interact with colleagues and opponents. It should put my aspirations and disappointments into perspective.

The mission of The Lawyers' Christian Fellowship is to bring the whole Good News of Jesus Christ within the legal world. As LCF members, we are ultimately seeking to direct people in the legal profession to Christ – and thus to pleasure, and to joy. It is an astounding truth that we are proclaiming – whether that is in the context of evangelism, or discipleship – we are pointing lawyers to Christ, and equipping them to be overjoyed.

Many lawyers I meet seem thoroughly miserable. Wouldn't it be wonderful if we, as Christian lawyers, were known as being overjoyed!

- *Pray that we would spend time in God's presence, and that we would become ever more joyful.*
- *Pray for opportunities to show that joy to others – and tell them why we are overjoyed!*

– Gavin Callaghan (2018)

25 MAR Are you GDPT ready?

*For who is God besides the LORD?
And who is the Rock except our God?
It is God who arms me with strength
and keeps my way secure.*

Psalm 18:31-32 (NIV)

King David knew the power of God's equipping and transforming strength. Murderous enemies pursued David, yet he stood strong in the end and was delivered because of his confidence in God.

David described his dire circumstances as "cords of death" and "torrents of destruction" which entangled and overwhelmed him (v 4). However, David knew the answer to his problem lay in the strength of his God, so he cried out to Him (v 6). Once God heard David's cries, He "parted the heavens and came down" (v 9). God then reached down and drew David out of his "deep waters" and brought him "into a spacious place" (vs 16, 19).

Why did God do this? Because He delighted in David (v 19).

Can you recall a situation when you felt totally helpless, overwhelmed and could see no way out? Be it balancing law exams alongside summer applications, time-consuming tasks, such as GDPR compliance, or the continued wait for a new member of staff, Psalm 18 screams Jesus to us! Whilst David's righteousness reflected his devotion to God (vs 20-24), post-Christ, we are seen by God through Jesus' righteousness, not our own. What a sacrifice Christ made for us, so that we could know God's power to shield, strengthen, move forward and equip us for whatever lies ahead (vs 30-36).

Are you ready for a God who Delights in you and Powerfully Transforms?

- *Thank God for delighting in you! (v 19) Praise Him for His power to transform us from inside out by His Spirit.*
- *Pray that in overwhelming and difficult circumstances you will learn to cry out to Him, your firm foundation, your deliverer, your protector (vs 2-3; 31).*
- *Pray to be armed and equipped by His strength for whatever you face this week (vs 32-34).*

– Fiona Mahendran-Gilliland (2018)

For who is God besides the LORD?
And who is the Rock except our God?
It is God who arms me with strength
and keeps my way secure.

Psalm 18:31-32 (NIV)

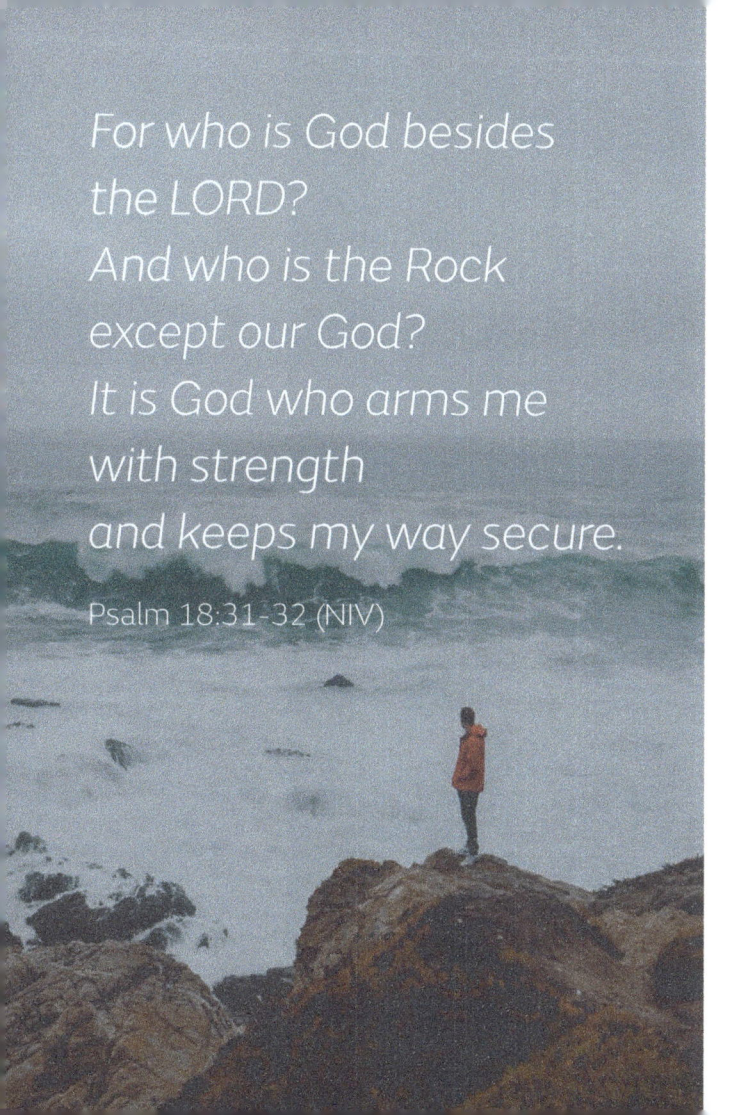

26 MAR — Happy talk…

The heavens declare the glory of God,
and the sky above proclaims his handiwork.
Day to day pours out speech,
and night to night reveals knowledge.
There is no speech, nor are there words,
whose voice is not heard.
Psalm 19:1-3 (ESV)

A happy joy of living in Mozambique was that most days, when I opened the curtains, the sun was out, the sky was blue, with hardly a cloud to spoil the view! As spring approaches, I suspect you too will be hopeful of better mornings, or to enjoy more in the summer.

Psalm 19 reminds us that the sun, alongside all creation, joyfully declares, proclaims and pours forth speech and knowledge about the glory of our creator. As lawyers, we love both speech and knowledge – using them all day long in the pursuit of justice. King David prompts us to remember that all we say and know needs to be put into perspective.

Our words are nothing compared to the one whose word and law is perfect and pure, true and sure, that revives, delights and endures forever. Sadly, the world may reject the Word of God and so injustice is inevitable. But rather than discourage us, may that drive our minds to ponder anew the Word of God that is firm and let our hearts rejoice in 'the Word' who saves us.

Whatever the weather be joyful and say, like David (v 14), the perfect Christian lawyer's prayer:

"Let the words of my mouth and the meditation of my heart be acceptable in your sight, O LORD, my rock and my redeemer." Psalm 19:14

- If you have time, read all of Psalm 19 now.
- Pray verse 14, above.
- Ask God to give you a renewed sense of his joy in his Word.

– Mark Barrell (2018)

27 MAR Hard wired to self-deception

Who can discern his errors?
Declare me innocent from hidden faults.
Keep back your servant also from presumptuous sins;
let them not have dominion over me!
Then I shall be blameless,
and innocent of great transgression.
Let the words of my mouth and the meditation of my heart be acceptable in your sight,
O LORD, my rock and my redeemer.

Psalm 19:12-14 (ESV)

Moving to a new firm involved a short period when I was between jobs, and for a short time I was living outside the 'skin' of a lawyer. This time taught me a few things about myself that I did not find very attractive. My identity was more wrapped up with what and who I was in the law than I had ever realised.

We might deny it, but the human heart is drawn to the trappings of status and identity, and we are hard wired to self-deception. Eugene Peterson paraphrases part of verse 13 as "Keep me from stupid sins, from thinking I can take over your work". Sometimes it is good to look in the mirror and say, "That's stupid".

As I draft up my new web profile and look to 'market' my offering, it provides a moment to pause and ask, "Who am I and in whom do I first seek to be identified?".

- Pray that the Lord may reveal those 'presumptuous' or 'stupid' sins and challenge us to deal with them.
- Pray for right motivations as we hunt down the work we are given to do.
- Pray for colleagues wrapped up in the law who may have lost touch with who they are and what they are doing.
- Pray that your 'words' and 'mediations' are acceptable in His sight.

– Brent Haywood (2015)

28 MAR What are you trusting in this morning?

Some trust in chariots and some in horses, but we trust in the name of the LORD our God. Psalm 20:7 (ESV)

Psalm 20 is an eve of battle Psalm. We might envisage David and his armies ready to march off to war. The people pray for the King, and he responds. All are confident that God will deliver the King, and through him, them. The background to verse 7 can be found in Deuteronomy 17:14-16. There, God said He would allow his people to have a King 'of His choosing', subject to the caveat that the King 'must not acquire many horses for himself' (ESV).

Some interpret this as a prohibition on keeping horses or chariots full stop, but I disagree. Rather, I think God was warning against accumulating resources in which the King and his people would anchor their trust, rather than relying on God.

In truth, do we not often trust in the wrong things: our expertise, our fee income, or our reputation? These are not bad things, but they must always be understood in terms of our paramount relationship: with God.

David could rightly be confident, because that wasn't where he was placing his trust. No, his trust was in God.

Where are you anchoring your trust this morning?

- *Pray that our hope wouldn't be in earthly things but that we would instead entrust everything to God.*

– Gavin Callaghan (2016)

29 MAR Lent for lawyers

Seven days from now I will send rain on the earth for forty days and forty nights …
And he stayed on the mountain forty days and forty nights.
At the end of forty days they returned from exploring the land …
 … and he was in the wilderness forty days, being tempted by Satan…

Genesis 7:4a, Exodus 24:18b, Numbers 13:25, Mark 1:13a (all NIV)

You may have been observing the season of Lent.

It is, of course, no accident that Lent lasts for about 40 days. Periods of 40 days (or 40 years) regularly occur in different contexts in the Bible, and there is often a special significance to the number 40.

Even if your church does not have a tradition of acknowledging Lent, is it something that would help your walk with the Lord this year?

John Piper calls Lent "the last blast of cold before the warm green is here to stay", and he advises us to "break a bad habit before Good Friday". [a]

What one or two bad habits can we pick on and seek to break before Easter?

But we also need to keep firmly in mind why we are doing this. As lawyers we perhaps easily fall into the trap of thinking that it is our works or our own efforts that solve things. To counteract this, it would probably be better for us if Lent was observed after Easter [b]: we would then first see that Jesus' death on the cross brought us salvation and then – out of thanks for that – we would seek God's help in observing Lent thereafter.

If you are observing some form of Lent this year, I hope and pray it would deepen your walk with the Lord and that He would use the time to break some bad habits. And I pray also that our hearts may recognise that our own attempts at breaking bad habits are (thankfully) not what saves us.

- Thank the Lord that He fixes the biggest problem in our lives – our sin.
- Pick one or two bad habits and pray that the Lord by His Holy Spirit would break the hold they have on you this Lent.

a. www.desiringgod.org/articles/lenten-preparations-for-good-friday-and-easter

b. I gratefully acknowledge Rev Glen Scrivener (www.christthetruth.net) for this idea. He also reminds us that the Feast of Unleavened Bread begins with Passover.

– Dominic Hughes (2016)

30 MAR The Lord has need of you!

… then Jesus sent two disciples, saying to them, "Go into the village opposite you, and immediately you will find a donkey tied, and a colt with her. Loose them and bring them to Me. And if anyone says anything to you, you shall say, 'The Lord has need of them,' and immediately he will send them." All this was done that it might be fulfilled which was spoken by the prophet … Matthew 21:1-4 (NKJV)

Meditating on this part of the Palm Sunday narrative, I was struck by two things. First, that God's sovereign intention to introduce His Son in fulfilment of great promises in the Old Testament, depended on an unnamed servant of God and his resources being in the right place at the right time. We get so caught up in our own lives that we sometimes forget to step back and see that God is at work in eternity and we have a part to play in His plan. As lawyers, we have the immense privilege of being involved in seeking justice; whether it be to draft a statute or a will, to sit on the High Court bench or to represent a mother accused of shoplifting in a Magistrates' Court.

The second thing is to be ready to serve whenever God calls us and in whatever capacity. We may think we're too busy or sometimes if we're honest, too important to carry out humble tasks: free legal advice to a Christian charity, being a driver for the youth meeting, standing with an open-air speaker in our lunch break.

"Immediately", in our reading, brooks no hesitation or questions, but rather faithful obedience.

Our Saviour didn't let importance, busyness or self-regard get in the way of obedience to His Father by dying for sinners.

- *In this season of Lent and Easter, take time to reflect on God's sovereign plan and the wonderful gift of reconciliation we have through His Son.*
- *Ask the Lord to show you where he wants you to serve Him, in whatever capacity that might be in the next week.*

– Esther Harrison (2017)

31 MAR Take courage!

Jesus answered and said unto them, Destroy this temple, and in three days I will raise it up. Then said the Jews, Forty and six years was this temple in building, and wilt thou rear it up in three days? But he spake of the temple of his body. **John 2:19-21 (KJV)**

This is the crowning proof of the Lord Jesus' divinity, for it was God who raised the Lord Jesus from the dead (Colossians 2:19). The Lord Jesus was claiming that, as God, He would raise up his own body from the grave after his death on the cross. The Father and the Holy Spirit raised Christ from the dead (Galatians 1:1 and Romans 8:11). There is nothing that one person of the Trinity does which does not involve the others since all are One and yet distinct persons.

By rejecting Christ's claim of divinity and crucifying him instead, the Jews proved the truth of it. They also unwittingly offered the only acceptable sacrifice for sin to which their temple sacrifices pointed.

Ironically, it was the Jews who lost their temple. God not only raised up the temple the Jews had destroyed but built many more in the hearts of every believer (1 Corinthians 6:19).

Does it seem as though evil triumphs in your work as a lawyer? If God can turn even the execution of his beloved Son to His and our advantage, nothing is too difficult for Him. Let us take courage!

- *Praise God for the hope we have in the resurrection of our divine Lord.*
- *Pray that this Easter time we would take every opportunity to point others to that sure and certain hope of eternal life in Christ.*

– Mark Mullins (2018)

1 APR Are you really in control?

… Jesus answered, "You are right in saying I am a king. In fact, for this reason I was born, and for this I came into the world, to testify to the truth. Everyone on the side of truth listens to me." **John 18:37 (NIV 1984)**

In one of the most significant court scenes in history the powerful Roman governor, Pilate, stood in judgment on Jesus deciding whether he was to live or die. The scene is deeply paradoxical: Pilate only had power because it had been conferred on him by God (Romans 13:1), he was playing his part in God's pre-ordained plan, and he had no notion that he was judging the ultimate judge of all mankind.

Pilate's own eternal destiny was decided by whether or not he would listen to Jesus, whether he would accept Jesus' testimony about the truth and whether he was prepared to accept him as king – whether during Jesus' trial or subsequently. The prisoner was in fact the judge, the judge was appointed by the prisoner, and the judge's response to the prisoner's own questions would ultimately determine his future.

How humbling for lawyers who appear to be in control and what a spur to testify to others of the truth about Jesus.

- *Give thanks to the Lord for His wonderful gift of grace, and recommit yourself and all you do into the hands of the King of Kings this morning.*
- *Ask the Lord to guide you in all truth this week and for a willingness to share the truth with others.*

– Rev. Ian Miller (2016)

2 APR A lawyer's greatest problem

And you, who were dead in your trespasses and the uncircumcision of your flesh, God made alive together with him, having forgiven us all our trespasses, by cancelling the record of debt that stood against us with its legal demands. This he set aside, nailing it to the cross. He disarmed the rulers and authorities and put them to open shame, by triumphing over them in him.
Colossians 2:13-15 (ESV)

What's your greatest problem? Fee targets? Too much work, or too little? A difficult boss or client? All of these can have a big impact on us. But for any lawyer, the greatest problem is sin. Everything else pales into insignificance in comparison.

But praise God that in Christ Jesus, our sins can be forgiven. On the cross, the record of our sin was cancelled, and our forgiveness was secured. Horatio Spafford reflected this so beautifully when he wrote:

"My sin, oh, the bliss of this glorious thought!
My sin, not in part but the whole,
Is nailed to the cross and I bear it no more,
Praise the Lord, praise the Lord, O my soul!" *

This Easter, amid all the pressures we face, let's rejoice in the forgiveness secured for us on the cross, and be sure to tell others of it too. The news is far too good to keep to ourselves!

*From 'When peace, like a river' by Horatio Spafford.
- Give thanks for God's indescribable gift of grace in Jesus.
- Ask that the Lord will over this Easter time give you the peace and joy of knowing that everything is safe in His hands, whatever the problem or pressure you face.

– Gavin Callaghan (2016)

3 APR Turning Points

Stand at the crossroads and look, ask for the ancient paths, ask where the good way is and walk in it, and you will find rest for your souls. **Jeremiah 6:16 (NIV)**

"At the next junction turn left" says the voice from the dashboard. We know where we want to get to – our destination – but often we are not sure which way to turn. We stand at the crossroads and look. Which way now we wonder?

If you are at a crossroads – perhaps not sure how to advise a client or how to present her case to the Court or how to cope with some unexpected happening at work – why not follow the wisdom of Jeremiah by asking God where the good way is, then be guided by Him, follow His advice and find rest.

- Ask God to guide you in all the decisions that you make this week and seek His wisdom in all that you do.

– John Head (2015)

4 APR Hope in hard times

Restore us to yourself, LORD, that we may return; renew our days as of old unless you have utterly rejected us and are angry with us beyond measure. **Lamentations 5:21-22 (NIV)**

The book of Lamentations is a book about faith in the hard times, about trust in God in the face of overwhelming circumstances. It describes the raw grief, deep anguish and tortured desperation of existence in the ruins of a city which has fallen to ruthless conquerors. The writer calls out to God to restore God's people, and he does so in faith because he knows that God's compassion never fails (Lamentations 3:22).

All of us face difficult circumstances, sometimes at home, sometimes at work, sometimes because of our own fault and sometimes because of the unreasonable behaviour of others. Lamentations reminds us that God's ears are open to our honest prayers about how tough we are finding it, that God is capable of bringing renewal where all hope is gone, and that even when we feel that what we have done is unforgiveable, God reaches out in Christ to all who truly repent.

- Offer your difficult circumstances to God this morning and ask him to bring renewal into those situations. If repentance is needed then seek the Lord's forgiveness, and remember he is faithful and just.

- Pray for your clients – especially those whose situation needs restoration and renewal – and for opportunities to share the good news of Christ.

– Dr David McIlroy (2015)

5 APR 'The truth, the whole truth and nothing but the truth'?

I am the way and the truth and the life. John 14:6a (NIV 1984)

Jesus claims to be 'the truth'. It is clear from his statement that there is no independent truth which exists outside God (Father, Son and Spirit). You cannot ask the question how God or Christianity match up to some independently existing and freestanding truth because God is truth.

Take away absolute truth and you take away the only secure foundation for a system of morality or a legal system. Take away absolute truth and you take away the foundations of society: kingdoms will break up, political systems will fragment, dishonesty will abound, and everyone will do as they see fit (Judges 21:25).

As we see so many of these things occurring around us, Christian lawyers must look to God in every situation we deal with as there is no truth outside Him. May God help us to work for truth, for Him, this week in all that we do.

- Ask God to guide you in His truth in your work for Him this week.

– Rev. Ian Miller (2015)

6 APR Captivated witnesses to Jesus' love

When Jesus saw his mother and the disciple whom he loved standing nearby, he said to his mother, "Woman, behold, your son!" Then he said to the disciple, "Behold, your mother!" And from that hour the disciple took her to his own home. John 19:26-27 (ESV)

When Jesus was crucified, he saw Mary his mother and one of his disciples standing nearby. The disciple whom Jesus saw is referred to here in John's Gospel, not by his name, but by the fact that Jesus loved him; he was the disciple whom Jesus loved.

It is apparent from other references in John's Gospel that this anonymous disciple was the Gospel writer. When writing his Jesus biography, the author chose to define his witness identity not by his name, nor by his achievements, but by his relationship to Christ – He loved me!

As the Gospel author remembers Jesus on the Cross – the place where Jesus demonstrated the extent of God's love for His people, by suffering the punishment for our sin in our place – he is captivated by his realisation of Jesus' love towards him.

Lawyers can so easily trade on their name and their achievements. This Easter time, as we reflect on the Cross, and all that this event tells us about who Jesus is and what He has done, may we like the Gospel author be captivated by Jesus and His love for us. As a result, may God help us to esteem Jesus above our own reputation and ambitions, so that through our witness to Him, others may come to believe that Jesus is the Son of God, God's Saviour-King, and by believing have life in His name.

- *Confess times when you have put your name and reputation as a lawyer before your commission to be a witness for Christ. Ask God to renew and enlarge your love for Jesus, and your appreciation for all that He has done.*
- *Ask God to give you opportunities this Easter time to speak to colleagues about the hope that you have in Jesus, that they may have life in His name.*

– Mark Bainbridge (2019)

7 APR — Jesus' sacrificial atonement – the permanent solution

… but God shows his love for us in that while we were still sinners, Christ died for us. Since, therefore, we have now been justified by his blood, much more shall we be saved by him from the wrath of God. For if while we were enemies we were reconciled to God by the death of his Son, much more, now that we are reconciled, shall we be saved by his life. Romans 5:8-10 (ESV)

As lawyers, we are often called upon to provide water-tight solutions that will stand the test of time to our clients' legal problems. Of course, most of our solutions only ever remain valid for as long as the applicable legal and cultural rules remain unchanged, or until technological advances force a re-think.

The greatest problem facing humanity is the wrath of, and separation from, God, caused by our sin – for all have sinned and fallen short of the glory of God (Romans 3:23). In His loving mercy, whilst we were still sinners, God gave his only Son as the atoning sacrifice for our sins (1 John 4:9-10). As He hung on the cross, bruised, beaten and forsaken, Jesus paid the price for your sin and mine, once and for all.

As we ponder the events that took place in Golgotha in Jerusalem many years ago, let us give thanks to God that He offers the permanent (and only) solution. For those who put their trust in Him, Jesus Christ's death on the cross and resurrection three days later achieves that which humanity so greatly needs – forgiveness of our sins and eternal reconciliation with God the Father.

- *Thank God for His loving mercy in rescuing us from our sinful nature and redeeming us through the blood of Christ.*

- *Ask God for boldness in sharing the true Easter message and the free offer of forgiveness and salvation made possible only as a result of Jesus' atoning sacrifice.*

– Kiki Alo (2019)

8 APR — Hope in the midst of a pandemic

God raised him up, loosing the pangs of death, because it was not possible for him to be held by it. **Acts 2:24 (ESV)**

As someone who temperamentally does not readily tolerate uncertainty, the uncertain days of the pandemic were challenging. During recent medical difficulties (in simpler times, before Covid-19) I found myself repeatedly peppering hospital staff with leading questions, the sole purpose of which being to manoeuvre them into reassuring me that all would be well health-wise.

As humans, we treasure our health, because the fear of death so often stalks us. Consequently, the uncertainties of a pandemic can seem unbearable.

Will we, or those precious to us, fall victim to a virus? Will we stand by our loved ones' graves, or will they stand by ours? Will we have jobs, or firms, or practices to return to when it is over?

At Easter, we utter those familiar words: Christ is risen – he is risen indeed!

Amidst all uncertainty, we hold this certainty above all. Christ came. He lived a sinless life. He died an atoning death. He rose again.

And because of that, as Christians we can look with confidence beyond a pandemic. We know that death for the Christian is not the end. Illness and death ultimately do not control our destiny.

Because of Easter, Christ does. And in him, we have the promise of being in the place where *"death shall be no more"* (Rev 21:4).

- *Pray for those within our profession facing financial and health concerns.*
- *Pray that during uncertain and challenging times we would have confidence in Christ, and for opportunities to share our faith, and the courage to take them!*

– Gavin Callaghan (2020)

9 APR — Silent witness

He who saw it has borne witness – his testimony is true, and he knows that he is telling the truth – that you also may believe. **John 19:35, 21:24, 19:38 (ESV)**

Direct evidence is powerful. A witness relates what he/she has seen, heard or experienced so that others may know the truth about what happened.

The gospel of John is eyewitness evidence of both the death and resurrection of Jesus – the central core of our faith. Joseph of Arimathea was a secret follower of Jesus until the death of Jesus drove him to reveal his discipleship to the cynical governor who had condemned Jesus to death.

No silent witnesses.

Are we seeking to be silent witnesses? It can't be done, can it?

May our lives and our words give evidence of the risen Jesus and His Lordship over us. May we be able to point others to the direct eyewitness evidence of his death and resurrection so that they may believe that Jesus is the Christ, the Son of God and by believing have life in His Name (John 20:31, ESV).

- *Praise God for the hope we have in the resurrection of the Lord Jesus.*
- *Pray that this Easter time we would take every opportunity to point others to the evidence of Jesus' death and resurrection, so that they may believe in Him and have life in His name.*

– Sir Jeremy Cooke (2019)

10 APR St Patrick – the Patron Saint of Ireland & Grand Slams

Surely, Lord, you bless the righteous; you surround them with your favour as with a shield. **Psalm 5:12 (NIV)**

I presume it is a coincidence that the only contributor from Ireland is submitting his Word for the Week for Easter Monday on St Patrick's Day, coinciding with another Irish Six Nations Grand Slam?

The story of St Patrick is well known – his capture in his youth, escape from slavery in Ireland, voluntary return after a vision to evangelise his former captors (though not the secondary motive of ensuring his eligibility for their rugby team under the residency rule!), and his subsequent banishing of the snakes and illustration of the trinity with the shamrock (before his audience drowned it).

Perhaps his most enduring spiritual legacy for the modern church, however, is St Patrick's Breastplate, his prayer of protection.

As we hopefully enjoy a short break from work after the spiritual refreshment of the celebration of Easter, as the Psalm above reminds us, we should continue to bind ourselves to the virtue of the crucifixion and resurrection. Also, echoing St Patrick's, we can pray that Christ is with us, before us, behind us, within us, beneath us, above us, at our right and at our left, and also in the heart of everyone who thinks of us, the mouth of everyone who speaks to us, the eye of everyone who sees us and the ear of everyone who hears us, both today and when many of us return to our legal roles later this week.

- *Pray that we would be conscious of God surrounding us individually and corporately in everything we do at work, at home and at church this week.*
- *Pray that all those with whom we come into contact in all those contexts should see, hear and experience God in us.*

– Peter Brown (2018)

11 APR — Thine be the glory, risen conquering Son

For in Christ all the fullness of the Deity lives in bodily form, and in Christ you have been brought to fullness. He is the head over every power and authority.
Colossians 2:9-10 (NIV)

This Easter time I hope you are able to celebrate again the amazing truth of Jesus' resurrection, whether online or in person. As St Paul goes on to tell us, the cross has taken away the sin that condemned us before God, and has confirmed Jesus' complete victory over the "powers and authorities" mentioned above (vs 13-15). What good news!

Perhaps we can nevertheless feel discouraged that we do not yet experience the fullness of Jesus' triumph in our lives and practices. Relationships with colleagues, clients and other professionals can be fraught. The weight and pressures of our work can feel immense, the cases we deal with intractable. Jesus may not be honoured, or even acknowledged, in our workplaces, where financial targets and personalities seem to rule.

If so, let us be encouraged by Paul's reminder of how the universe really is. Jesus is supreme and has triumphed over all of His enemies, and all powers and authorities, through the cross. In the same way, we have been made alive in Him (v 13).

Therefore, let us lift up our eyes again to Jesus, and give Him His rightful place of supremacy as we go about the legal work that He has given us to do. Let us also ask Him for all that we need to do it, from the fullness to which He has brought us.

- *Give thanks to God for Jesus' complete victory over sin and death, and every power and authority, through the cross.*
- *Lift your week up to God, and ask Him to help you live it in light of Jesus' supremacy, and in the fullness to which He has brought you.*

The title of this contribution is derived from the name of the well-known hymn which was written by Edmond Louis Budry and translated by Richard Birch Hoyle.

– Jon Hyde (2021)

12 APR — Beyond redemption

Two others, who were criminals, were led away to be put to death with him ... One of the criminals who were hanged railed at him, saying, 'Are you not the Christ? Save yourself and us!' But the other rebuked him, saying, 'Do you not fear God, since you are under the same sentence of condemnation? And we indeed justly, for we are receiving the due reward of our deeds; but this man has done nothing wrong.' And he said, 'Jesus, remember me when you come into your kingdom.' And he said to him, 'Truly, I say to you, today you will be with me in Paradise.' **Luke 23:32, 39-43 (ESV)**

Meditating about the Cross last Good Friday, I was particularly drawn to Luke's account of the two criminals who died with Jesus. The two criminals were bound (as we all are) to either reject Jesus or embrace him. Whatever our earthly misdemeanours and fate, we can call on Jesus' name, and, if we do so, we have the assurance of eternal life with Jesus in Paradise. It is not (and is never) too late for anybody to put their faith in Jesus and repent – so long as they do!

It is a feature of many of our lives as lawyers that we have to deal with some very wicked people who have done awful things, or who appear to have rejected Jesus. It is all too easy for us to write them off as beyond redemption, and for us to consider ourselves superior to them in the eyes of God forgetting our own sins. To do so is, of course, quite wrong. The Kingdom of God is open to all who turn to Jesus.

- *Pray that prisoners and other offenders, and those who appear to have rejected Jesus, might come to fear God, and call on Jesus' name, and that God will strengthen and support all those involved in ministry to prisoners and other offenders;*
- *Be grateful that we have so much to thank God for in sending his Son to die on the Cross for our sins so that all who believe might have the sure hope of eternal life in Paradise, and that we might use every opportunity that we have to share this Gospel message.*

– HHJ Mark Cawson KC (2016)

13 APR — Reporting for Duty

Simon Peter said to them, 'I am going fishing.' **John 21:3a (NKJV)**

In our legal careers we experience high spots, low spots and ordinary spots. There are memorable cases, important clients and interesting experiences; but at other times, professional life can appear somewhat dull. At the first Easter, the disciples had an amazing and unforgettable experience; but a week after the resurrection Jesus disappeared. Then we read in John

21 that sometime after that some of the disciples were together when Peter said he was going fishing. So, following all that had happened, life had to continue as normal for the time being. (The disciples were not to know that there would be another momentous experience the following morning.)

In the course of our professional work, life has to continue regardless of the importance of the work at hand. We need to report for duty, so to speak. It is the same in the Christian life. There will be some uplifting and memorable experiences when we see God at work. At other times when nothing of real interest seems to be happening, we need to go forward in obedience and faith, reporting for duty, knowing that He is in control, come what may, day by day.

God is still on the throne,
And He will remember his own,
Though trials may press us and burdens distress us,
He never will leave us alone.
God is still on the throne,
He will never forsake his own,
His promise is true, he will not forget you,
God is still on the throne.

Words & Music: Kittie Suffield, 1929

The LORD is my shepherd, I lack nothing.

Psalm 23:1 (NIV)

- Help us, Lord, to report for duty willingly no matter the task at hand each day, whether it be interesting, important or dull and keep us faithfully to our calling.
- Pray for members of the profession who working in difficult circumstances.

– HH Alan Taylor (2021)

14 APR A refreshed soul

The LORD is my shepherd, I lack nothing. He makes me lie down in green pastures, he leads me beside quiet waters, he refreshes my soul. **Psalm 23:1-3 (NIV)**

Perhaps this passage from the psalms is familiar, but it is easy to rush past. Many of us work or study in pressurised, busy environments, where anxiety and stress have become the norm, where moaning is commonplace, and where peace is not easily found.

We are not immune to such things, but we do have a shepherd who wants to lead us to places and spaces where he can refresh us from the inside out. Learning to follow him there and 'lie down' can be challenging if your mind is still on the 'to-do' list. Perhaps we need to be more intentional about making that time to be still and spend time with our risen Lord.

Even as David struggled with internal and external battles, he found the Lord leading him to green pastures and quiet waters – places where he could be refreshed and regain focus, being reminded of who God is, even in the midst of surrounding chaos. As we still ourselves, sit for a moment, take the time to rest, we may find ourselves similarly reminded that God is the Lord Almighty, our shepherd, and He is with us.

Do you need to make time to allow God to refresh your soul?

- Thank God for the refreshment that he offers (and take the time to receive it!)
- Ask God for opportunities to share the soul-refreshing hope that we have in Jesus with colleagues and friends.

– Naomi Cooke (2019)

15 APR Clean hands and a pure heart

Who may ascend the mountain of the LORD? Who may stand in His holy place? The one who has clean hands and a pure heart …
… if we walk in the light, as He is in the light, we have fellowship with one another, and the blood of Jesus, His Son, purifies us from all sin.
Psalm 24:3-4a (NIV) and 1 John 1:7 (NIV)

What does it mean to have 'clean hands and a pure heart'?

Whatever your view about politicians in the light of recent developments, we are reminded of the need to be honest and act properly. To have 'clean hands and a pure heart', we need to be honest, humbly admitting our wrongs. We then must demonstrate the sincerity of that honesty by our changed attitude and conduct.

It's one thing to recognise those needs in others. But do we live that way ourselves, both in our professional lives as lawyers and in our personal lives as Christians? Are we good examples to others? It is easy to criticise politicians of all parties. But how brightly does our light shine?

God uses those principles of honesty and humility to bring a sinner to repentance and forgiveness. But we are not just forgiven: the 'blood of Jesus, His Son, purifies us from all sin'. And no Christian need live for Christ daily without continuing to be honest: we are offered purification both from wrong things we do ('hands') and also the downward drag of sin in our hearts that we allow too often to control or influence our lives.

So, fellow Christian lawyers, are you and I seeking to live to please our Sovereign Lord from a 'pure heart' and with 'clean hands' in full view of all with whom we meet or deal each day?

- *How often do we stand back and take an objective look at what we have done in the last 24 hours that did not come from 'clean hands' or was as a result of our hearts not being pure?*
- *Do we seek wholeheartedly God's cleansing and purification in humbly confessing our sins and forsaking them?*

– Gerard Chrispin (2022)

16 APR Asking God for "one thing"

One thing have I asked of the Lord, that I will seek after: that I may dwell in the house of the LORD all the days of my life, to gaze upon the beauty of the LORD and to enquire in his temple. **Psalm 27:4 (ESV, 2001)**

What are we to pray at the beginning of another busy week with all the pressures which come with being a lawyer? You may have many things on your mind as David did in this Psalm: from the first few verses it would seem he struggled with evil men advancing on him, enemies and foes attacking, the prospect of a siege and war breaking out against him.

David prays "one thing", namely, to gaze upon the beauty of the Lord and to enquire of Him. He is preoccupied with God's Person and His will. Paul reminds us that if we seek to gaze upon God then we should look to the gospel which reveals the face of Jesus (2 Cor 4:4,6).

There is no better starting point for our prayer this week than David's "one thing": desiring God for who He is – for his beauty, light, holiness, goodness, graciousness, for all those qualities which cannot be reduced to mere words – and desiring his will.

- At vs 8-9 David prays: *"Your face, LORD, do I seek. Hide not your face from me."* Pray that we might know the blessing of God's face shining upon us this week and that His will would be done in our lives.
- In the light of Psalm 27:4, pray for the particular tasks and issues you face this week.

– Rev. Ian Miller (2016)

17 APR Your times are in His hands

Into your hands, I commit my Spirit, redeem me O LORD, the God of truth.
But I trust in you, O LORD; I say, "You are my God."
My times are in your hands …

Psalm 31:5, 14-15a (NIV 1984)

When there is no other source of help, consolation or hope, the writer of this Psalm places himself in the hands of His God in words that Jesus later echoes on the cross. He expresses his confidence in the Lord, the one who remains true, who can be trusted and who is in control of all that happens and redeems by using even the evil acts of those opposed to Him to achieve His purposes.

Our times are in His hands too. The terrible things that happened to you years ago; what happened yesterday; what happens today; what will happen tomorrow and every day until He calls you home. Wherever God has placed you this Monday morning – law firm, chambers, university – and whatever lies ahead this week, remember, your times are in His hands and He will bring you through. Be strong and take heart, all you who hope in the Lord (v 24).

Praise God that he is in control of all things at all times.

– Sir Jeremy Cooke (2020)

18 APR Be bold, be strong

Be strong, and let your heart take courage, all you who wait for the LORD! **Psalm 31:24 (ESV)**

There are periods in our personal and professional lives that are shrouded in uncertainty, disappointment and, sometimes, pain. These periods (whether it be marked by the loss of employment or a training opportunity, a toxic environment in the office or in chambers or stress induced health issues) can be overwhelming, lead to deep anxiety and cause us to question if, and when, God will intervene.

The Bible is full of accounts of God taking seemingly hopeless situations and using them for His glory. It is often in the impossible moments, and when all is surrendered to God, that He breaks in and does something extraordinary. We see that in the accounts of David and Goliath, Gideon and the Midianites, Joshua and the walls of Jericho and, most significantly, in the death and resurrection of Jesus Christ.

Recent times have presented challenges for many of us. For some, these challenges did not start with the pandemic and have not ended. Today's passage reminds all of us who put our hope in the Lord to be strong and courageous. This is not a call to take up more exercise (as important as that is in maintaining physical and mental health), but to face all challenges in life with spiritual strength and courage, for the Lord our God is with us (Judges 6:16; Joshua 1:9; Isaiah 41:10).

Whatever age, stage or circumstance that we are in, may we bold, be strong and take heart, for our Heavenly Father is with us.

- *Thank God that He is with us in every circumstance in our lives.*
- *Ask God to help us not to lean on our human understanding and strength, but to fully place our hope and trust in Him at all times.*
- *Ask God to help us to be bold and courageous in our thinking and doing, that His name be glorified as a result.*

– Kiki Alo (2020)

19 APR — May counsel receive counsel

You are my hiding place;
you will protect me from trouble
and surround me with songs of deliverance.
I will instruct you and teach you in the way you should go;
I will counsel you with my loving eye on you.
Do not be like the horse or the mule,
which have no understanding
but must be controlled by bit and bridle
or they will not come to you.

Psalm 32:7-9 (NIV)

It is perhaps encouraging to know that "making a difference to people's lives" is still one of the top 10 reasons my students give for wanting to become lawyers. Indeed, many lawyers will continue to use their God-given gifts to advise clients on law and processes, and on making wise decisions for relationships and projects alike. Praise God.

Psalm 32 contains an important reminder to those who counsel others, that they must also be counselled. How reassuring it is that the God of the universe wants to instruct us and teach us in the way we should go – and with His loving eye on us (v 8).

But there is also a warning to us in verse 9. We are not to become like the horse or the mule who have no understanding in the things of God and who must be controlled by bit and bridle. We have a God who wants to instruct and teach us, but do we make ourselves teachable or ready to be guided?

In the beginning of Psalm 32, David experiences the deep relief of knowing God's complete forgiveness of his confessed sin, so fully covered that he could call God his "hiding place" (v 7). Let us make sure we hear His voice as we read His Word daily; allow His Spirit to convict us of our sin; know the blessing of forgiveness through Jesus Christ's covering of our sin and respond in humility in service of Christ in the law.

Let's pray
- *That whether we are experienced advisers or just beginning a career in the law, we would always look to surrender our wills to be instructed, taught and counselled by God himself.*
- *That we would all know the blessing of forgiveness through Jesus Christ's covering of our sin, and that we would respond in humility in service of Christ in the law.*

– Debbie Woods (2018)

20 APR Be still and know

God is our refuge and strength, an ever-present help in trouble. Therefore we will not fear …. Psalm 46:1-2a (NIV)

Dover Castle, with its great Norman keep, stands on top of Castle Hill overlooking the town and ferry port far below. Additions were made to protect against the French in Napoleonic times with an underground hospital and operations centre built during the last war.

It has never been breached.

The Psalmist reminds us that God is our refuge and strength – an idea used in more than one Psalm (see Psalm 62) – therefore we will not fear.

Later in the same Psalm we are exhorted to "Be still and know that I am God".

It is good to take this Psalm to heart. When you get into your workplace this morning, and before you switch on your computer and get involved in the often frantic pace of a lawyer's life, why not be still, and reflect on the refuge God provides, especially in times of trouble?

Unlike the man-made castle standing proudly on the hill above Dover, we have something far better – a heavenly fortress as an ever-present refuge in times of trouble.

- *Praise God that He is our refuge and strength.*
- *Pray that God would help you to be still this morning.*
- *Consider situations this week where you may need peace, and commit them to the Lord.*

– John Head (2020)

21 APR — God is still on the throne

God is our refuge and strength, an ever-present help in trouble. Therefore we will not fear, though the earth give way and the mountains fall into the heart of the sea, though its waters roar and foam and the mountains quake with their surging. **Psalm 46:1-3 (NIV)**

Over the past few weeks [In October 2017] we have heard of several enormous storms which have affected the Caribbean areas, causing untold physical destruction and loss. As lawyers in England, we seldom have to deal with the aftermath of these events but we do often have to deal with people whose lifestyles and livelihoods are just as badly affected; people who have "lost everything" or whose lives have been changed beyond measure due to totally unexpected events. Do we try to imagine what it must it be like to experience such devastating changes?

The Psalmist takes shelter in his belief that God is ever present, a refuge and strong enough to uphold us come what may. If you have recently experienced such a blow or if you have a client who has, we know that we cannot turn the clock back. We have to go forward in faith, knowing that God is in control of our lives and trusting that he knows best. Can people see this in our personal and professional lives?

Jesus faced the ultimate change in circumstances on the cross, committing his spirit into his Father's hands (Luke 23:46). In the final analysis this is all a believer can do, but in the meantime we can show by our lives where we stand. "Therefore put on the full armour of God, so that when the day of evil comes, you may be able to stand your ground, and after you have done everything, to stand." (Ephesians 6:13)

- *Give praise to our loving heavenly Father, for who He is and that whatever the situation He remains sovereign.*
- *Pray for those known to you who are going through troubled times: clients, colleagues and friends. Ask that in the midst they may discover the peace that only comes from making Christ Jesus the Lord of their life.*

– HH Alan Taylor (2017)

22 APR — The ultimate peacemaker

He maketh wars to cease unto the end of the earth; he breaketh the bow, and cutteth the spear in sunder; he burneth the chariot in the fire. **Psalm 46:9 (KJV)**

This verse reminds us that it is God who brings wars to an end. That is why Parliament attended a service of thanksgiving on the day of the Armistice in 1918.

But how did such a terrible war begin in the first place? James 4:1 gives us the answer: "From whence come wars and fightings among you? Come they not hence, even of your lusts that war in your members?"

The First World War started in the hearts of the rulers of the great nations of the world just as every war does.

The principle that governs wars applies equally to litigation which is of course war on a different front.

The same God who stops war also brings an end to litigation. I hope we all pray for our cases remembering that, for those cases that end up before a judge/jury, the heart of the king is in the Lord's hand (Proverbs 21:1).

Litigation, like wars, will be with us until the human heart is changed in this life by the New Birth, and finally at the Second Coming of the Lord Jesus Christ.

- *Pray for your caseload this week, that God's will would be done and peace would be accomplished.*
- *Pray for opportunities to tell our clients and colleagues the Gospel, so that they would come to a saving knowledge of the Lord Jesus Christ.*
- *Pray that we would all be living our lives in readiness for the Second Coming of the Lord Jesus Christ.*

– Mark Mullins (2018)

23 APR — Get off the phone, and from behind your desk and look outside …

He says, 'Be still, and know that I am God; I will be exalted among the nations, I will be exalted in the earth.' **Psalm 46:10 (NIV)**

As busy lawyers, we find it difficult to be still and hard to remember who is God. It is all too easy for us to think that we are God, on a mission to save our clients or capable of controlling everything. Or we can treat our clients or our bosses as God, crossing the line from serving them well to letting them impose unreasonable demands on us.

Take some time this week to be still, to get away from your desk and to put away your smartphone, and to go outside. Look at the beauty of creation as summer gives way to autumn and remember: remember that we serve the Lord God, who loves us, and who is glorious.

- *Give thanks that the Lord of hosts, the creator, is with you and that you serve Him in all His glorious splendour.*
- *Pray for your fellow Christian lawyers who today are stressed and worried, and ask that they may know the peace and presence of God.*

– Dr David McIlroy (2016)

24 APR — The dangerous side of risk management

Why should I fear when evil days come,
when wicked deceivers surround me –
those who trust in their wealth and boast of their
great riches?
No one can redeem the life of another
or give to God a ransom for them –
the ransom for a life is costly,
no payment is ever enough –
so that they should live on for ever
and not see decay.

Psalm 49:5-9 (NIV)

In these verses "wealth" is shorthand for self-sufficiency and independence. Those who are rich are more likely to feel safe, and to think they can buy their way out of difficulty. Later on in the psalm, the writer talks about the wealthy as "those who trust in themselves".

Much of the practice of law involves helping people to avoid or minimise risk. But the continual practice of risk mitigation can have dangerous side-effects. We can easily develop habits of mind and heart that lead us to believe we can protect ourselves from harm – that we can trust in our own strategies for life, and to secure what is good.

The psalm reminds us that nothing – no amount of wealth or other form of earthly security – can protect us from death, or buy us eternal life. It is a brutal reality. But the psalm also gives us a beautiful glimpse of the gospel. Confronted by our incapacity in the face of death, we are thrown into dependence on God who alone can rescue us, and on his Son who gave himself up for us, paying the price of his own life so that we might live for ever. We are humbled by the rebuke to our pretence at self-sufficiency. And we are prompted to praise him for the free gift of eternal life that he has bought for us, at such great cost to himself.

- *Pray that God would guard us against the deceitfulness of wealth (whether we have it or not!).*
- *Pray that we would keep on putting our trust in God who rescues us, rather than in the earthly things we think will make us safe.*
- *Pray that this Easter we would take every opportunity to point others to the hope of eternal life in Christ.*

– Caroline Eade (2016)

25 APR — The hardest word?

The sacrifices of God are a broken spirit;
A broken and contrite heart, O God, you will not despise.

Psalm 51:17 (ESV)

Apologising or saying "sorry" is not something that tends to come easily to lawyers. We live and work in a world where weakness is not meant to be shown and mistakes are rarely acknowledged.

King David also initially found it difficult to admit to his mistakes: it was only after he was confronted by the prophet Nathan that he confessed to adultery with Bathsheba and the murder of her husband, Uriah. Yet what David eventually realised is that no mistake or sin can ever be covered up from an omniscient God. Even as a mature believer, David had committed a serious offence against God and needed to come clean and confess his guilt.

But David also knew that God is full of love and mercy (v 1) and forgives all who truly repent. When we confess our sins with a broken and contrite heart (v 17) then our gracious God will wash and cleanse us (v 2) and amazingly we shall become whiter than snow (v 7): as if nothing had ever happened! Having then experienced His forgiveness, we can confidently pray to our loving Heavenly Father that He will restore to us the joy of his salvation (v 12).

- *What might you need to confess to God this week? Pray that we would truly repent in areas we need to change.*
- *Ask that God would restore to us the joy of His salvation and make us eager to share the message of forgiveness with friends and colleagues.*

– Adam McRae-Taylor (2016)

26 APR Fearless faith for fearless times

When I am afraid, I put my trust in you. Psalm 56:3 (ESV)

During the pandemic many of us will have lived with more fear than we have likely known in our lifetimes. We questioned: what if I contract the virus? Will I survive? What will the long-term impact be? What if a loved one becomes ill?

Maybe some of us now have fears for the future when we see instructions drying up, fee targets missed, or face redundancy.

Such feelings are, of course, a natural and legitimate response to the frightening situation.

Some of us will have become ill, some of us have died. My own church grieved the loss of a much-loved and inspirational Deacon who died of Covid-19. We grieved his loss and for his family. But we grieved knowing that, for him, he has ultimately been healed and is now safe with the Saviour he loved.

We may be afraid, but we can lift our eyes to our Saviour who will never let us be snatched from his hands. To our sovereign God who is working out his purposes – even in the midst of this pandemic.

None of us can guarantee, in a worldly sense, that it will all be all right. But as Christians, in an eternal sense, we know it will be.

- Pray that, amid the fear and uncertainty of these times, that you would act as a faithful and fearless witness to the hope we have in Christ.
- Pray specifically for two or three colleagues, that you will have (and take) the opportunity to tell them of the hope you have in Christ.

– Gavin Callaghan (2021)

27 APR Bottled tears

You have kept count of my tossings;
put my tears in your bottle.
Are they not in your book?
Then my enemies will turn back
in the day when I call.
This I know, that God is for me.

Psalm 56:8-9 (ESV)

The Covid-19 lockdown saw courts closed and lives put on hold. We surveyed damage all around. There were redundancies, businesses lost and much misery. And the consequences are still with us.

David wrote Psalm 56 from lockdown. He was a prisoner in enemy hands. Yet he was confident that God saw his troubles. His distress mattered enough to God for his tears to be collected up and bottled. He put his case before the Lord, not in written pleadings, but in tears, and God recorded the plea in His book. David was confident that God would make His judgment and act. Escape was at hand.

Tears are not futile. Our Saviour wept over Jerusalem. He wept at the graveside of his friend Lazarus, and most significantly he was in agony in the garden of Gethsemane as he contemplated the death he would die for our redemption. In the end, as we are assured in Revelation 21:4, after the judgment is pronounced, God will wipe away every tear from our eyes.

So with the Psalmist we can cry out to our Lord, we can cast our cares on Him, confident that He hears, He cares and He acts. We are ultimately rescued by the saving work of Jesus. God is for us.

- *Pray for those in the legal world who are suffering as a result of difficult circumstances.*
- *Praise God that He is for each one of us now, that we are redeemed and that in the end every tear will be wiped away from our eyes.*

– Janys Scott KC (2020)

28 APR On rocky ground?

Hear my cry, O God; attend unto my prayer. From the end of the earth will I cry unto Thee, when my heart is overwhelmed: lead me to the rock that is higher than I.
Psalm 61:1-2 (KJV)

There are days – and nights – when we feel completely overwhelmed. Whether it's the pressures of work or study, deadlines looming, circumstances at home, ill health, spiritual warfare or the many other challenges of life.

In these verses, the Psalmist uses the word "cry" twice. It emphasises the heartfelt desperation that he experienced and perhaps how we feel at times. No-one else can help. No-one else understands.

But we are not alone. In fact, we have a Rock that is solid.

He is our foundation (Matt 7:24). He is our rescuer (Ps 40:2). He is our provider (Numbers 20:8). He is our security (Ps 61:2). Most of all, our Rock left heaven to experience life, overcome in all things, die for our sins, rise gloriously to defeat our greatest enemies of sin, death and hell. He is enthroned in glory ready to receive us, if we trust in Him, in an eternal place of bliss.

Let the storm surges of life and waves of care lift you onto the Rock that is Jesus.

- *Bring to God today the cry of your heart, and know that he will lift you up because he cares for you.*
- *If there are those known to you today, especially in your workplace, who are going through difficult times lift then before the Lord, and ask for opportunities to share Christ with them.*

– Esther Harrison (2016)

29 APR Good witnesses in difficult times

Let not those who seek You be confounded because of me, O God of Israel. **Psalm 69:6b (NKJV),**
Only let your conduct be worthy of the gospel of Christ … **Philippians 1:27 (NKJV)**

In these times of division, if we have ventured an opinion about current events, we may have experienced hostility, particularly since respect for individuals is now often equated with agreement (and vice versa).

Or, in our work, we may have a potentially incendiary negotiation to navigate where tempers may become frayed. Our clients (and those on the other side of the negotiation) may have a lot at stake and in these situations emotions can run high.

The Apostle Paul tells us: "Let your gentleness be evident to all" (Philippians 4:5 (NIV)) and in the same verse he gives us a context: "The Lord is near". We should not take offence at what others say, even if it is personal and unfair. The important thing is how God sees us and He can give us the resources to respond appropriately and with generosity of spirit so that we are worthy witnesses for Him.

- *Let us pray that, even in the most challenging encounters, the peace of God (which is beyond all human understanding) will rest upon us and that we will be worthy witnesses for Him.*

– John Scriven (2019)

30 APR — Don't slip, keep your footing

Surely God is good to Israel,
to those who are pure in heart.
But as for me, my feet had almost slipped;
I had nearly lost my foothold.
For I envied the arrogant
when I saw the prosperity of the wicked.
… till I entered the sanctuary of God; …
Psalm 73:1-3; 17a (NIV)

The legal profession is highly competitive. How quick we can be in believing the lies Satan first told to Eve in the garden, that God doesn't want the best for us, doesn't love us, or perhaps has forgotten us.

Are we tempted to envy those fellow law students who have a training contract or pupillage already sorted? Do we resent clients who are seeming to prosper despite dubious business practices, or who treat others in their family or workplace oppressively? The psalmist was despondent to the point where his feet, or faith, "had almost slipped" (v 2), until he "entered the sanctuary of God" (v 17), focused his gaze heavenwards and was reminded of the amazing blessings that were his. The God of the Universe, whom we get to call Father, is with him, holding him by his right hand, guiding him with His counsel, and afterward taking him into glory (vs 23-24). We, with Paul, can learn to be content in all circumstances when we "enter the sanctuary of God" and recall our blessing. Let us enter daily through reading His word, speaking to Him in prayer and meeting in the fellowship of believers. "Surely God is good" (v 1) to those who trust in the work the Lord Jesus has already done for them on the cross; let us tell of all His deeds.

- *Pray that we will focus on the blessings that are ours in Christ and not envy the false attractions of this world.*
- *Pray for opportunities this week to tell of His deeds.*

– Debbie Woods (2019)

1 MAY — Where would you rather be?

Better is one day in your courts than a thousand elsewhere; I would rather be a doorkeeper in the house of my God than dwell in the tents of the wicked. Psalm 84:10 (NIV)

I have learned to be content whatever the circumstances. I know what it is to be in need, and I know what it is to have plenty. I have learned the secret of being content in any and every situation, whether well fed or hungry, whether living in plenty or in want. I can do all this through him who gives me strength. Philippians 4:11-13 (NIV)

For lawyers who are used to attending meetings or going to court, it is a very strange experience to be limited to spending almost all of every day at home. It's easy to develop "cabin fever" and to become preoccupied with thoughts of the places and activities which we are missing out on.

David lived through all sorts of circumstances: life in the outdoors as a young shepherd, travelling around with an army, hiding in caves when on the run from Saul, and enjoying the pleasant atmosphere of the palace in Jerusalem. The Psalmist probably had David's experiences in mind when he declared that being near God (even if only as a watchman standing at the entrance to the Temple) was far better than being anywhere else.

Let us praise the Lord that even though we are isolation from one another at the moment, God does not socially distance from us but has come near in the person of Jesus and has made us into the temple of the Holy Spirit, dwelling with us during this time when we cannot meet together in person.

- *Please pray for those lawyers working at home on their own, that they would know the presence of the Lord with them.*
- *Pray for those lawyers trying to juggle the continuing demands of practice with responsibilities for children or looking after vulnerable people.*
- *Pray for those lawyers who are anxious about their lack of work or fearful about the future of their jobs.*

– Dr David McIlroy (2020)

2 MAY — What can we do that will truly last?

Before the mountains were born or you brought forth the whole world, from everlasting to everlasting you are God. You turn people back to dust, saying, 'Return to dust, you mortals.'…

May your deeds be shown to your servants, your splendour to their children. May the favour of the Lord our God rest on us; establish the work of our hands for us – yes, establish the work of our hands.

Psalm 90:2-3a, 16-17 (NIV)

Every now and again something happens to remind us of our frailty and transience – the failure of a major project that we have invested much in; sudden ill-health; the death of a loved one.

Only the Lord is "from everlasting to everlasting". Unless he saves and sustains us, everything we do – and even who we are – gets swept away in the end. More than that, he's the one that blows over us and uproots us. It is what we deserve at his hand.

But in his mercy, the Lord our God rescues those he calls his servants, and gives them permanence. He not only shows them his own deeds, but also enables their work to become bound up with his actions on earth, so that it is established and secure.

Praise God that by his grace we are given eternal hope and significance. Pray that as you seek his will, he would enable your work for him to result in everlasting praise to his name.

- *Pray for Christian lawyers facing difficult circumstances, that they may be able to trust that the Lord is at work in their lives for their good and his eternal glory.*
- *Pray for lawyers' Christian outreach events: that many non-Christians will come, hear the gospel clearly explained and respond.*

– Caroline Eade (2017)

3 MAY Everything will be alright?

Because he loves me,' says the LORD, 'I will rescue him;
I will protect him, for he acknowledges my name.
He will call on me, and I will answer him;
I will be with him in trouble,
I will deliver him and honour him.
With long life I will satisfy him
and show him my salvation.
Psalm 91:14-16 (NIV)

Psalm 91 seems to promise God's protection both against enemies and against disease and other natural disasters. Sometimes we enjoy God's deliverance from such troubles, but at other times Christians go through the most horrendous experiences. Where is God in such moments?

The devil quoted Psalm 91 verses 11 and 12 to Jesus as part of the second temptation following Jesus' baptism, suggesting that God was offering immunity from suffering. Jesus' rejection of the devil's temptation to throw himself down from the roof of the Temple, and the whole of Jesus' life, show us a more profound truth. God's promise is that God will be with us in our troubles in this life and assures us that we will enjoy the fullness of salvation one day. Whether we are spared a particular trial or are put through a very painful and draining experience, God is with us.

Thank God for those times when he has spared us from disaster where, even though we have made a mistake in our professional or personal life, the worst hasn't happened. Thank God that he is with us even when we have to face something that seems too hard for us to handle, whether illness, opposition at work, or having to take responsibility for something bad that has happened. Rest in the truth that our status and our identity comes from our relationship to God, and not from the job that we happen to do.

- *Thank God that He is with you even in the toughest times.*
- *Ask God to protect and deliver you from evil this week.*

- Ask God to reveal his presence and his blessings to you whatever your circumstances.
- Ask God to deepen your love for him and your dependence on him.

– Dr David McIlroy (2019)

4 MAY — Steadfast in the storms

He will have no fear of evil tidings.
His heart is steadfast, trusting in the LORD.
Psalm 112:7 (NKJV)

You could be waiting for a medical diagnosis for a loved one or for yourself. Or you might be anticipating the outcome of a serious issue at work which could affect your career. Understandably you are very worried. The storms of life take myriad forms, seeming to engulf us, and the greatest storm of all is death.

But, whatever our circumstances may be, we can bring these to our Heavenly Father in prayer. We have a refuge. We can trust that He will, just at the time when we need it most, give us the strength to face whatever challenges beset us. And we should not be reticent in asking our Christian friends and colleagues for their prayer and support.

- *Heavenly Father, give me confidence that I can face the uncertainties and crises of life in your strength.*

- *May I be a friend to those who need my prayer and help in testing times.*

– John Scriven (2018)

5 MAY — Seeking rest?

I love the LORD, for he heard my voice; he heard my cry for mercy. **Psalm 116:1 (NIV)**

It can seem at times that a lawyer's life is a mixture of famine and feast, and we often worry where the work will come from. Yet when there is too much of it and when it comes with responsibility, it can feel as though there can be too much to cope with. Pressures from life outside work sometimes only add to this. We can fear being overwhelmed, either because we believe we can rely only on ourselves to cope or because we focus too much on our ambitions rather than on God's will.

God does not promise us that we will never feel overwhelmed. What He does promise is that we can always turn to Him and that in doing so our soul may find rest. This is what the Psalmist found after his tribulations. And Jesus makes the same promise to us (Matt 11:29).

In accepting this promise and turning to our Saviour (in good times as well as bad), we will begin to recognise when we have been protected from stumbling (Ps 116:8) and, like the Psalmist, our hearts will turn in praise and thanksgiving (Ps 116:17-19). And we will see that the support we get from our colleagues, family and friends is itself in God's providence.

- *Pray that we and our Christian colleagues will turn to Jesus with whatever we find difficult to deal with this week.*
- *Ask God for opportunities to speak to colleagues about Jesus who is gently and lowly in heart, and in whom they can find rest for their souls.*

– James Brightwell (2019)

6 MAY Overwhelmed

Let my soul be at rest again, for the Lord has been good to me. Psalm 116:7 (NLT)

As we return to work this morning – client appointments; drafting challenging documents; studying for exams; court hearings (or those most precious of Mondays: the empty diary and time to catch up) – it may seem strange to focus on rest, rather than activity. However, when I transitioned to a new job, in a new country, I reflected on 'busyness' and its cost to my soul – the bone-deep weariness that seems immoveable; how hard it can be to speak to God when my mind is so full; and the rising tide of panic that threatens to overwhelm me when I look at all that needs to be done.

Teach me knowledge and good judgment, for I trust your commands.

Psalm 119:66 (NIV)

This verse from Psalm 116 spoke powerfully to me. Truly I can say, "… the Lord has been good to me". God pours out His abundant blessings on our lives all of the time – but often I fail to stop to appreciate them. Importantly, the Psalmist does not see rest as an achievement or another activity to fit in – rather, it is surrender to the LORD who has been good to us: "Let my soul be at rest …" or, as the NIV and NKJV have it, "Return to your rest, O my soul…"

So, this morning, take some time to reflect on all of the ways that God has been good to you. Return, once more, to your soul-rest in Him, surrendering all of the week's activities to the mighty power of our God, for whom all things are possible (Matthew 19:26).

- Be at rest now and ask the Lord to show you where you can take a step back and rest in him.
- Pray for those working for justice, in the name of Christ, around the world, in particular for The Lawyers' Christian Fellowship CLEAR partners in Kenya, Uganda and Rwanda.

– Claire Wilkinson (2015)

7 MAY — Knowledge and good judgment come from God and his Word

Do good to your servant according to your word, LORD. Teach me knowledge and good judgment, for I trust your commands. **Psalm 119:65-66 (NIV)**

These two verses from the longest of the Psalms highlight that our knowledge and our ability to exercise sound judgement ultimately come from God; from obeying his commands, and more importantly trusting in his commands and his Word. This is of particular practical significance to us as lawyers given that knowledge and the exercise of sound judgment are central to virtually all that we are called upon to do, whether we are acting for clients or serving in a judicial capacity.

As we immerse ourselves in daily life, and seek to tackle difficult problems at work, it is all too easy to overlook the true source of our knowledge and judgment, and believe that we can get by trusting in our own abilities and human insight, forgetting that we serve under a sovereign Lord. However, this passage makes the clear link between a belief in God's commands and God's Word, and knowledge and the exercise of good judgment. It therefore how important it is for us, as we go about our practices or otherwise seek to deploy our skills in a way that furthers the interests of justice in a way pleasing to God, to embrace and place our trust in God's Word, and to have real belief and confidence in his commands.

- Pray that, as we conduct our practices or otherwise seek to further the interests of justice in our work, God will

deepen our knowledge of Him and His Word, and teach us knowledge and good judgment.
- Keep us strong in our faith and help us to obey God's commands, so that we might be blessed with knowledge, and exercise sound judgment in the decisions that we are required to make each day.

– HHJ Mark Cawson KC (2019)

8 MAY Our all-seeing God

My help comes from the LORD,
Who made heaven and earth.
He will not allow your foot to be moved;
He who keeps you will not slumber.
Behold, He who keeps Israel
Shall neither slumber nor sleep.
The LORD is your keeper;
Psalm 121:2-5a (NKJV)

I was prosecuting in front of a bench of three lay magistrates an alleged assault case. If true, it was serious, nasty and messy. The lunch break came and went. The case continued. I noticed the 'right hand winger' (the magistrate on the right) evidently had too good a lunch! He started nodding off. I drew this, first, to the attention of the excellent defence lawyer. I will draw a veil over what happened next!

Are you not glad and grateful that our holy, saving, keeping God never sleeps? He never misses anything. He never ignores a sin. He never cannot hear a prayer. He is never off duty.

When we trust and follow Christ as our personal Saviour, Redeemer and Lord, we know He lives and watches over us forever. He sees and hates all sins, bore them all in His death on the cross for us and forgives us for them all. Similarly, He knows all that we think, say and do. That is both comforting and challenging. Our watchful, caring keeper never slumbers nor sleeps!

Prayerfully ask:
- *How conscious are you that 'the eyes of the Lord are in every place beholding the evil and the good?'*
- *What comfort can we take from God's watching over us when we have that problem that we cannot solve, or that unattainable deadline, or that difficult client, or that tricky Court situation?*
- *What challenge do we face when we wish we could do something that we really would not like God to see or hear, but know He does?*

– Gerard Chrispin (2020)

9 MAY The joy of meeting in person

I rejoiced with those who said to me, "Let us go to the house of the LORD." **Psalm 122:1 (NIV)**

The great 19th Century preacher, D.L. Moody, said that:

> "Church attendance is as vital to a disciple as an infusion of rich, healthy blood is to a sick man."

During the pandemic there was an enforced absence of corporate worship. One of my previous minister's sermon illustrations was about a regular church attender who had suddenly stopped coming to Sunday services. His minister visited him and used the companion set tongs to remove a red hot coal from the blazing fire in the grate. He let it cool and turn black and lifeless on the hearth before returning it to the other coals in the grate where, within a short time, it glowed red hot again. He left without further comment.

My church completed renovations just prior to lockdown and our old front doors inscribed with this verse were used as a wall panel in our vestibule and greeted us on our return to the building. We have arguably taken our inalienable right and the invaluable opportunity to worship God together for granted – has Covid-19 taught us a valuable lesson?

- *Pray for those who in their work or church life are responsible for the safety of others through their involvement in developing and/or implementing safe working or worshipping protocols.*
- *Pray that believers who are isolated or discouraged would soon find encouragement from Christian fellowship.*

– Peter Brown (2021)

10 MAY — Do You Pray About Your Work?

Unless the LORD builds the house, the builders labour in vain. Unless the LORD watches over the city, the guards stand watch in vain. Psalm 127:1 (NIV)

You do not have because you do not ask God. James 4:2b (NIV)

Legal work takes mental effort, and most lawyers soon realise there are only so many decisions we can make in a given day and only so many tasks we can do in a day.

But is there space in our schedule to pray about the work that lies in front of us?

Psalm 127:1 shows us that we need to integrate our faith in God into our daily work. And one key way of doing that is to pray about our work.

In his book *Don't Just Stand There ... Pray Something!*, Ronald Dunn underlines the importance of prayer: "There are some things God will do if we ask Him that He will not do if we do not ask Him ... James says it plainly enough: ... James 4:2".

Sometimes our legal workload is beyond our control – but we need to do what we can to leave time and energy in our day to pray about our work.

Sometimes our prayers about our work may be short and brief (God doesn't need a detailed explanation of the facts), but at other times we may need to wrestle in prayer (especially where our motives are awry). And what this looks like may differ depending on our precise context. But one way or another we need to invite Him in.

Taken from *Don't Just Stand There...Pray Something!* by Ronald Dunn Copyright © 1992 by Ronald Dunn. Used by permission of HarperCollins Christian Publishing. www.harpercollinschristian.com

- *Father, forgive us for when we have failed to integrate our work with our faith in You.*
- *Lord Jesus, thank You that You are interested in our work. Please help us to be better at knowing what it looks like to bring our work before You in prayer.*

– Dominic Hughes (2021)

11 MAY Pay attention!

You know when I sit and when I rise; you perceive my thoughts from afar ...
... How precious to me are your thoughts, God! How vast is the sum of them!

Psalm 139:2 and 17 (NIV)

As lawyers we are accustomed to court sittings. The usher's call to "All rise!" heralds the arrival of the Judge to start the hearing. Do on-line hearings have the same impact I wonder?

The psalmist marvels at the fact that God knows exactly the moment when we sit down and when we rise up again. Nothing escapes His notice. He hears what we say, but He even knows what we are thinking at any moment. God's attention is upon us always.

A question from verse 17 is this: am I paying attention to God? Are our prayers one-sided? All petition and no listening? As we read our Bibles are we asking: "What is God saying to me through this passage?

We will be extremely busy today, but before we set off let us pay attention to our Lord, seek His wisdom, and allow His light to shine through us to those He wants to reach.

- *Pray that we retain awareness of our Lord's presence with us through the working day and afterwards.*
- *Pray that we remain responsive to His prompting and leading in our work and witness.*

– Michael Hawthorne (2017)

12 MAY Working for God's purposes

I know that the LORD secures justice for the poor and upholds the cause of the needy. **Psalm 140:12 (NIV)**

The Psalmist prays to the Lord for help in keeping him safe from the hands of the wicked. He knows that it is part of God's character to protect His people and that one of the ways He does this is in securing justice for those who know they are dependent on Him.

Knowing that our Father secures justice for His people, we pray that He will use us to help Him fulfil this purpose in the world. For some lawyers, such as those working directly to serve the disadvantaged, God's purpose in their work may at times be very clear. All of us, however, should pray that He may use our work and our professional relationships to his greater glory and all the more so when it may not be immediately apparent where our day-to-day work may fit into that purpose.

Having expressed his great fears, David shows confidence that he is heard and so he can pray with assurance that the plans of the wicked do not succeed (Psalm 140:8). We also can be confident that God will use us for His purposes if we are faithful, and we should therefore not be afraid to let others know of this confidence so that it is a witness to them.

- *Pray for God's guidance for all those involved in the administration of justice, and that we may be aware of His greater purposes as we do our work.*
- *Pray for The Lawyers' Christian Fellowship CLEAR partners, seeking to bring justice in the developing world.*

– James Brightwell (2018)

13 MAY Abound in love!

This is my prayer: that your love may abound more and more in knowledge and depth of insight, so that you may be able to discern what is best and may be pure and blameless for the day of Christ, filled with the fruit of righteousness that comes through Jesus Christ – to the glory and praise of God. **Philippians 1:9-11 (NIV)**

Lawyers like to be known for having 'knowledge and depth of insight' – about relevant case law, litigation strategy, or professional conduct issues. To be regarded, by our colleagues and clients, as someone who has 'depth of insight' is a worthy aim indeed.

But here, for Paul, knowledge-with-insight, in itself, isn't the goal he has in mind. Rather they're the tramlines, the perimeter, which give shape to his big goal: a love which abounds. He longs for Christians to be marked by an ever-growing love for the Lord and his ways, for His people, and for His world. As the great Day approaches – not a great wedding or our salary review day, but the Day of Christ – what an incentive that is to pursue the most excellent way of love.

So as a new financial year gets underway, where there will be expectations to be abounding in fees or clients or legal excellence, let's be those who are known, too, and above all, for abounding in love. We're called not to a wishy-washy, inoffensive niceness but an insightful, constructive, Spirit-borne love which engages with real people – to the glory and praise of God.

- *Praise God that through Jesus Christ, we have experienced God's abounding love and grace, that we might become pure and blameless in His sight.*
- *Pray that our love may abound more and more to engage more effectively with those around us.*
- *Pray for opportunities to share the good news of Jesus Christ with our colleagues.*

– Rev. Ed Veale (2018)

14 MAY Trust in the Lord

Trust in the LORD with all your heart, and do not lean on your own understanding. In all your ways acknowledge him, and he will make straight your paths. Do not be wise in your own eyes, fear the LORD and turn away from evil.
Proverbs 3:5-7 (ESV)

For those caught up in a busy and hectic practice, it can be all too easy to forget God's presence in our lives, and to rely simply upon our own understanding as to the right thing to do in the various situations that confront us, and to set our own standards by being wise in our own eyes rather than God's eyes.

This passage is a helpful and powerful reminder to trust in the Lord in all that we do, and to be guided by how he speaks to us through his Word, and not to pit our own understanding against his.

If we do place our trust and confidence in the Lord and his Word, and acknowledge his presence in all aspects of our lives, then we have the magnificent assurance that God will keep us on the right path, help us to make the right decisions, and guide us through the difficulties that life throws in our way.

- *Give thanks to God that we can place our trust in him, and that if we do we have the magnificent assurance that he will keep us on a straight path.*
- *Pray that God might help us get the balance of our lives right so that we do not allow our busy and hectic practices and lifestyles to distract us from recognising God's presence in all aspects of our lives, but to place our trust and confidence in him rather than simply our own understanding of matters.*

– HHJ Mark Cawson KC (2017)

15 MAY The principal thing

Wisdom is the principal thing;
Therefore get wisdom.
And in all your getting, get understanding.
Proverbs 4:7 (NKJV)

As Christians, we can be filled with biblical knowledge – and that is good. We are called to study God's Word. As lawyers, we are also filled with legal knowledge – and that, too, is good. It is why our clients both instruct and trust us.

But knowledge and wisdom are two very different things. Wisdom is not found through years of studying and learning, nor through many years in practice. It is found not in ourselves but in God alone ("Behold, the fear of the Lord, that is wisdom …" Job 28:28) through His Word. Not merely in the knowledge of God's Word, but in the applying of the Word in our daily lives.

How much more effective we can be for Christ when we step beyond merely 'knowledge' and begin to walk daily in His wisdom, actively seeking spiritual discernment in the realities of our lives and those around us. When His wisdom is embedded in our hearts, the Holy Spirit will enable us to navigate the difficult and complex situations of life with clarity and illumination. It is when we, as Christian lawyers, bring not only our legal knowledge but also God's wisdom to bear on the situations that our clients are facing, that we see God's supernatural power at work to transform, renew and restore even the most dire of earthly situations … and we begin to see His Kingdom come.

- *Pray that we would prioritise the 'getting' of wisdom above all else and be willing to discipline ourselves to actively seek to study and apply God's Word.*
- *Pray for boldness to step out into the application of God's wisdom not only in our own personal lives, but in the lives of those whose legal situations God has entrusted to us, knowing this is not by coincidence but by God's design.*

– Hilary Underwood (2021)

16 MAY Dispensing with justice

Honest scales and balances belong to the LORD; all the weights in the bag are of his making. **Proverbs 16:11 (NIV)**

Do I love justice? When there's a personal cost, do I want justice to be done or perhaps just be seen to be done? When did I last have my scales and balances calibrated or have light shone on the darkest corners of my work bag to check what lurks within?

How about in the areas of:

- Loving justice, rather than vindication
- Working/studying diligently, but neglecting the Lord
- Prioritising client and employer over the needs of family or others
- Working for the Lord, rather than to please men
- Giving others credit
- Accepting responsibility for failures and shortcomings
- Apologising to clients/colleagues
- Being accountable to clients/colleagues
- Taking refuge in the true-ish, the half-truth and nothing like the truth

- Honesty in time recording
- Honesty in finances
- Over-charging and over-claiming.
- Charging different rates, or not charging for work out of favouritism
- Compassion for the undeserving as well as the deserving
- Giving the Lord the honour for success
- Trusting Him through challenges
- Loving those clients/colleagues I have no affinity for
- Honouring timescales and promises
- Praying for and with clients/colleagues
- Overcoming fear of bringing light to areas where there is darkness

Where might Christians lawyers be challenged? Where do I need to allow the Holy Spirit to recalibrate and spring clean what weighs me down?

- *Put aside 10 minutes to ponder and pray. Do I desire this transformation, or am I content to conform to the pattern of the world?*
- *Being honest about the burden of our failings, approach the cross in prayer and place them there, trusting in the one whose nature is to forgive. Lord have mercy, Christ have mercy.*

– Mark Jones (2021)

17 MAY — The best laid plans...

Many are the plans in a person's heart, but it is the LORD'S purpose that prevails. **Proverbs 19:21 (NIV)**

We may make a lot of plans, but the LORD will do what he has decided. **Proverbs 19:21 (CEV)**

When you woke this morning and you saw the day stretching out in front of you, you probably had some idea of how you thought the day would work out. Clients to see, opinions to write, decisions to take, judgments to give.

You settle into the routine of another busy day, and then that unexpected telephone call or email can throw everything into confusion. How do you react? There is an old Yiddish proverb: "We plan, God laughs."

It is at times like this that we need to remember that God is in control whatever we may feel – He is working His purposes out through us.

Therefore, let go and let God direct.

- *Take time to stop and offer afresh the day and the week ahead of you to the Lord and ask him to direct your paths.*
- *Pray for those Christian lawyers for whom the road is uncertain, or who are experiencing difficult times, that they may know the truth that God is their rock in times of trouble.*

– John Head (2016)

18 MAY — A Question of sovereignty

The king's heart is in the hand of the LORD, as the rivers of water: he turneth it whithersoever he will. **Proverbs 21:1 (KJV)**

Do you remember those gut-wrenchingly challenging days as a pupil or trainee? Possibly as a student doing your final exams or facing a crucial interview? Those days when the task ahead seemed overwhelming and one for which all your training and experience of life could not equip you?

As we go on in our practices and learn more, those days fade away. We gain in confidence, experience, knowledge and wisdom. We become complacent. We forget. Then something comes along for which we have no resources. The fear rises up.

This happened recently to me. And God met my need with this scripture. It first became precious to me years ago at a Lawyers' Christian Fellowship conference. It reminded me that our God is sovereign. In Him, we have all the resources of the cosmos and more. There is no situation beyond Him because our times are in His hands, as is the heart of the greatest earthly ruler. He has dealt with our most difficult problems – those of sin, death and hell – through Christ's death and resurrection. By faith in Him, we're saved and on our way to heaven!

So when the fear begins, fix your eyes upon Jesus; meditate on who He is and all that He has done for you. To quote the old hymn: "And the things of earth will grow strangely dim, in the light of His glory and grace." *

*From 'Turn your eyes upon Jesus', by Helen Howarth Lemmel.

- *Give thanks for all that the Lord Jesus Christ has done for you in his death, resurrection and ascension; and for His saving grace. As you do so, commit any difficult situation you face into His hands.*
- *Pray for those in authority, that they may understand that it is God, the maker of heaven and earth, who has the ultimate authority and pray that they may rule according to His word.*

– Esther Harrison (2017)

19 MAY — Keeping cool as others vent

Fools give full vent to their rage, but the wise bring calm in the end. **Proverbs 29:11 (NIV)**

As lawyers, we will have experienced seeing people give vent to rage. Fear, disappointment and anger can all cause it. No doubt we feel it sometimes ourselves. But anger prevents clear thinking and can lead to bad decisions.

It is one of our tasks as lawyers to enable our clients to think clearly and calmly so that they reach decisions which are good for them. This will often be difficult because the decision they need to make will often be contrary to their inclination.

Keeping our cool when discussion gets heated is essential. This is not something we do naturally, it is one of the gifts of the Holy Spirit and we must pray that we receive it.

- *Pray for grace when dealing with rage in others.*
- *Pray for grace in dealing with your own anger.*
- *Pray for wisdom to enable good decisions to be reached.*
- *Pray for guidance by the Holy Spirit when dealing with angry or difficult clients.*

– Michael Hawthorne (2016)

20 MAY — A lawyer and an honest man

Two things I ask of you, LORD;
Do not refuse me before I die:
Keep falsehood and keep lies far from me;
Give me neither poverty nor riches,
but give me only my daily bread.
Otherwise I may have too much and disown you
and say 'Who is the LORD?'
Or I may become poor and steal,
and so dishonour the name of my God.
Proverbs 30:7-9 (NIV)

If you had two things to ask of God before you died, what might they be?

Two men were walking through a country churchyard noting the inscriptions on the gravestones and observed one which read "A lawyer and an honest man." "Gracious me", said one to the other, "I see that they are burying them in pairs here!"

Honesty should be a seminal part of everyone's life. Absolute honesty should be expected of a lawyer even if one's client might not appreciate being told the truth, especially if it would appear to be to their disadvantage.

Both riches and poverty are potentially dangerous. I suspect that for most lawyers aspiring to be rich is the real challenge. Will the love of money get in the way of our love for the Lord?

Perhaps this is a good time to stop and reflect on our own priorities. Are they dishonouring the name of God in any way?

- *Praise God that He gives us our daily bread, all that we need.*
- *Pray that our priorities would reflect the Lord's priorities, that we may honour His name.*

– John Head (2018)

21 MAY — Stand up, speak up!

Speak up for those who cannot speak for themselves, for the rights of all who are destitute. Speak up and judge fairly; defend the rights of the poor and needy.
Proverbs 31:8-9 (NIV)

Our God loves justice and has a special heart for the poor and needy, the widow and orphan. Whilst all Christians should share such concerns, lawyers have a special responsibility to ensure that the voice of the poor is heard. We need to pray for those who serve the poor and needy in court, and out of it.

Our judges too at all levels need our prayers if they are to judge fairly. Is God calling you to consider applying for judicial office?

With the growing awareness of climate change in our world, we see that so often it is the most needy who are impacted hugely by the effects of global warming. From increasingly intense storms and floods to the opposite extreme of drought and famine, those who have the least and cause the least damage, suffer the greatest.

Whilst doing what we can as individuals to reduce our carbon footprint we should also support the Christian agencies which are seeking to mitigate the effects being felt by those who have contributed least to the problem.

But there is another form of poverty: spiritual poverty. We cannot be unaware that our nation has become largely secular in outlook, with little or no thought for eternity and where they will spend it. We need to pray that our nation will turn back to God and seek His power in their lives.

- *Pray for all who represent the poor before court and tribunals.*
- *Pray for our Judges at all levels, that they may judge fairly and with integrity.*
- *Pray for those most affected by climate change and all who seek to bring them help in their need.*
- *Pray for the Holy Spirit to inspire the church to reach out to those without Christ and without hope in our nation.*

– Michael Hawthorne (2022)

22 MAY — Everything has its time

Everything on earth has its own time and its own season. There is a time for birth and death, planting and reaping.
Ecclesiastes 3:1-2 (CEV)

The passing of a beloved wife, husband, child or friend is inevitably a sad event, but out of it can come a new birth, a new chapter in the life of the bereaved.

News that a colleague is moving to something new can bring a mixed reaction – a sadness on our part as we shall miss them, but an exciting prospect for them, even if there is uncertainty about how things will work out.

Maybe you are facing change in life – a new job beckons, redundancy is looming or some other unforeseen event has occurred. How might we – and you – respond to change? Who can understand the ways of God? Despite all the changes that life might throw at us, the writer of Ecclesiastes understood that God has power over everyone.

The following quotation may be of help:

> "I said to the man who stood at the gate of the year: 'Give me a light that I may tread safely into the unknown.' And he replied, 'Go out into the darkness and put your hand into the hand of God. That shall be to you better than light and safer than a known way!' So I went forth and, finding the hand of God, trod gladly into the night …" (Minnie Louise Haskins)

If this thought resonates with you, be encouraged – you are not alone.

- *Consider whose hands you are trusting your life to at present, your own or the Lord. Recommit yourself into His hands at the start of this week.*
- *Pray for those known to you who are facing changes or uncertain futures, that they may know the peace that comes only from trusting in the Lord.*

– John Head (2017)

23 MAY — The gift of time

Sow your seed in the morning, and at evening let not your hands be idle, for you do not know which will succeed, whether this or that, or whether both will do equally well.
Ecclesiastes 11:6 (NIV)

These words, coming at the end of the writer's wisdom about God's great gift of life, remind us of the urgency of the tasks we have been given.

Even though we do not understand the mysteries of all of God's ways (Ecclesiastes 11:5), we can have confidence that in doing the tasks entrusted to us we will enable His will to be done. This will encompass not only professional responsibilities but also the way in which we respond to the people whom we encounter in life. This will involve both carrying out the everyday duties within our jobs assiduously as well as being aware of opportunities to speak and act in a way in which our faith will shine.

We will not win every case, even those we believe we should have won, or understand why some of those whose paths we cross are hostile to us. But we can have an assurance that God wants us to play our role fully today, however small it may be in His bigger plans.

- *Pray that each of us may have a keen awareness of the fragility and beauty of life and a desire to carry out God's purposes with that gift, without too much delay.*

- *Give thanks for opportunities to come alongside young lawyers and students within legal and church fellowships. Pray for them and that we can encourage them to be salt and light in the profession.*

– James Brightwell (2016)

24 MAY — Scrub it out...

Wash yourselves; make yourselves clean;
remove the evil of your deeds from before my eyes;
cease to do evil,
learn to do good;
seek justice,
correct oppression;
bring justice to the fatherless,
plead the widow's cause.

Isaiah 1:16-17 (ESV)

None of us likes to be judged, but judgment is part and parcel of our profession. Clients often don't like it when we tell them they are in the wrong, but giving that advice when needed is crucial to being a good lawyer.

Isaiah starts with a damning summing up of the facts before God. Things were not as they should be. Evil, oppression, discrimination, and blatant sin were rife. Judgment was coming and repentance needed.

But how can we wash ourselves and make ourselves clean? Isaiah prophesied a coming redemption, and for those of us living in the New Covenant that was made possible, as the writer to the Hebrews says, "by the blood of Jesus" (10:19). Only because of His sacrifice and in our repentance can we "draw near with a true heart in full assurance of faith, with our hearts sprinkled clean from an evil conscience and our bodies washed with pure water." (10:22).

In times of crisis, we must all be attentive to what the word of God says directly to us. When it convicts us of evil, oppression and discrimination that abides in our hearts, we must draw near to God asking for forgiveness, and seek forgiveness and reconciliation with those we have hurt, whilst using our God given skills to advocate for those caught up in oppression and injustice.

- *Give thanks to Father for the Lord Jesus, and His sacrifice.*
- *Ask God to reveal to you circumstances, people or situations where you have fallen into discrimination or oppression. Seek His forgiveness and ask how you might reconcile with those you have hurt.*
- *Pray for Christian legal fellowships throughout the world: that God will give them strength to stand alongside the widow and the fatherless to plead their cause and bring justice, while offering eternal hope in Jesus.*

– Mark Barrell (2020)

25 MAY — The goodness of God's law

Woe to those who call evil good, and good evil; who put darkness for light, and light for darkness; who put bitter for sweet, and sweet for bitter!
Woe to those who are wise in their own eyes, And prudent in their own sight!
Woe to men mighty at drinking wine, woe to men valiant for mixing intoxicating drink, who justify the wicked for a bribe, and take away justice from the righteous man!
Therefore, as the fire devours the stubble, and the flame consumes the chaff,
So their root will be as rottenness, and their blossom will ascend like dust;
Because they have rejected the law of the LORD of hosts, and despised the word of the Holy One of Israel.
Therefore the anger of the LORD is aroused against His people ...

Isaiah 5:20-25 (NKJV)

Isaiah's prophetic voice proclaims the reality of the true order of things, as determined by the Lord of the universe. The message is striking, characterised by sharp contrasts. It also stands as a grave warning to the church today, having been directed at God's disobedient people in Isaiah's time.

The revealed divine order consists of good (as opposed to evil), light (as distinct from darkness), the law of God (contrasting the wisdom of man) and just judgment (unlike the corrupt subterfuges of sinful man).

Our instinctive tendency is to re-direct the force of these words elsewhere; to excuse ourselves from attitudes and conduct which would offend the Lord of the divine order revealed here. Yes, Isaiah's words do accurately describe and therefore remind us of the fallen world under God's judgment. Shockingly, however, their primary application is to God's people. Thankfully, Isaiah later provides hope, speaking of a servant who would be pierced for our transgressions, taking the punishment we deserve and bringing us peace with God (53:5).

In the light of Christ let us be eager to examine our own lives and to promote his life-giving order. Israel was called to be a light to the nations: as Christians too, it will only be our faithfulness to God's Word and His ways which enables us to live in true godly obedience in this world, both privately and in the public sphere.

- *Pray that we ourselves would live and work according to an enriched understanding of God's eternal order and value system.*
- *Pray that today's church would act upon Isaiah's prophetic warnings, living obediently in a disobedient world.*
- *Pray that the legal profession would remember and not reject God's laws which he has given as a path for human flourishing.*

- *Pray that we turn daily to the living God, confessing our sin and receiving forgiveness and strength to walk in His ways.*

– James Crabtree (2017)

26 MAY A portrait of justice

There shall come forth a Rod from the stem of Jesse,
And a Branch shall grow out of his roots.
The Spirit of the LORD shall rest upon Him,
The Spirit of wisdom and understanding,
The Spirit of counsel and might,
The Spirit of knowledge and of the fear of the LORD.
His delight is in the fear of the LORD,
And He shall not judge by the sight of His eyes,
Nor decide by the hearing of His ears;
But with righteousness He shall judge the poor,
And decide with equity for the meek of the earth;
He shall strike the earth with the rod of His mouth,
And with the breath of His lips He shall slay the wicked.

Isaiah 11:1-4 (NKJV)

In this fallen world, everyone longs for justice, and cries of injustice reach our ears every week. Human justice is imperfect, often unreliable and frequently of limited scope and duration. To the extent that we see true justice done, then it is in circumstances where wisdom, understanding and knowledge are on display. Just and equitable outcomes presuppose that such qualities are breathed into life and put to work on the often very troubling and difficult problems and disputes of this world.

Isaiah gives us a portrait of the coming King, the model Judge. For Him, wisdom, understanding and knowledge are part and parcel of his character, and His actions reflect the exercise of power consistent with wise counsel. The fear of the LORD is the prevailing benchmark, and this judge is never deceived by appearances which entice the eyes and ears away from reality. His just decisions reflect righteousness and equity.

As we wait for the return of the Lord, we can be thankful for and, despite our limitations, work to achieve just outcomes in all spheres of life. However, we should recognise that perfect and unquestionable justice lies in the future, when as King, the returning Lord and perfect Judge vanquishes all who stand opposed to His eternal rule.

- *Give thanks for the Bible's clear teaching on the characteristics of true justice derived from the perfect Lord and Judge.*
- *Pray that Christian lawyers would model their lives and legal practices on principles which reflect biblical justice.*

- *Give thanks for the returning King and Judge of all mankind, praying in the meantime for just outcomes in this world which display a genuine fear of the Lord.*

– James Crabtree (2022)

27 MAY The foundation of true security

In mercy the throne will be established;
And One will sit on it in truth, in the tabernacle of David,
Judging and seeking justice and hastening righteousness.
Isaiah 16:5 (NKJV)

As we look back through history, as well as observe our world today, it is difficult not to be struck by the contrast between worldly kingship and government and the characteristics of the everlasting kingdom foreseen by the prophet, Isaiah. Echoing Isaiah 9:6-7, this prophecy reminds us that ultimate security is only to be found in the promised Messiah, the Son of David, in fulfilment of the Davidic promises. Such security is for all who take refuge in Him.

So often, we look in vain for truth, justice and righteousness in the temporary rule of sinful leaders, whether captured in the pages of history, or on display across our daily news bulletins. Instead, we find the exercise of power often accompanied by lies, injustice and godlessness. It is therefore striking that Isaiah describes the establishment of divine government as 'mercy', providing relief from destruction and oppression.

As Christian lawyers, we are called to live in obedience to the future king, whose eternal reign of truth, justice and righteousness will be established for ever and yet, in striving to do so, we are out of step with the fallen world and its systems, which almost invariably manifest a rejection of the eternal Lord and King.

Yet we have the confidence that Isaiah's prophecy represents God's certain promise, providing hope, strength and security now, as we await its complete fulfilment in the final manifestation of the Lord's divine government.

- *Pray that we should continue to look to the Lord for strength and wisdom as we battle for obedience in a sinful world.*
- *Pray that we should continue to confess our own sin as we reflect on the moral perfection of God's character and coming rule.*
- *Pray that our nation and its institutions would find their security in Christ and the perfect laws of His kingly rule, not temporal things and human standards.*

– James Crabtree (2018)

28 MAY Great accomplishments?

LORD, you establish peace for us: all that we have accomplished you have done for us. **Isaiah 26:12 (NIV)**

There are days when I find the practice of law perplexing. I have been in a strange season which has involved cases where the outcomes have been remarkably successful for clients. I have been in no doubt that this has been the hand of the Lord and that my involvement, though necessary, has been as his servant. Ephesians tell us that we are "God's workmanship, created in Christ Jesus to do good works, which God prepared in advance for us to do." (Eph 2:10).

Why am I perplexed? Because, in this season my workload has also included situations that are not going well, despite what I hope are my best efforts.

As I hold on to this verse, contained within a song of praise, I am only too aware that it is the Lord who brings peace and that anything we think we have accomplished, he has done for us. At the start of each day of work, my challenge and, I am sure, the challenge for all in the law, is to act and walk humbly, whatever is accomplished.

- Thank God for the work he has given you to do.
- Pray for the work that sits before you as you start your day; that you would apply yourself; that you would be consistent and that you would give it back to the Lord.
- Meditate on the role the Lord has you in, whatever your position and whatever are you 'accomplishing'.
- Pray for those you know who are wrestling with 'success' and 'failure', or with too much work, or too little. Include yourself in that prayer.

– Brent Haywood (2021)

29 MAY What do you value most?

Behold, I lay in Zion a stone for a foundation, a tried stone, a precious cornerstone, a sure foundation.
Isaiah 28:16 (NKJV)

Therefore, to you who believe, He is precious ... "The stone which the builders rejected has become the chief cornerstone." 1 Peter 2:7 (part) (NKJV)

This fundamental question is often asked in sermons or Christian books. If you're like me, you take it for granted and think to yourself "Well, God of course."

Is that really true? Whatever we value most affects every aspect of our lives: what we say and do; where we go; how we spend our time and expend our energies and resources. Often as busy lawyers, these commodities are even more precious. You never hear a lawyer or student bemoaning an abundance of time! As we seek to prioritise, our value system is our guide.

Time and again this year, the words of 1 Peter 2:7 have come to challenge and to probe me. Is Jesus precious

> Behold, I lay in Zion
> a stone for a foundation,
> a tried stone,
> a precious cornerstone,
> a sure foundation
>
> Isaiah 28:16 (NKJV)

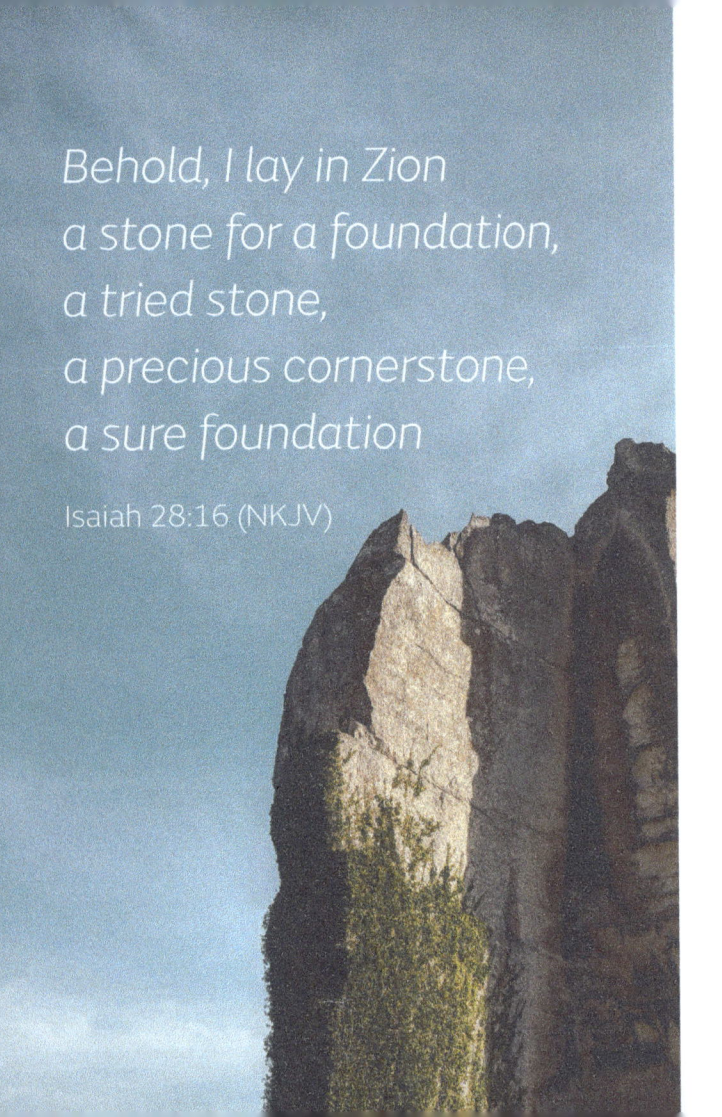

to me? Does the fact that He left heaven and shed His precious blood to atone for my sins break my heart and lead me to worship, love and serve Him more?

This week let our heart song truly be "All that thrills my soul is Jesus, He is more than life to me." *

*From 'All that thrills my soul is Jesus', by Thoro Harris.

- Thank You Jesus for giving up the glory of heaven and Your precious life to save me.

– Esther Harrison (2015)

30 MAY Whose power do you trust?

You are in for trouble if you go to Egypt for help, or if you depend on an army of chariots or a powerful cavalry. Instead you should depend on and trust the holy LORD God of Israel. **Isaiah 31:1 (CEV)**

It's the start of another working week. Sunday was great – worshipping God in the company of Christian friends – great hymns/songs, an uplifting sermon, a chance to meet with other Christians – but now it's the working week! How will we cope with the stresses and strains that work can bring, often in a lonely place?

Isaiah reminds us that when the going is tough we must eschew looking to earthly things to sustain us – relying on others who appear to have the things we lack.

Rather a prayer to the Holy One of Israel – a cry to the Lord – is a better way of getting the help and strength we need to take us through the day.

We need to put our trust in the Lord who knows us and will never forsake us.

- Ask that, rather than relying on your own strength, you will be aware of the leading of the Lord throughout this week.
- Recollect the message you last heard at church and give thanks to God for the one who gave it and ask how you might apply it to your work or study.

– John Head (2015)

31 MAY — "Walls and peace": the real story of international reconciliation

For he himself is our peace, who has made us [Jew and Gentile] both one and has broken down in his flesh the dividing wall of hostility by abolishing the law of commandments expressed in ordinances, that he might create in himself one new man in place of the two, so making peace ... Ephesians 2:14-15 (ESV)

Physical walls and fences recur in international politics – building them against migrants, or bringing them down for unification. Legal systems and treaties too can either unify peoples together or, as they benefit some peoples more than others, foster hostility and calls for independence.

But the Christian lawyer remembers how limited these rearrangements really are. The New Testament takes for granted that all international political activity had been ultimately futile for thousands of years – "separated from Christ, alienated from the commonwealth of Israel and strangers to the covenants of promise, having no hope and without God in the world" (2:12). Endless strife, treaty, and boundary changes were never able to heal hearts and minds regardless of which sides of the various walls we were on.

But Christ's coming internationalised the unique hope of old Israel's political commonwealth. The death of the Jews' Messiah thereby killed their ethnic privilege over Gentiles, and his physical resurrection in an upgraded and glorified human body trumped ethnicity and changed everything. As a second Adam offering his life-giving Spirit to all, he now offers universal and direct membership of one new race, in place of many.

Praise God that we have joined the Prince of Peace in his work of international reconciliation. But there's room for more to join him, and this is the great political hope of the world.

- *As political conversation continues to dominate, let's pray we'll not only keep our own hopes in the right place, but take the opportunity to speak naturally and boldly to colleagues of the real story of hope and international peace.*
- *Remember Christian law students as they come into the exam season. Pray that they will be aware of God's peace and strength, and that they find time to focus on Him amongst the exam angst.*

– Tim Laurence (2016)

1 JUN A bigger picture

Look at my servant, whom I strengthen. He is my chosen one, who pleases me. I have put my Spirit upon him. He will bring justice to the nations. He will not shout or raise his voice in public. He will not crush the weakest reed or put out a flickering candle. He will bring justice to all who have been wronged. He will not falter or lose heart until justice prevails throughout the earth. Even distant lands beyond the sea will wait for his instruction. Isaiah 42:1-4 (NLT)

Sometimes we get those moments that really remind us of why we went into law. But, much more often, it is easy to get bogged down with day-to-day tasks and constant pressure from deadlines, clients, billing targets … We can often forget that we are all part of a bigger picture of God bringing His justice to the world.

The passage above is one of the prophecies in the Old Testament about Jesus, made a few hundred years before his birth. Note that the prophecy says that Jesus will bring justice. And He will not only bring justice to Israel, where He mainly physically lived and worked, but to the nations: His justice will spread throughout the whole earth.

During His ministry on earth, He gave strength to the weakest reed and the flickering candle when He went out of His way to care for the downtrodden and oppressed in society. And as His church today, this is now our mission to continue and take forward.

So let us be encouraged that we are part of God's purpose in bringing justice to the nations (although, of course, true justice will not be achieved until Jesus' second coming). We do this in lots of ways: by our day-to-day work in the law, and also by praying and asking God for justice to prevail not only where we are, but throughout the earth.

- *Pray for God's justice to prevail throughout the earth, especially in countries where access to justice is more restricted.*
- *Pray that we would not "falter or lose heart" in our role in God's mission to bring justice.*

– Jane Edwards (2022)

2 JUN — Sing to the Lord a new song

Sing to the LORD a new song, his praise from the end of the earth, you who go down to the sea, and all that fills it, the coastlands and their inhabitants. Isaiah 42:10 (ESV)

During 2020 and 2021, many of us missed the joy of singing together. But why, and to whom, do we sing?

Isaiah writes to a rebellious Israel, prophesying defeat by their enemies, and exile in Babylon. Thankfully, the story doesn't end there. Our God is ever gracious and merciful – so, to the repentant and humble remnant, hope is offered. The Messiah will come with compassion, bringing justice and salvation to the nations (42:1-9).

What response does this provoke? "Sing to the Lord a new song." Praise, gratitude, and reverence bubble up inside and overflow – how can it not? It may not be tuneful, but it is a heart-filled response of praise, which fills the earth.

The times of 'lockdown were challenging – personally, professionally, spiritually. There have been extraordinary pressures across our justice system, struggling to provide certainty in ever-changing circumstances; delays with court cases; difficulties accessing justice.

The future is uncertain and unclear. Yet the Lord remains faithful, just and merciful.

"He will not grow faint or be discouraged, till he has established justice in the earth; and the coastlands wait for his law." (42:4)

Unlike Isaiah, we have the joy of knowing the risen Jesus, the Messiah. Take heart! Today, whatever your circumstances, make time to meditate on Him, our sure and certain hope – and reflect on who He is, allowing a new song of worship to arise, and overflow, for He is worthy of our praise.

- *Pray for those in our fellowship who are burdened and struggling with their circumstances today, may they find their hope and strength in Jesus;*
- *Pray for those in desperate need of justice in their situation that they might be able to access legal advice and support, but also encounter the transformative power of knowing Christ as Lord;*
- *Pray for our justice system, and all who are a part of it. May it reflect justice, truth and mercy and may those working within it be sustained and strengthened.*

– Mhairi Hamilton (2021)

3 JUN — An incredible burden lifted

Listen to me … you whom I have upheld since you were conceived, and have carried since your birth. Even to your old age and grey hairs I am he, I am he who will sustain

you. I have made you and I will carry you; I will sustain you and I will rescue you. **Isaiah 46:3-4 (NIV 1984)**

In the face of judgment from God – invasion by Persia – Bel and Nebo, the gods of the Babylonians, do not just fail to save the people, but they are heavy burdens that they must carry as they flee (vs 1-2).

Often, we think that we work to please God and that we carry Him to places that He needs to go. That can become an incredible burden, driving us away from rest and twisting our perception of work. It is a lie. The truth is that we are the Beloved. Even before our work begins, and regardless of how well it goes, our loving Father carries us. We do not carry or sustain God – although truthfully, I often act like I do.

What great peace there is, therefore, at the start of another busy week, in remembering that God carries us – from the womb, until old age. He, who never fails, will carry, rescue and sustain each of us, wherever we are.

- *Take your work and the week ahead to the Lord in prayer, and give him thanks that he will carry you through it and know his peace in this.*
- *Give thanks for opportunities Christian lawyers have had to gather together over this last year, and ask the Lord to remind us of the things he has taught us through this and to remember each other as we witness for him this week.*

– Claire Wilkinson (2015)

4 JUN Do you consider yourself beautiful?

How beautiful upon the mountains are the feet of him who brings good news, who publishes peace, who brings good news of happiness, who publishes salvation, who says to Zion, "Your God reigns." **Isaiah 52:7 (ESV)**

News is constantly being made as law is enacted, advice is given and judgments are handed out. It represents good news, peace and happiness for some, and very bad news, including loss and incarceration for others. As lawyers we are often the voice bringing that news.

The prophet Isaiah, in the midst of the pain of exile, spoke of a time when the coming news would be so good that those who heard it would be set free to rejoice and sing. God's salvation, by His sovereign rule and reign, would not be held back. He would bring restoration.

Isaiah's words are a precursor to chapter 53, where we are introduced to the servant who, by his sacrifice, grace and mercy, brings salvation to all who believe it as true. This suffering servant will one day return in redemptive power and glory. This news – good news of peace and joy – needs to be told.

As a Fellowship, our challenge is to speak about Jesus Christ and live out the gospel in our profession. Are we prepared then to speak up and be heralds of this good news with the extraordinary thought that there is something beautiful about us as we do so?

- *Ask God for boldness to speak up and bring the message of Good News to your family, friends, neighbours and colleagues.*
- *Give thanks for your freedom to speak about your faith and trust in Jesus. Pray for those who do not enjoy such freedom in our world today.*

– Mark Barrell (2016)

5 JUN — You do know the word "overwhelmed" is in the Bible, don't you?

**"...the torrents of destruction overwhelmed me."
2 Samuel 22:5b (NIV)**

As lawyers, we can very easily get overwhelmed. Sometimes we have too many different things demanding our attention all at the same time and we feel completely overrun.

In the scripture above, David recalls pressures he faced. Reflecting on this helps us in the pressures we face, for at least 3 reasons:

1. It's a comfort to know that the Bible is "real" about the pressures we face. In it we read of the pressures that David, Moses, Paul and a whole host of others felt. The God who we meet in the Bible is a God who understands what we're going through.

2. More than that, God Himself – in Jesus – faced all kinds of pressures personally Himself whilst on earth. As Hebrews 4:15 says, "For we do not have a high priest who is unable to empathize with our weaknesses, but we have one who has been tempted in every way, just as we are – yet he did not sin."

3. And in the midst of our pressures, we can learn a lesson from David. After reciting how he felt overwhelmed, he continues in verse 7 by saying: "In my distress I called to the LORD; I called out to my God." When we feel assailed, let's do what David did and call out to the God who understands and hears.

- *Thank God that He understands what we face and that He hears us when we pray.*
- *Take time to lay before the Lord the pressures you face today.*

– Dominic Hughes (2012, revised 2023)

6 JUN — The unexpected friend

All of us have become like one who is unclean, and all our righteous acts are like filthy rags ... **Isaiah 64:6a (NIV)**

I often think that the doctrine of total depravity is a great friend for lawyers. Let me explain what I mean ...

You don't need to work as a lawyer for very long to figure out that, every time you lift a rock, you'll find some kind of wrongdoing lurking there. When you examine the affairs of even the most decent clients you'll find something that was wrong or messy.

By the phrase "doctrine of total depravity" I do not of course, mean that everything is as bad as it can be. Instead, I mean that sin affects every part of our lives.

It's actually a comfort that the Bible warns us to expect to find sin lurking everywhere like this.

But how do we respond to such ubiquitous sin?

Sometimes we are tempted to throw our hands up in despair and say "What's the point? This is all a mess!"

But despair is not the answer.

Instead, the problem of widespread sin should drive us to seek the help of the Only One who is big enough to deal with it: the Lord Jesus. He is the One who offers forgiveness for sin. He is the One who will heal and restore the whole of creation. And He hears the prayers of those who are stuck in this messy world and who call out to Him for help.

- Thank the Lord that He is big enough to deal with ubiquitous sin.
- Bring before the Lord some of the mess and sin you are aware of in your cases or work, and seek His help.

– Dominic Hughes (2018)

7 JUN What now?

... Stand at the crossroads and look; ask for the ancient paths, ask where the good way is, and walk in it ... But you said, 'We will not walk in it.' Jeremiah 6:16 (NIV)

The Judeans whom Jeremiah was warning were at a crossroads. They had incurred God's displeasure and were facing his severe punishment.

In the pandemic, we also found ourselves at a crossroads. The pandemic changed how we live, how we communicate, how we behave, how we see the world. Justice was delayed and denied, courts and tribunals closed, emergency laws passed, backlogs created. Church meetings migrated online, gatherings were cancelled, and programmes were obliterated.

Now lockdown has lifted, what now?

We should beware of 'back to normal'! Was God in every aspect of our 'normal' before? Were our lives, our routines, our programmes, truly dependent upon His Spirit? What was the reality?

Let us ask for the ancient paths! The book of Acts is as sobering as it is inspiring. The early church was given to prayer, fasting, preaching the gospel, teaching and being taught the Word of God. They showed us the 'good way'. God walked it with them, with salvations, miracles and persecutions accompanying them throughout.

Before our Heavenly Father, what is our resolution?

Let us pray
- *For hunger and thirst for righteousness – God's good way.*
- *For grace to seek, find and walk in it.*
- *That God would cause our lives to bear good fruit as we do so.*

– Niazi Fetto KC (2020)

8 JUN — Where do you see yourself in five years' time?

Thus says the LORD: "Let not the wise man boast in his wisdom, let not the mighty man boast in his might, let not the rich man boast in his riches, but let him who boasts boast in this, that he understands and knows me, that I am the LORD who practices steadfast love, justice, and righteousness in the earth. For in these things I delight, declares the LORD." Jeremiah 9:23-24 (ESV)

Let's face it: law is so often a business all about getting on, getting up the ladder, and so it's all too easy to boast and over-egg the pudding when it comes to describing our abilities and achievements.

Where do you see yourself in five years' time? Partner, or Managing Partner? Silk, or Head of Chambers?

None of these things is wrong in and of itself, but I wonder whether our aspirations, and the boastfulness that can go with them, betray a desire and focus that is failing to make God and His glory paramount?

We should of course strive for excellence in our work, though our definition of excellence might be different from that of the world. One might be an excellent lawyer, while never 'great' as the world might define it.

As Christian lawyers, our striving for excellence should be based on a desire to please and serve the Lord, rather than simply to achieve worldly success. Indeed, as we make career decisions, do we consider the impact these might have on our families, or on our ability to serve in the local church?

How about we make these verses our priority and let them define our approach to our professional (and personal) lives, and leave the next five years to Him?

- *Praise God for his steadfast love, justice and righteousness!*
- *Pray that we would be humble and boast in the Lord alone.*

– Gavin Callaghan (2019)

9 JUN — Running with horses or struggling at the back of the pack?

*Righteous are you, O LORD,
when I complain to you;*

yet I would plead my case before you.
Why does the way of the wicked prosper?
Why do all who are treacherous thrive?
You plant them, and they take root;
they grow and produce fruit;
you are near in their mouth
and far from their heart.
But you, O LORD, know me;
you see me, and test my heart toward you.
Pull them out like sheep for the slaughter,
and set them apart for the day of slaughter.
…
"If you have raced with men on foot, and they have wearied you,
how will you compete with horses?
And if in a safe land you are so trusting,
what will you do in the thicket of the Jordan?"

Jeremiah 12:1-3 & 5 (ESV)

I think I have developed a bad habit. When commuting home from work I've taken to catching up on the news with the BBC radio app. Maybe it is just a season, but the news is rarely all that encouraging. My bad habit is not listening to the news; it is my reaction to what I hear: it has affected my 'mindset'. As a litigator, I need to be alive to the danger of developing a negative mindset. It is very easy to fall into that trap, particularly when the surrounding cultural narrative seems so unhelpful. This holds true in many areas of the law; it can grind us down.

In reflecting on my poor attitude, I was reminded of the remarkable exchange in this passage. Jeremiah is praying with despondency and despair. He is honest enough to tell the Lord what he makes of the situation. Having got a few things off his chest, I wonder what he expected in response. Verse 5 sees a robust and honest response from the Lord: "You think this is hard?" I wonder for how long did Jeremiah reflect on this answer.

It is right to take all our concerns to the Lord. When we do that, how good are we at listening to his response? Strong relationships allow for honest exchanges. We serve a compassionate God, but he is the 'Almighty', not the 'All Matey'. Sometimes he does tell us that we have got things out of all proportion; at other times that we need to face up to the hard things.

- *This passage is a challenge to 'excellence'. Ask the Lord to reveal to you in what ways might you be struggling along when in fact you can be running with horses.*
- *Pray for the mind of Christ: the gospel protects us from a negative mindset.*
- *Pray for those around you who might be locked into a negative mindset – that they might be liberated from their chains by the gospel of Jesus Christ.*

– Brent Haywood (2018)

10 JUN — In whose strength?

Thus says the Lord: "Cursed is the man who trusts in man and makes flesh his strength, whose heart turns away from the LORD. He is like a shrub in the desert, and shall not see any good come.

He shall dwell in the parched places of the wilderness, in an uninhabited salt land.

Blessed is the man who trusts in the LORD, whose trust is the LORD. He is like a tree planted by water, that sends out its roots by the stream, and does not fear when heat comes, for its leaves remain green, and is not anxious in the year of drought, for it does not cease to bear fruit."

Jeremiah 17:5-8 (ESV)

Over recent times, much of what our clients and colleagues put their hope in has been shaken. As Christians, we have not been exempt – life has been up-ended. For some, this has brought increased personal time, but with uncertainty about the future – exams, training opportunities and job security; for others, the juggle of increased workloads, family and home, and a loss of personal space. The boundaries have become blurred, and the journey is unclear.

In whom do we trust? Jeremiah reminds us that we have a sure and certain hope in the Lord. He is trustworthy and faithful – when we truly trust in Him, and root ourselves in His Word, we don't need to be anxious. The tree flourishes, regardless of its circumstances (v 8). In contrast, those who "make flesh [their] strength" (v 5) find themselves caught in a perpetual cycle, pursuing prosperity, but never attaining fruitfulness.

Trusting in the Lord can be easier when times are uncertain, but what about when circumstances are going well? As lawyers, we could certainly do much within our own strength. However, may I encourage you to use this time to build good habits of trusting the Lord with all aspects of your work, big and small, so that when circumstances change, as they will, you will continue to focus on the Lord, and trust Him with whatever comes your way.

- *Give thanks that in Christ we have a sure and certain hope. May we be bold in offering this good news to those around us.*
- *Let's pray for one another that we would be intentional this week in building the habit of trusting God with all aspects of our work, regardless of our circumstances.*
- *Please remember our Christian lawyer partners across Africa, as they seek to respond to natural disasters and continued challenges around access to justice. May they continue to be rooted in Christ and a beacon of hope for those most in need in their communities.*

– Mhairi Hamilton (2020)

11 JUN — Confidence in uncertainty

"I know the plans I have for you", declares the Lord, "plans to prosper you and not to harm you, plans to give you hope and a future". **Jeremiah 29:11 (NIV)**

Does it ever feel that nothing is ever going to go right at work? Times where there is not enough work, a threat of redundancy, or just a lack of motivation to do the job, can be destabilising.

In these inspiring words, Jeremiah speaks to those in exile from Judah, giving God's hope to them in their captivity. The hope and future they were promised was to bring them back to Judah.

These timeless words are also very relevant to us today. However uncertain the future may seem, we can be confident that God knows of the issues we face and has a plan for that future, whether it may involve staying where we are at present or something completely different.

The key to understanding God's plans for us, when they may not be apparent or when things are difficult or demanding, is that they are in His hands and not ours. It is when we stop looking for all the answers ourselves, and bring our hopes, frustrations and disappointments to the foot of the cross, that we may discover answers to our questions. As the Lord said, "You will seek me and find me when you seek me with all your heart." (Jer 29:13).

- Pray that each one of us may cherish our God-given work, and delight in the fact that He knows each of us and our problems and has plans to use what we do for His glory.

– James Brightwell (2016)

12 JUN — Covenant, Regulation and Reform

"This is the covenant I will make with the people of Israel after that time," declares the Lord. "I will put my law in their minds and write it on their hearts. I will be their God, and they will be my people". **Jeremiah 31:33 (NIV)**

This is one of my favourite Old Testament passages, as it may be for you. The verse above is a snippet from a wonderful promise of restoration by God to His people, given at a very difficult time for them. The particular promise is fulfilled in the new covenant that God has made with us through Christ. By His Spirit, God enables us to internalise and live out His commands with joy.

The Solicitors Regulation Authority has been wrestling with the impact of rules on behaviour, as the latest reforms to its Handbook come into force. The days of detailed rules are long gone. Instead, solicitors and firms have high-level principles and a short code of conduct that they must follow. It is hoped this will encourage solicitors to think more about their actions, and imbibe the principles set down in the Handbook as they do.

However, that can seem a daunting task as guidance on precisely what to do in any given situation is limited.

As Christians, we are not alone navigating the complex and sometimes choppy waters of our work or studies. God has promised to settle His commands, which bring life, deep within us, and enable us to follow them. As we start this week let's commit ourselves afresh to follow God through it, and grow in our understanding of His word.

- Give thanks that God desires to be our God, and us His people, giving us life, purpose and joy.
- Lift your week up to God, and ask that He enables you to follow Him closely through it.

– Jon Hyde (2019)

13 JUN Jeremiah attends a completion meeting

"… my cousin Hanamel came to me in the courtyard of the guard and said, 'Buy my field at Anathoth in the territory of Benjamin. Since it is your right to redeem it and possess it, buy it for yourself.'

I knew that this was the word of the LORD; so I bought the field at Anathoth from my cousin Hanamel and weighed out for him seventeen shekels of silver. I signed and sealed the deed, had it witnessed, and weighed out the silver on the scales. I took the deed of purchase – the sealed copy containing the terms and conditions, as well as the unsealed copy – and I gave this deed to Baruch son of Neriah, the son of Mahseiah, in the presence of my cousin Hanamel and of the witnesses who had signed the deed and of all the Jews sitting in the courtyard of the guard.

In their presence I gave Baruch these instructions: 'This is what the LORD Almighty, the God of Israel, says: Take these documents … and put them in a clay jar so they will last a long time. For this is what the LORD Almighty, the God of Israel, says: Houses, fields and vineyards will again be bought in this land.'"

Jeremiah 32:8-15 (NIV)

This passage should be a favourite for all Christian conveyancing lawyers: the exercise of a right of pre-emption, the public payment of the sale price and then the deed of conveyance containing all the contractual terms – signed, sealed, delivered, witnessed and then preserved, with a duplicate, for future generations to view.

Fantastic though it is to see the intricacies of a 6th century BC real estate completion meeting recorded in holy writ, there is actually a spiritual point to all this: the Babylonian army was already besieging Jerusalem. The field being sold is already in enemy-occupied territory. Only a fool would buy it. Or someone who thought long-term, because he was convinced that what God said about the future would indeed happen. God had promised that people would one day return from their imminent exile to this land. By his purchase Jeremiah demonstrated that he was prepared to put his money where his mouth was. It showed that he trusted God.

As should what we do.

- *Ask God to show you areas in your life where you need to be trusting God more, and for the courage to do so.*
- *Pray for those who are struggling in their workplace and studies this week, that they may know the Lord's guidance and peace.*

– Andrew M (2015)

14 JUN Hope in unsettled times

Yet this I call to mind and therefore I have hope: Because of the LORD's great love we are not consumed, for his compassions never fail. Lamentations 3:21-22 (NIV)

For some, when we reflect upon the uncertain times we live in, it is hard to avoid a deep sense of insecurity, and particular events will be the subject of workplace conversations.

Just as the writer of Lamentations surveyed the destruction around him, including of the temple, the destruction in our own country is a visible reminder of the fallen world we live in and can make us feel that we walk in darkness rather than light (Lam 3:2). Yet it is also a reminder of our need for God.

When we focus on the difficulties of the world, or in our own lives, we are at risk of being consumed by doubt or despair. This can affect every aspect of our lives, including our professional relationships. When we remind ourselves of God's covenant love for his people, we can be assured of His compassion and that we can find our strength in Him. We should seek to be an example to those with whom we work, Christian and non-Christian alike, not of being without uncertainty or suffering, but in surrendering it to the Lord who sustains us.

Great indeed is His faithfulness.

- *Pray for our witness to the country in the face of present uncertainties, and that we may be a sign of God's hope revealed in Jesus Christ.*

– James Brightwell (2017)

15 JUN Heart of stone

I will give you a new heart and put a new spirit in you; I will remove from you your heart of stone and give you a heart of flesh. And I will put my Spirit in you and move you to follow my decrees and be careful to keep my laws. Ezekiel 36: 26-27 (NIV)

It was an album by Cher in 1989 and it is a song in the *SIX* musical, but with a difference of meaning. In Ezekiel, it means the hardness of heart that does not respond to the God of Israel in loving obedience – that does not want to walk in the ways of the Lord. He sent the Holy Spirit to deal with that.

Lawyers may have to be cool, objective, analytical and passion free in giving opinions and advice. As Christian lawyers, however, we need God's law written on our heart and our heart moved to follow His ways and to keep His commands. The effect of the Holy Spirit in us should be to change our heart to make us want to obey Jesus. Not a heart of stone, but a heart of love which leads us to keep His commands. How much is that true of me? How much do I really want Him to change me in that way?

"Search me, O God, and know my heart; test me and know my anxious thoughts. See if there is any offensive way in me, and lead me in the way everlasting."
Psalm 139: 23-24 (NIV 1984)

- *Take a few moments to pray over the words of the Psalm above, to make it your own prayer, asking the Holy Spirit to touch your heart and lead you in the week ahead.*

– Sir Jeremy Cooke (2021)

16 JUN Are you prepared to take a stand?

Daniel then said to the guard whom the chief official had appointed over Daniel, Hananiah, Mishael and Azariah, "Please test your servants for ten days: Give us nothing but vegetables to eat and water to drink. Then compare our appearance with that of the young men who eat the royal food, and treat your servants in accordance with what you see". So he agreed to this and tested them for ten days. At the end of the ten days they looked healthier and better nourished than any of the young men who ate the royal food. So the guard took away their choice food and the wine they were to drink and gave them vegetables instead. **Daniel 1:11-16 (NIV)**

What would your response be if you were asked to do something that you knew went against your beliefs? Would you risk speaking up to challenge the status quo?

In this passage, Daniel faced one of these tough situations where the stakes were very high. Serving in the Babylonian king's court would have required Daniel to be involved in many activities that he might have disagreed with. He was given a new name connecting him with a Babylonian god, and had to study Babylonian literature, but he drew a line where it came to defiling himself with the king's food.

Daniel risked life and limb by asking for an exception to the rule, but notice how he approached the situation in a winsome and tactful way. He knew that honouring God had objectively positive consequences, and in taking a stand he influenced the way in which the hostile Babylonian court operated.

The passage also shows that we might be required to choose where we draw our lines. While we can't always expect to see our objections handled as smoothly as this (NB chapter 6 and Daniel's trip to the Lion's Den!) we shouldn't let our fear of the consequences stop us from speaking up where God calls us to do so. And when we do speak up, we need to be sensitive and wise about how we present our arguments.

- *Praise God that He is with us through whatever trials and tribulations we find ourselves in.*
- *Ask the Lord to strengthen our resolve ahead of any storms we might find ourselves in.*
- *Pray that we would conduct ourselves with the wisdom and integrity of Daniel in the face of testing circumstances.*
- *Pray for opportunities to lead others to God through our obedience to Him.*

– Laurence Wilkinson (2019)

The Lord roars from Zion and thunders from Jerusalem;

Amos 1:2a (NIV)

17 JUN — Right praying for justice

And he hath confirmed his words, which he spake against us, and against our judges that judged us, by bringing upon us a great evil: for under the whole heaven hath not been done as hath been done upon Jerusalem. Daniel 9:12 (KJV)

Daniel prayed these words towards the end of the 70 years of the Babylonian exile. For God to fulfil his promise to restore the people of Israel to Jerusalem, the people needed to repent of the sins that had caused the captivity in the first place. These included the sins of the judges. Too often in our own land we see the wicked acquitted and innocent victims walking away empty handed. Blame can lie anywhere within the system from police officers, jurors, judges, advocates and those involved in the administration of justice generally.

Let us pray for our judicial system and those involved in it, confessing the sins of those responsible for its failings and praying that God would turn away his judgment from our land. God's justice is perfect and God's eternal judgment – hell for those who remain dead in their sins and heaven for the ones justified by Christ – is to be rightly feared.

May justice in our land reflect God's justice. Like Daniel, let us therefore pray to the Lord our God, to whom belong mercy and forgiveness, that all involved in the criminal justice system, from the accused to the Lord Chief Justice and everyone in between, would be turned from their own sins and be justified by the blood of the Lord Jesus Christ, shed for the many whom the Lord has called.

- *Let us give thanks for the just laws that are still on our statute books and wherever justice is done.*
- *Let us confess our own part in injustice, and also pray for those areas where injustice is present in our judicial system.*
- *Let us pray that the Lord would move the hearts of ministers to reform our system and in particular remove ungodly laws and introduce righteous ones in their place.*
- *Let us pray for opportunities to witness to the gospel of our Lord Jesus Christ to those involved in the law that God would turn hearts to His Son.*

– Mark Mullins (2021)

18 JUN — The lion will roar

The Lord roars from Zion and thunders from Jerusalem; Amos 1:2a (NIV)

At a conference for Christian students and young lawyers in 2018, there was an opportunity for joyful fellowship and reflection on the book of Amos. Amos is shot through with the theme of God's anger and frustration at his people for the injustices they are perpetrating. Justice and righteousness should flow from genuine relationship with God, Amos says, but the Israelites' actions have revealed their contempt for both God and other people.

Israel had fallen into the trap of seeing God as weak and powerless to act or (depending on the viewpoint,) as indifferent to injustice. But, in the very first verses, Amos demonstrates the foolishness of this view – the voice of God will be as fierce and powerful as a lion's roar; as vast and deafening as a clap of thunder. God cannot be contained, controlled or overlooked.

Whether we are encountering the real injustice and oppression so often seen in this world for the first time at the start of legal careers, or have many years' experience behind us, it is easy to feel like God is either too powerless to intervene or too distant to care. Let Amos remind us this week that the Lord we serve is deeply, deeply concerned with the lives of the people he created, and more awesome than we can comprehend to act.

- Thank God that he is a powerful and compassionate God, who cares deeply about injustice and the ways people of this world treat each other, and is able to bring about his will.
- Pray that, as we work in the legal world, God would give us a genuine heart for righteousness and justice.

– Elsa Glauert (2018)

19 JUN Wisdom from within the whale

"Those who cling to worthless idols
turn away from God's love for them.
But I, with shouts of grateful praise,
will sacrifice to you.
What I have vowed I will make good.
I will say, 'Salvation comes from the LORD.'"
Jonah 2:8-9 (NIV)

As a lawyer, it's all too easy to think that everything depends on you. Do a good job, find a clever argument, make an eloquent speech and your client will win. Make a mistake and your client may lose.

It's tempting to think that it was this very same attitude that led Jonah to flee from God and end up in the belly of a fish, from where he made this cry. Indeed, I am too often put off sharing the gospel with friends and colleagues because I do not think I have what it takes to persuade them. I forget that salvation comes from the Lord.

However, this was not actually Jonah's problem. In 4:2 he explains that he disobeyed God's instruction to preach in Nineveh because he knew that God is "gracious and compassionate" and "relents from sending calamity". In other words, Jonah knew that God could save the Ninevites but didn't think that those who clung to worthless idols deserved His grace.

Are there people in your life with whom you have not shared the life-giving news of Jesus Christ because you do not think that they are worthy of God's love?

- *Thank God that salvation comes from Him*
- *Praise God that he can save anyone he pleases, no matter how indifferent or even hostile they seem.*
- *Ask God for opportunities to share the gospel this week.*

– Ben Fullbrook (2019)

20 JUN Rolling down rather than limping on

But let justice roll down like waters, and righteousness like an ever-flowing stream. **Amos 5:24 (NRSV)**

Amos faced a situation in which, because of bribery and oppression, justice was not upheld in the courts (Amos 5:10, 12). He called for justice to roll down like a river, righteousness like a never-failing stream. It may not be bribery which prevents justice happening in the British courts, but costs, delays and inefficient administration mean that it can feel as if justice is limping rather than rolling on.

Amos' vision was for a community in which people's righteousness (*tsedeqah*: their right relationship to God and to their fellows) would be expressed in right decisions (*mishpatim*) when conflicts or questions arose, both in and outside of the courtroom.

Let us pray that God will give us wisdom this week to discern how we may promote the resolution of conflict and collaboration which puts relationships right.

- *Consider those situations, whether in relation to clients, family or church, that need reconciliation. Pray now for Godly wisdom, justice and right relationships to prevail.*
- *Pray for all those who are involved in the administration of justice in our nation, and for wise decisions to be made.*

– Dr David McIlroy (2017)

21 JUN Compassion for our colleagues

But it displeased Jonah exceedingly, and he was angry. And he prayed to the LORD and said, "O LORD, is not this what I said when I was yet in my country? That is why I made haste to flee to Tarshish; for I knew that you are a gracious God and merciful, slow to anger and abounding in steadfast love, and relenting from disaster." **Jonah 4:1-2 (ESV)**

Do we long for our colleagues and clients to come to know, and follow, Christ? What about those who perhaps irritate or frustrate us – a difficult boss, an obstructive opposing counsel, a demanding client – do we really believe they deserve the radical salvation of the gospel?

God sent the prophet Jonah to Nineveh to call them to repent but Jonah went in the opposite direction. The

Ninevites were a fearsome people, known for their evil and wickedness. And yet God loved them and longed for them to turn to Him.

It would have been understandable if Jonah had felt scared. Do we let the fear of others, and their reactions, hinder our gospel witness?

However, here we see another emotion: Jonah was angry. He didn't want to share God's word with the Ninevites in case they did repent and turn to God. He didn't think they deserved God's grace and salvation. In our hearts, do we sometimes make a similar call?

The good news of the gospel is that Jesus Christ died for the sins of each and every one of us – none of us deserve God's grace, and yet we all can enjoy this gift if we repent and choose to follow Him.

- *Ask God to give you a heart of compassion for your colleagues and clients this week and seek opportunities to show God's grace and to share the gospel.*

– Mhairi Hamilton (2019)

22 JUN Tantrums or thankfulness?

But the LORD said, "You have been concerned about this vine, though you did not tend it or make it grow." Jonah 4:10a (NIV 1984)

For many people the story of Jonah is a supernatural story about a man who gets swallowed by a fish for three days and is then spat out. 'Jonah, fish, land' and the story is over.

Readers will be familiar with some of the big themes in Jonah beyond this, e.g. the repentance and salvation of the Ninevites or Jonah's 3 days in the fish being a pre-figuring of Jesus' 3 days in the earth or (as we will focus on here) God's provision.

Chapter 4 begins with Jonah throwing a childlike tantrum about God saving the people of Nineveh. After his tantrum, God provides a shelter for him: a shelter Jonah put no work towards. When the Lord takes it away, Jonah is very upset which is when the Lord reminds Jonah he did nothing to earn the shelter.

How often do we find ourselves in the same situation complaining to the Lord despite his abundant provision in our lives? When we are facing hardship at work, do we forget to give thanks for our job? When we are stuck in a rut with our studies, do we forget the privilege it is to be studying at all? This may be particularly if we find ourselves at a point in our lives where we didn't imagine ourselves – e.g. trainee not solicitor, solicitor not senior associate, senior associate not partner.

- *Spend a moment repenting of the times when you might be ungrateful or complaining.*

- *Take time to think about the things for which you are grateful and where God has abundantly provided – perhaps even jot them down on a post-it note at your desk to encourage you as you go through the week.*
- *And for everything else, the worries around us, the things going on, the people on our minds, let's raise them up in prayer.*

– Esther Wade (2021)

23 JUN Watch, and be amazed

How long, LORD, must I call for help, but you do not listen? Or cry out to you, 'Violence!' but you do not save? Why do you make me look at injustice? Why do you tolerate wrongdoing? Destruction and violence are before me; there is strife, and conflict abounds. Therefore the law is paralysed, and justice never prevails. The wicked hem in the righteous, so that justice is perverted.

"Look at the nations and watch – and be utterly amazed. For I am going to do something in your days that you would not believe, even if you were told."

Habakkuk 1:2-5 (NIV)

Lawyers can often be faced with the day-to-day reality of injustice, wrong-doing and conflict in the world. Many among the legal community will spend their working lives battling against the injustices and violence we see in the world around us. For all of us, life can feel uncertain.

It can be tempting sometimes to cry out, as Habakkuk did – God, why do you not listen? Or not act? And rather than call Habakkuk out on the audaciousness of questioning God in this way, God is gracious and responds – watch what I will do, and be utterly amazed.

God was not deaf or blind to the injustice in Israel that Habakkuk despaired at. We have a God who is never unaware of the realities of the world we live in. He may be acting in ways that we don't yet perceive or understand but, ultimately, we can be supremely confident that he is acting. This side of the cross we even have the privilege of seeing his ultimate plan for the salvation of the world through Jesus Christ. And just as the prophet learnt to rejoice in God despite his circumstances, when we or others around us encounter situations in life that make us feel hopeless we can take comfort and strength in knowing that our God is able and willing to act.

- *Pray that Christian lawyers would have confidence even in difficult circumstances that our God is able and willing to act.*
- *Pray for those struggling with the brokenness of the world around us, that they would take comfort that our God is in control.*

– Elsa Glauert (2021)

24 JUN — Waiting for the Lord's answer

I will stand upon my watch, and set me upon the tower, and will watch to see what he will say unto me, and what I shall answer when I am reproved. **Habakkuk 2:1 (KJV)**

Habakkuk had a burden (1:1) which arose from the state of the Nation of Israel and which led him to bring that burden to the Lord in the form of a complaint. His first complaint was about injustice in the nation: "Therefore the law is slacked, and judgment doth never go forth: for the wicked doth compass about the righteous; therefore wrong judgment proceedeth" (1:4). The Lord's answer in verses 5 to 11 that He would raise up the Babylonians to invade the land resulted in Habakkuk's second complaint that the Lord was using an even more wicked people to devour men more righteous than them.

Our own nation sadly contains its own injustice within the legal system and we increasingly depart from biblical laws. We should follow Habakkuk's example and bring our burdens to the Lord in prayer. National burdens should form part of our prayers, but so too should the burden to see our friends, families and work colleagues saved.

Habakkuk isolated himself in a tower. The weight of his burden caused him to watch and wait for the Lord to answer. Can I encourage you, with the different burdens that you carry, to take them first to the Lord Jesus, and then to wait for Him to answer through and according to His Word.

- *Let us pray for unjust laws to be repealed and just laws to take their place remembering that righteousness exalts a nation, but sin is a reproach to any people (Proverbs 14:34); and*
- *Let us pray for the salvation of our friends, families and work colleagues.*

– Mark Mullins (2020)

25 JUN — Why our service is never futile

"You have said harsh things against me," says the LORD. "You have said, 'It is futile to serve God. What did we gain by carrying out His requirements ... now we call the arrogant blessed. Certainly the evildoers prosper, and even those who challenge God escape.'"

Then those who feared the LORD talked with each other, and the LORD listened and heard. A scroll of remembrance was written in His presence concerning those who feared the LORD and honoured His Name.

"They will be mine", says the LORD Almighty, "in the day when I make up my treasured possession ... you will again see the distinction between the righteous and the wicked, between those who serve God and those who do not."

Malachi 3:13-18 (NIV 1984)

Why might it seem futile to serve God? Because we appear to get nothing out of it? Is that a good reason or merely evidence of our self-centred nature – our old self – looking for what God will do for us?

It is easy to be discouraged as we see the arrogant, the self-promoting and the self-centred flourish in the competitive legal sphere which we inhabit, whilst our attempts to serve God in the law appear neither to be recognised nor to bear fruit, whether in the eyes of the world or in what we perceive as the effect of our witness to Him.

So what does Malachi say in verse 16 (italics)? *Then those who feared the Lord talked with each other.* They met with each other to share their pain. They must have encouraged one another and talked in such a way that *the Lord listened and heard.* The ensuing picture is yet more encouraging – *a scroll of remembrance was written in His presence of all those who feared Him and honoured His Name.*

The Lord knows what is happening to us and we are to be *His treasured possession* (v 17). That should be enough for us. It is our relationship to Him and our loyalty and fidelity in living for Him that matters most.

What do I get out of serving Him? Not the right question, surely? The Lord knows who are His, and He treasures us as we should surely treasure Him.

- *Give thanks for the wonderful promises we have in Christ and the knowledge that whatever happens to us, as we serve him, we are his treasured possession.*

– Sir Jeremy Cooke (2017)

26 JUN Calling all peacemakers!

Blessed are the peacemakers, for they will be called children of God. **Matthew 5:9 (NIV)**

If you stopped someone in the street and asked them to describe a lawyer in one word, what odds would you give to them using 'peacemaker'? I think we could agree that the prospects of success would be poor!

However, as He opens the Sermon on the Mount with the Beatitudes, Jesus is clear that His disciples should be known as precisely that. In fact, it is evidence that they are children of God. Children reflect their father, and God is the supreme peacemaker. Jesus says that those who emulate God in this way are blessed.

How might we reflect Him as lawyers?

One way is by being His instrument as He leads us to make peace between people, particularly in our cases and also in our workplaces. Moreover, God made peace with us through the cross when we were His enemies and thereby reconciled us to Himself. Accordingly, we can also seek to emulate Him by His Spirit in loving and making peace with our 'enemies' insofar as we can, be they opponents in our cases or even colleagues at work. Let us be known and distinctive by reflecting our Heavenly Father in this way.

- *Give thanks to God for making peace possible between Him and us through the cross.*
- *Ask God to show you ways in which you can make peace this week and to empower you by His Spirit to do so.*

– Jon Hyde (2015)

27 JUN Flavour of the week!

You are like salt for everyone on earth. But if salt no longer tastes like salt how can it make food salty? All it is good for is to be thrown out and walked on. **Matthew 5:13 (CEV)**

Let me tell you why you are here. You're here to be salt-seasoning that brings out the God-flavours of this earth. If you lose your saltiness, how will people taste godliness? You've lost your usefulness and will end up in the garbage. **Matthew 5:13 (MSG).**

Salt which remains in a jar by the cooker is useless. To be useful it has to be used to season the food. Salt has a number of uses, but serves mainly to give flavour and to prevent corruption (purify).

Christian lawyers, if they are true to their calling, should make the office, chambers or courtroom a purer and more palatable place. But they can only do so if they preserve their distinctive character. Unsalty salt has no value.

To be salty may well mean being counter cultural – something that St Paul touches on in Romans 12:2: "Do not be conformed to this world" (ESV).

So here's the thought: are we flavoursome Christian lawyers? Is the way we act or react in the workplace salty and counter cultural or is it flavourless and bland?

- *Pray that this week you might by God's grace be the salt which brings a Christ-like distinctive to your place of work and study.*
- *Give thanks for gatherings of Christian law students and young lawyers and pray that, with the help of the Holy Spirit, they might build on and implement in their own lives what they heard and learnt.*

– John Head (2016)

28 JUN The great commission

"You are the light of the world. A town built on a hill cannot be hidden. Neither do people light a lamp and put it under a bowl. Instead they put it on its stand, and it gives light to everyone in the house. In the same way, let your light shine before others, that they may see your good deeds and glorify your Father in heaven." **Matthew 5:14-16 (NIV)**

As the Attorney General for Northern Ireland reminded those at a meeting recently, unlike those of some other (more inwardly looking) religions: "A Christian must preach the gospel. A Christian cannot keep Christianity to themselves. A Christian who does not spread the good news acts inconsistently with his or her Christian faith".

He went on to say "There is no one way to spread the good news. Good preaching is often done outside the pulpit and the best preaching is sometimes wordless." In other words, as Jesus himself put it in the passage above from Matthew's gospel: "You are the light of the world … let your light shine before others, that they may see your good deeds and glorify your Father in heaven". We need to be telling people about Jesus Christ, and living lives that reflect that too.

Our lives, both our words and actions, are a constant sermon to those around us, even if we think no one is listening or indeed watching. Let us hope and indeed pray that they are always a proclamation of the gospel and that we are not failing in our great commission to make disciples of all because we are not letting our light shine.

- *Ask for wisdom this week to know when and how to speak up about your faith in Christ.*

– Peter Brown (2017)

29 JUN Sugar-coating the merits

"Again, you have heard that it was said to the people long ago, 'Do not break your oath, but fulfil to the Lord the vows you have made.' But I tell you, do not swear an oath at all: either by heaven, for it is God's throne; or by the earth, for it is his footstool … All you need to say is simply 'Yes' or 'No'; anything beyond this comes from the evil one." Matthew 5:33-37 (NIV)

The blessed simplicity of Jesus' teaching! The Jewish leaders had developed elaborate ways of deceiving people whilst retaining a clear conscience: one example was that if they swore by the temple altar they considered themselves not to be bound by it, but if they swore by the gift on the altar, they were bound (Matt 23:18). Jesus cut straight through it: all you need to say is simply 'yes' or 'no. Then there is no room for slippery behaviour.

Although we may see some oaths in our professional work (the witness who says "I swear on my life I didn't see it!"), it may be rare for the average Christian lawyer to resort to swearing in this way. That does not mean this passage is irrelevant. It may have got to the point where we've made so many broken promises that colleagues or clients or our families (or God) no longer believe or expect us to abide by our 'yes' and our 'no'.

And what about a sugar-coated assessment of the merits of a case? Or a deliberately ambiguous e-mail intended to buy you wriggle-room? Or the agreement to an impossibly optimistic deadline? Even if these are well-intentioned, they all have the capacity to deceive.

Today is an opportunity to start afresh. Let's start making our 'yes', our 'yes' and our 'no', our 'no'.

- *If there are areas where a fresh start is needed in your own life, bring them the Lord and seek his mercy, forgiveness and wisdom.*
- *Give thanks for Christian young lawyers and pray for them as they make decisions in their working life, often against the prevailing culture, that they may be able to honour God without compromise.*

– Thomas Cordrey (2017)

30 JUN A completely different way

You have heard that it was said, 'You shall love your neighbour and hate your enemy.' But I say to you: love your enemies, bless those who curse you, do good to those who hate you, and pray for those who spitefully use you and persecute you, that you may be sons of your Father in heaven. **Matthew 5:43-45 (NKJV)**

Therefore you shall be perfect, just as your Father in heaven is perfect. **Matthew 5:48 (NKJV)**

We do not follow the world's teaching, religious views, godless dictates of certain 'political correctness', or immoral attacks on the Bible. We follow Jesus, 'the Way the Truth and the Life'. Lawyers are the same as anyone else – no godly power or status has come from an LL.B, further degree, or the Bar Council, or the Law Society.

We live in the same world as others. Some people can become our enemies, despite our lives honouring the Lord. Have you ever been sworn at? Join the club! Some hate the nicest Christians, especially when they resolutely honour God and His standards. We can be ostracised or marginalised (an old expression is 'spitefully used') by others.

The world says: 'Hit back'. Note the verbs that Jesus uses to give each of us our marching orders as 'a soldier of the cross'* and 'a follower of the Lamb': 'love', 'do good to', and 'pray for'. The reason is because everyone who receives Christ as Saviour becomes a child of God (John 1:12) and begins to show the family characteristics as 'sons of your Father in heaven'. We also now have as our goal, though never achieved fully on earth, to 'be perfect, just as your Father in heaven is perfect'.

The Saviour we trust, follow and obey displayed these qualities without fault when He came to die for our sins on the cross. We need to keep close to Him.

*From 'Am I a soldier of the cross?' by Isaac Watts.

- Am I ready to be opposed unreasonably without getting personal with my would-be adversary?
- Could I make a prayer list now of people who have 'spitefully used' me and for whose good and blessing I should earnestly pray?

– Gerard Chrispin (2018)

1 JUL Disagreeing well

"But I say to you, love your enemies, bless those who curse you, do good to those who hate you, and pray for those who spitefully use you and persecute you …"
Matthew 5:44 (NKJV)

Jesus challenges us to trust in Him in the midst of conflict – not to repay hate with hate and to bless our enemies. To do so, we will need to have God's love for them in our hearts.

Applying these words in our lives, how should we deal with people with whom we disagree? These may be friends, neighbours or even fellow church members. At work they may be colleagues, clients, those on the other side of a negotiation, or even a judge who you believe has made a mistake in law. We will need God's grace and His wisdom, while holding fast to the truth.

Depending upon the situation, this may look something like the following:
- Listening carefully to the argument of the other person
- Not interrupting
- Not pre-judging what you think they are going to say
- Asking questions to clarify what they are saying
- Endeavouring to understand what is at stake for the other person – thinking of yourself in their position
- Not assuming that the disagreement goes wider than the point(s) under discussion
- Being tactful and gracious in pointing out what you think is incorrect
- Not needlessly repeating a point that you have already made, though you may need to ask a question to clarify why your point has been rejected
- While not compromising a principle, looking for ways to work together

Heavenly Father, when we are in disagreement with others:
- *Calm our spirit and give us inward peace, trusting in You.*
- *Help us to love the other person(s), however difficult or unreasonable they may appear (to us) to be.*
- *Give us wisdom to look for constructive ways forward, while not compromising the truth.*
- *And in these situations, may Your kingdom come and Your will be done.*

– John Scriven (2022)

2 JUL — Forgiven to forgive

And forgive us our debts,
As we forgive our debtors.
And do not lead us into temptation,
But deliver us from the evil one.
For Yours is the kingdom and the power and the glory forever. Amen.
"For if you forgive men their trespasses, your heavenly Father will also forgive you. But if you do not forgive men their trespasses, neither will your Father forgive your trespasses."
Matthew 6:12-15 (NKJV)

The glorious good news of the Gospel is that our sins are forgiven. We don't have to engage in the impossible, exhausting task of trying to do enough good works to outweigh the wrongs we have done. God in Christ offers His forgiveness to all who truly repent. But … there is a catch. Those who have been forgiven by God are called to forgive those who have sinned against us. Not only did Jesus expressly link our forgiveness by God with our forgiveness of others, it is the one point in the Lord's Prayer which he immediately re-emphasised. Jesus made the same point at greater length in the Parable of the Unmerciful Servant (Matthew 18:21-35), in answer to Peter's question about how many times we should forgive one another. God's forgiveness of us is without limit, and the acknowledgment of the true depth of our need for forgiveness should inspire us to, with the help of the Holy Spirit, keep on forgiving those who wrong us.

Forgiveness isn't easy or cheap; it doesn't bypass judgment. Forgiveness can only come after something has been named as wrong and condemned as such. The law is powerless to offer forgiveness, but as lawyers we need to practise forgiveness in our relationships in order to stay in a healthy relationship with our heavenly Father. We should be encouraging our clients to forgive, but we cannot make that decision for them.

As we begin this week, let's take a moment to search our hearts.
- *Are there any unconfessed sins for which we need to ask God's forgiveness?*
- *Are there any wrongs others have done to us which we are nursing?*
- *Who are the people in our workplaces, our families, our churches, our communities that we need to forgive?*
- *Are there clients who need to forgive, or to be forgiven?*

– Dr David McIlroy (2022)

3 JUL — Getting our priorities right

No one can serve two masters, for either he will hate the one and love the other, or he will be devoted to the one and despise the other. You cannot serve God and money.
Matthew 6:24 (ESV)

For too many of us, the legal profession has become a pressured commercial environment where the drive to achieve financial and other targets is in danger of becoming a greater priority than achieving justice for our clients. It is all too easy to be driven by the fees that one is getting for a case rather than the privilege of being able to help a client to achieve the right and fair result.

Jesus spoke about the risks of developing a love of money on several occasions. In this passage from the Sermon on the Mount, Jesus warns us of the serious dangers if we develop an unhealthy subservience to money because we cannot serve both God and money. It is important therefore to keep this warning at the forefront of our minds at all times and to strive to get our priorities right, at work and throughout our lives, to place our love of our glorious sovereign God above all else, and not to allow our lives to be driven by a love of money.

- *Pray that we will not allow a love of money to prevail in our work or to otherwise prevail in our lives.*
- *Pray that in all that we do, working as lawyers and more widely in our lives, we might get our priorities right and allow our love for our glorious and sovereign God to prevail above all else, so that we might best strive to achieve justice.*

– HHJ Mark Cawson KC (2018)

4 JUL — Are you dressed properly?

"Which of you by being anxious can add a single hour to his span of life? And why are you anxious about clothing? Consider the lilies of the field, how they grow: they neither toil nor spin, yet I tell you, even Solomon in all his glory was not arrayed like one of these." Matthew 6:27-29 (ESV)

What do you worry about? Maintaining the image of doing it all? Winning or losing the case? Impressing your boss, colleagues or client? Or is it the next steps – Training contract? Tenancy? Partnership? Maybe your anxiety is more deep-seated – are you a "worrier"?

This is not what God has planned for us.

If you clothe yourself in worry, your core focus is not on God but on your fears, causing you to act from a place of insecurity and defensiveness – diverted from a love for others to self-protection. Staying late at work, missing time with Christian friends or skipping time with God for fear of missing out, not succeeding, or somehow not being able to do it all – without God, it's a lonely place to be.

Clothing ourselves in Christ (Gal. 3:27), we can find peace. The challenges that face us remain, but we are able to respond from a place of confidence and love, reflecting God into our situation; secure in the knowledge that "as we seek first the kingdom of God and his righteousness" (Matt. 6:33), God will meet us and give us all that we need.

What and who are you clothed in today?

- *Give thanks that we do not need to act out of fear or anxiety, but that we can have confidence in God, for He has overcome.*
- *Pray that the Holy Spirit would change our hearts, that we may be clothed with God's righteousness and know His peace.*

– Mhairi Hamilton (2015)

5 JUL Ask, seek, knock, and…!

"Ask, and it will be given to you; seek, and you will find; knock, and it will be opened to you." **Matthew 7:7 (NKJV)**

No-one has been entirely unaffected by the Covid-19 pandemic. I had the pleasure of sending an email to a young man to inform him that his pupillage would finally start, seven months late. A rare moment of joy in all the difficulties besetting the justice system and legal practice.

For some, it has been a time to make lifestyle changes. For others, there has been the joy (or frustration) of working from home. On a deeper level, there have been worries over job security, care for employees, loss of income, and reduced access to justice for many desperate people. For the students among us, the future of a career in law may look challenging.

This verse, known well to many, reminds us that our God cares about every aspect of our lives. He longs for us to come to Him; to seek His will, His direction, His perfect plan for our lives. When we "ask", "seek" and "knock" on our knees, and at times in tears, He promises us "AND" it will be given, found and opened to us.

Whatever the future holds, trust in a loving Heavenly Father, who gave His Son to die on the cross for our sins and who longs to bless His redeemed people. Have confidence in His promises. Commit your way to Him.

- *Please pray for clients and colleagues carrying any additional worries: that they would come to Jesus and find rest for their souls.*
- *Please pray for Christian lawyers making big life choices, that they would have the grace and wisdom they need.*

– Esther Harrison (2020)

6 JUL Applying the golden rule

'So whatever you wish that others would do to you, do also to them, for this is the Law and the Prophets. Enter by the narrow gate. For the gate is wide and the way is easy that leads to destruction, and those who enter by it are many. For the gate is narrow and the way is hard that leads to life, and those who find it are few.' **Matthew 7:12-14 (ESV)**

In creating the world, God's plan was to bring order out of disorder and provide for his creation. To function as

God intended, this created order fundamentally depends upon justice being done (Proverbs 21:15 and Psalm 89:14). It is only if justice can be done that commerce can be conducted on a proper and beneficial footing, and wealth created to provide for our schools and hospitals etc., wrongs can be made right, and crimes can be punished. However, justice being done depends upon the rule of law being upheld and maintained.

Whatever area of law we, as lawyers, practice in, we are called by God to engage in furthering God's plan for his created order, and to facilitate this process by playing our part in upholding and maintaining the rule of law.

What this passage from the Sermon on the Mount helps us to remember is that if we are to do this properly and effectively, then we must always act in a godly way, in particular in our relations with others, and to remember that in all that we do, we are either firmly with Jesus or against him.

- *We pray that in all we do in our work as lawyers, and throughout our lives, we might act in a godly way, in particular in our relations with others, at all times doing to others what we would wish them to do to us.*
- *We pray that in all we do we might let Jesus into our lives and submit to him, remembering at all times that God has a plan for his creation and that Jesus is our Sovereign Lord.*

– HHJ Mark Cawson KC (2016)

7 JUL A matter of construction…

'Therefore everyone who hears these words of mine and puts them into practice is like a wise man who built his house on the rock. The rain came down, the streams rose, and the winds blew and beat against the house; yet it did not fall because it had its foundation on the rock.'
Matthew 7:24-27 (NIV)

The outward appearance of a building can be deceptive. A structure may seem grand, imposing and built to last. Rain and wind can quickly reveal the truth.

As lawyers, I expect most have the experience of trying to construct arguments which are not well founded on either the law or the evidence: cases which, at first sight, appear imposing and solid, but, in the scrutiny of correspondence or the storm of trial, turn out to be houses of straw which, despite our best efforts and intentions, collapse under the huffing and puffing from our opponent or judge.

The questions are left to us to answer:

- Upon what will you build your life? Will it be on Jesus and what he has done for you?
- How will you seek to build? With what, and for what purpose?

Jesus has given us the means (Himself), the method (the Gospel), and the strength (His Spirit), to build our lives upon Him. We would do well to listen to our Master Builder. For only that built on Him will last.

- Pray that God would convict you of the ways in which you seek to build houses of straw.
- Pray that all you build this week would be built on Jesus and His Gospel.
- Pray that the Lord would use you and your labours this week to build his Kingdom.

– Rob Horner (2020)

8 JUL Burdened or uplifted?

'Come to me, all you who are weary and burdened, and I will give you rest.' Matthew 11:28 (NIV)

When Jesus says this to us, he is not issuing a command. He is giving an invitation. But it is not an invitation alone. It is an invitation coupled with a promise. He wants us to respond willingly. There can be no force attached to putting our trust in him. We don't know where such a willing acceptance will lead throughout our lives; but that is the nature of faith. "Faith is the assurance of things hoped for, the conviction of things not seen" (Hebrews 11:1 (NRSV)).

So when we come to Jesus, we should expect to receive a blessing – a more modern word may be 'uplift' – and that blessing can be carried forward into our professional work and recreation. What form does the blessing take?

'Come to me, all you who are weary and burdened, and I will give you rest.'

Matthew 11:28 (NIV)

Sometimes it will provide peace and quiet as we commit our lives into the Lord's hands. At other times it will provide encouragement as we seek to obey him and to do his will. At yet other times we shall receive, through the Holy Spirit, the confidence to stand up for Jesus.

Let us rest in the knowledge that Jesus, through his death on the cross, has made it possible for us to be assured of salvation and to have eternal fellowship with him.

"Come to Jesus not because you must but because you may, Come not to express an opinion, but to seek a presence and pray for a spirit …" *

*Call to Worship. Book of Services' 4th ed. (page 165) printed 1938, by D. T. Patterson.

Bring the burdens of this week to the Lord and commit them into his hands, trusting in his sovereignty.

– HH Alan Taylor (2017)

9 JUL — How can wheat and weeds grow together?

Jesus told them another parable: 'The kingdom of heaven is like a man who sowed good seed in his field. But while everyone was sleeping, his enemy came and sowed weeds among the wheat, and went away. When the wheat sprouted and formed ears, then the weeds also appeared.' Matthew 13:24-26 (NIV UK)

This parable covers the whole of history under God's sovereign rule, addressing the tension of living in a fallen world.

The servants wanted to pull up the weeds, but the owner forbade this until the harvest, to avoid harming the crop. So we must respect God's decision to defer His judgment on unbelievers. Our role is to be peacemakers, to encourage fair dealing and mitigate the damage sinful people can inflict on God's world. We are His agents to help the wheat and the weeds to get on together until Jesus returns.

Our help as lawyers is needed in 'non-contentious' transactions and other business because people cannot trust each other to do what is right, and in litigation because something has gone wrong. Our profession may not therefore be needed in the new heaven and earth, which will be full of righteousness (2 Peter 3:13).

Therefore our role as lawyers is our calling but not our identity. At the time of harvest, our work as lawyers may end, but the Bible is clear that we will have work to do in the world to come. Whatever the nature of that work, we are being prepared for it now. Our identity is not as lawyers but as adopted children of God through faith in Christ – while we are practising, after retirement and beyond the grave.

- *Thank God for your new identity as His son or daughter through faith in Jesus and pray for that to motivate you as you serve Him in the practice or study of law and in the rest of your life.*
- *Pray for your clients to instruct you to deal fairly with the other parties to any business you are conducting for them and for a just and fair outcome of any negotiations or proceedings.*

– Graham Whitworth (2017)

10 JUL — Fermenting and flourishing across Europe

Another parable He spoke to them: 'The kingdom of heaven is like leaven, which a woman took and hid in three measures of meal till it was all leavened.' Matthew 13:33 (NKJV)

As with salt and light, a small amount of leaven (yeast) is enough to ensure its effect. The peculiarity of the sourdough is that it is living organisms (unicellular) which initiate a transformation process, in order to convert the starting material into a higher-value state: from dough comes bread; from grape juice, wine; from grain, beer; from milk, cheese.

And just as sourdough works in secret, Christians, even in times of persecution and underground networks, flourish – at that time within the Roman Empire, and still today around the world. Just as those living in the time of Jesus little understood the exact biological processes of fermentation, so the individual disciples often understood little about how the kingdom of God worked, but in both cases it works. Where Christians live their lives in a binding communion with our Living Lord and with each other, they work as such living cells, often only in twos or threes: in every law firm and government office, in regional groups and in prayer communities at the universities, and in our meetings with partners locally, nationally and internationally.

When preparing for the European Christian Lawyers Conference in Berlin, I was reminded that God is calling lawyers from all over Europe to worship Him, to encourage one another and to be equipped to speak His gospel truths, and to encourage them to trust in the power of the Kingdom of God.

Please pray:

- *When we meet as lawyers from different countries, that we may be open to hear from God, and encourage one another, testing what we hear against the Word of God.*
- *For all Christian lawyers, but especially for colleagues from countries where there is still no network of Christian lawyers, that they do not fall into the trap of thinking of themselves as too small.*

- *That we would all trust in the Word of Jesus, and remember that like yeast, God can work in and through us to transform our communities.*

– Martin Franke (2018)

11 JUL — What's the most valuable thing you have?

'The kingdom of heaven is like treasure hidden in a field. When a man found it, he hid it again, and then in his joy went and sold all he had and bought that field.' Matthew 13:44 (NIV)

Assumptions about value surround us in the legal profession. Many (though not all) lawyers are relatively well paid, and inhabit a culture in which comparisons about the value of our possessions or experiences are the norm. Conversation easily revolves around fairly unsubtle boasts about cars, houses, or holidays. In private practice, the idea that some people's time is more valuable than that of others is simply embedded in the way we work: an hour's work by a partner or KC is worth much more than that of a trainee or junior. Discussions about how to charge for legal services are loaded with terms such as 'added value' and 'value based' pricing.

In this world, it is easy to lose perspective on where ultimate value lies. Jesus' brief parable reminds us that what is most valuable – worth much more than everything else we have put together – is in knowing God as our Father, and being able to live under his loving rule. Christ's grace towards us in the gospel outweighs whatever any of us or our colleagues may otherwise prize.

Let us develop the habit of rightly treasuring this precious gift, so that we guard our hearts against the distortions of value that can creep into our thinking. And as we then see more clearly the spiritual poverty of those around us, let us take every opportunity to share with them the one thing that will make them truly rich – the knowledge of God in Jesus Christ.

- *Thanks be to God for his indescribable gift! (2 Cor 9:15, NIV)*
- *Pray that we would be able to stand against the consumerist mindset of our culture and profession, and that we would live and speak in a way that values Christ above everything else.*
- *Pray that, as we do so, we would be able to point others to Christ's infinite worth.*

– Caroline Eade (2015)

12 JUL — What's it worth?

'Again, the kingdom of heaven is like a merchant looking for fine pearls. When he found one of great value, he went away and sold everything he had and bought it.' Matthew 13:45-46 (NIV)

We rightly talk to clients a lot in civil litigation about cost-benefit analysis. We compare the amount in dispute to the costs of carrying on, in light of the chances of success. If there are good prospects, and it will cost less to fight than is at stake, we often plough on. But if the costs will outweigh the damages, then even with reasonable prospects we'll encourage the client to think hard about settling quickly. It's just not worth the money to carry on.

In this short parable Jesus tells of a sophisticated businessman, perhaps not unlike some of our clients, who did his own cost-benefit analysis. He desperately wanted fine pearls and, when he found one with great value, he sold everything he had to buy it. He weighed up the cost of what he would have to sell to buy the pearl, and happily paid it for what he would gain.

Jesus likens God's kingdom to that fine pearl of such value. However, day-to-day there is plenty around us in our legal work that can seem more valuable – what we're paid, our career, who our clients are, what our peers think of us, how successful we seem. These things do have a value, but it will always be less than the value of knowing and following God. What is that worth to you?

- *Take a moment to reflect again on God's majesty and holiness, and His awesome love for us. Let's give Him the rightful place ahead of everything else that's going on for us this week.*
- *Pray for God's perspective on all that you face this week, that you would know Him close to you in it, and that you would follow Him in all that you do.*

– Jon Hyde (2018)

13 JUL — DON'T PANIC!

Jesus immediately said to them: 'Take courage! It is I. Don't be afraid.' Matthew 14:27 (NIV)

When the disciples, towards the end of the night in a boat buffeted by waves and wind, saw someone walking towards them on the water, they can be pardoned for their natural fear. Jesus at once reassures them: "Don't be afraid!" Perhaps he might have said, "Don't panic!". Fear was banished, and Peter even had confidence to walk on water himself and go towards Jesus, until he looked away and saw the wind, fear returned, and he began to sink. Jesus caught him and helped him into the boat.

You may not be out in the dark in a boat this week, but there could be challenging times ahead as we are faced with problems which may seem to be overwhelming. Before leaving for chambers, office, court or studies each day, claim this word from the Lord Jesus. He has promised to be with us always. We can take courage and face whatever challenges lie ahead, for He is beside us.

- *Pray for a sense of Jesus beside you at all times.*
- *Pray for calm when tempted to panic in an emergency.*
- *Pray for opportunities to reassure others facing testing.*

– Michael Hawthorne (2018)

14 JUL Revelation

'But what about you?' he asked. 'Who do you say I am?' Simon Peter answered, 'You are the Messiah, the Son of the living God.' Jesus replied, 'Blessed are you, Simon son of Jonah, for this was not revealed to you by flesh and blood, but by my Father in heaven.' **Matthew 16:15-17 (NIV)**

As lawyers and members of today's society we deal almost constantly in information. We obtain it, share it, weigh it, give advice and make decisions based upon it. We look to inform ourselves better professionally and personally; we regard being well-informed as necessary to our competence and to our practical worth, both to clients within our work and to friends and family outside it.

It is necessary to be well-informed about the most important issue in life: the identity of the God of all creation. But it is not enough. Jesus was pleased with Simon Peter's response, not because he had reached a reasonable view on the available evidence, applying the correct standard of proof, but because he knew who Jesus was by revelation from God the Father.

I know a lot about Jesus of Nazareth. I believe the information and evidence I have seen about Him. But today do I know Him? Good information enables me to make good decisions; revelation drives me into wholehearted service.

Let us not just be mental assenters, well-informed about Jesus and able to argue His case, but people to whom He has been revealed, blessed in knowing who we are in Him and equipped by His Spirit to reveal Him to others.

- *Pray that we might know Jesus and the power of His resurrection.*
- *Pray that we might reveal Him in our daily lives to those around us.*
- *Pray that those around us might know and live for Him.*

– Niazi Fetto KC (2018)

15 JUL How's your hearing?

While he was still speaking, a bright cloud covered them, and a voice from the cloud said, 'This is my Son, whom I love; with him I am well pleased. Listen to him!' **Matthew 17:5 (NIV)**

There are few experiences in life as frustrating as feeling like someone is not listening to you properly.

As lawyers we end up listening to a wide range of people for a wide range of reasons. We listen to clients to identify concerns and come up with relevant solutions. We listen to opponents to find cracks and flaws in their answers. We listen in a different way if we are being given instructions by our bosses or inviting suggestions from our colleagues. Our ears are very flexible.

And despite this flexibility, I wonder how often we stop to check how we are listening to Jesus? In this verse the command couldn't be clearer: 'Listen to Him!' But before we reach the command, Jesus is declared to be God's Son; as the one whom God loves; and as the one with whom God is well pleased. These characteristics proclaim both the greatness of Jesus and his close proximity to the Father, and they give the command to 'Listen!' a whole new significance. Jesus is the one to whom we should be listening above all the other voices in this world that fight for our attention; and we should be listening not only to understand but to love and obey. So as we go into this week, let us be encouraged to keep listening to Jesus – with the right sort of ears.

- *Pray that in our busy lives as lawyers we would be listening to Jesus above all of the many other voices that we hear every day.*
- *Pray for students and younger lawyers just starting out in their careers, that they would get into good habits of putting Jesus before all else even in pressurised workplaces that try to distract them with the concerns of the world.*

– Elsa Glauert (2018)

16 JUL How can a loving God allow a beautiful child to suffer?

Then one of them, which was a lawyer, asked him a question ... **Matthew 22:35 (KJV)**

Recently I encountered another Lawyers' Christian Fellowship member at Court whom I had not seen for some time. We arranged to meet when we were both finished with our cases. As we sat chatting about Christian things, we were approached by another lawyer who suddenly asked us why a loving God would allow a beautiful child to suffer. We don't think he had heard our conversation.

There then developed a fruitful conversation about the Gospel, how no one is innocent, that we are all born with the same fallen nature as our first Father, Adam, even a beautiful child; that we needed another, perfect, Adam to redeem us which God provided by sending us his only Son to be a perfect sacrifice for our sins; that the resurrection is true and (implied but not said) the hope of a future without suffering is also true, and that if all turned to Christ the world would be a very different place. It seemed to make him think.

This encounter reminded me of the importance of meeting up with fellow Christian lawyers to encourage each other in the faith and to be ready to give a reason for the hope that is in us (1 Peter 3:15). This week let us all pray that we might be granted the opportunity to encourage another Christian and to share the Gospel with a soul who is seeking.

- Ask God for the opportunity to share the good news of the Gospel with someone who is seeking answers to the most important questions about life.
- Give thanks for your fellow Christian lawyers and ask whom you might encourage this week in their walk with Christ.

– Mark Mullins (2017)

17 JUL Loving lawyers

And he said to him, 'You shall love the Lord your God with all your heart and with all your soul and with all your mind. This is the great and first commandment. And a second is like it: You shall love your neighbour as yourself.'
Matthew 22:37-39 (ESV)

When Jesus was asked which was the greatest commandment in the law, his response was disarmingly straightforward: God's central command is to love.

First, we are to love God. Not in a buttoned-up, lawyerly way. Rather, love should be bursting out of us, through our hearts, our souls and our minds. It can be easy for lawyers to reduce everything to an intellectual exercise, but to do so misses out on the joy of surrendering ourselves in love towards God.

Second, we are to love our neighbour as ourselves. This commandment's scale and breadth are huge. We are to love the person in the office next to us or at the other end of a Teams call, our clients in difficult situations and their difficult counterparties. And we are to love them as much as we love ourselves.

This brings us on to our third point: that Jesus wants us to love ourselves. It would be no use treating others as we treat ourselves if we overwork ourselves, doubt ourselves and neglect our own wellbeing. It can be easy to be a martyr at a law firm, to push through late into the night and to take on more work and pressure. As Christians, we can feel that doing so means we are working as if working for the Lord. However, we should remember that part of God's command is to love ourselves. Doing so can, in turn, help give us the time and energy to love others and grow as disciples.

- Pray that we would renew our commitment to love God wholeheartedly.
- Pray that we would love others and care for ourselves.

– Owen Vanstone-Hallam (2022)

18 JUL Well done

His master replied, 'Well done, good and faithful servant! You have been faithful with a few things; I will put you in charge of many things. Come and share your master's happiness!' Matthew 25:21 (NIV)

As lawyers (perhaps like other professionals), we like to achieve things (and dare I say be seen to achieve them). For many of us, therefore, these past six months have been a time of deep frustration: BSB exams, firms not recruiting – or downsizing – and even just the de-personification of working from home have all taken away opportunities to progress and succeed.

In this, the parable of the talents, Jesus is telling us what success in the Kingdom of Heaven is like: the master has gone away and left his servants to look after his affairs. When he returns, he is pleased to see that this servant has been "good and faithful" by looking after the five talents of gold in his absence.

Jesus has left this earth – but has promised to return in glory. In the meantime, the things we have been really entrusted with, may seem small to us now – showing the fruit of the Spirit to individual colleagues, honouring our bosses, doing our studies or holding forth the words of life to those in our bubble who don't know – but if we are faithful with a few things, then when the Master returns we will know they were not small, after all. For his response will be this: 'Well done!'

- Therefore, pray that:
- We would all be strengthened and encouraged to keep serving in the little things.
- We would see fruit in the lives of those around us – in seeking justice and proclaiming the gospel.

– Robin Younghusband (2020)

19 JUL No contract required

The angel said to the women, 'Do not be afraid, for I know that you were looking for Jesus, who was crucified. He is not here; he has risen, just as he said. Come and see the place where he lay. Then go quickly and tell his disciples …' Matthew 28:5-7a (NIV)

We have contracts (and contract law) to govern contractual relationships between parties – what has A agreed to do for B and in return for what? And what happens if A or B fails to deliver for whatever reason? Contracts are necessary because we live in a fallen world. A may be inclined to over-promise or indeed to lie outright; B may find that someone else lets them down, meaning they cannot deliver.

In a world where so many don't do what they said they would do, let alone keep their promises, God's word is wholly reliable and true. We see this over and over again in the Bible: our God is a faithful God. Jesus promises us that "My Father's house has many rooms … I am going there to prepare a place for you … I will come back and take you to be with me" (John 14:2-3). He knows our weakness and doesn't require us to take everything on trust. There is historical evidence that Jesus was crucified, died and rose again and, if he can do that (defeat sin and death), what is to stop him from fulfilling his other promises, including the promise that we will one day make our home with him? But we aren't to keep this good news to ourselves; we are to go and tell others.

- We live in a culture which so often doesn't believe that God's word is reliable and true. This may cause us to doubt God's word. Did God really say …? Did God really mean …? Pray that we would all be able to stand firm on the promises of God's word, and make reading the Bible and spending time with God a daily priority.
- We know a God whose word is faithful and true. Pray that we would be people who are faithful and true, and who keep our word.
- So many people we know and love are building their lives on sand. Pray that we would be winsome as we seek to share the truth of God's word with others.

– Nat Johnson (2020)

20 JUL What bothers us in life?

Some men came, bringing to him [Jesus] a paralyzed man, carried by four of them … When Jesus saw their faith, he said to the paralyzed man, 'Son, your sins are forgiven.'

Now some teachers of the law were sitting there, thinking to themselves, 'Why does this fellow talk like that? He's blaspheming! Who can forgive sins but God alone?'

Immediately Jesus knew in his spirit that this was what they were thinking in their hearts, and he said to them, 'Why are you thinking these things? Which is easier: to say to this paralyzed man, "Your sins are forgiven", or to say, "Get up, take your mat and walk"? But I want you to know that the Son of Man has authority on earth to forgive sins.' So he said to the man, 'I tell you, get up, take your mat and go home.' He got up, took his mat and walked out in full view of them all ...

Mark 2:3-12a (NIV)

Many of my prayers and cries to God are about matters that are trivial compared to the difficulties that this man had to face.

The difficulties facing heavily paralysed people in the 1st century must have been enormous. Consider what it would be like to depend (like this man did here) on others to carry you. Or consider the difficulties you may have had in finding work. Or consider how difficult you would have found it to protect your family from physical threats.

Yet Jesus sees that forgiveness of sins is even more important than this.

Will we let this truth sink in? We might face all kinds of difficult situations in our work as lawyers this week – but our sin is a vastly bigger issue than them all.

And it's humbling to remember that Jesus offers hope and forgiveness to all of us today even though we're totally unaware of just how bad our sin is before our Holy God. To paraphrase Karl Barth – even our thinking about how crooked we are is itself crooked. But thank God that He sorted our biggest problem for us, even though we didn't know just how much it needed sorting.

- *Thank God that, even though we don't appreciate just how much we need His forgiveness of our sins, He still offers it to us all.*

- *Bring whatever difficulties you face before God, and also remember our brothers and sisters who have additional needs and how you might be able to respond to help their needs.*

– Dominic Hughes (2015)

21 JUL Don't rely on yourself

And he took the blind man by the hand and led him out of the village, and when he had spit on his eyes and laid his hands on him, he asked him, 'Do you see anything?' And he looked up and said, 'I see people, but they look like trees, walking.' Then Jesus laid his hands on his eyes again; and he opened his eyes, his sight was restored, and he saw everything clearly. Mark 8:23-25 (ESV)

You rarely find a lawyer lost for words! We are renowned for our confident communication skills. Whether it's drafting letters or skeleton arguments, negotiating deals or making submissions in court; day in, day out, we rely on our ability to explain, argue and persuade.

But my assurance in my own abilities has often left me feeling disappointed and disheartened. If I can persuade a judge to mitigate a difficult sentence, why I can't I persuade my friends and family to follow Jesus – especially when this is objectively true and deserving? Have I used the wrong words? Wasn't I clear enough?

Jesus' encounter with the blind man of Bethsaida should reassure us. Whilst our clients rely on us not just to convey, but to convince God doesn't. It is Jesus who opens eyes, who restores sight, who brings people from death to life. Every time a sinner repents and turns to put their trust in Christ, it is His doing, not ours.

How liberating! We have a commission to convey the gospel, but we know that the outcome of our evangelistic efforts doesn't depend on us. Instead, our confidence is in God, that He will use our words, and that He will open the eyes of those who do not yet see Jesus for who He is.

- Pray that we would boldly use words to speak of Christ Jesus.
- Humbly pray that God would use our words.
- Pray that more would come to see who Jesus is and put their trust in Him.

– Jen McKelvin (2019)

22 JUL Keep it simple!

Truly I tell you, anyone who will not receive the kingdom of God like a little child will never enter it. Mark 10:15 (NIV)

Children had been kept away from Jesus by His own disciples. How wrong they were! Jesus not only welcomed children, but also expected anyone wanting to enter the Kingdom of God to receive it like a child.

We lawyers are sophisticated and accustomed to argument. We spend much of our time with similar people. Do we complicate the Gospel, lest we insult their intelligence? Do we try to argue them into becoming Christians?

We belong to The Lawyers' Christian Fellowship because we believe the Gospel is for lawyers. It certainly is, but it is also for road sweepers, accountants, factory workers, the unemployed, people with learning disabilities, in fact everyone – the same Gospel. It calls for a simple, child-like trust in Jesus as Saviour and Lord.

Around us there may be a greater hunger for Gospel truth than we realise, especially at this time of uncertainty. Why not see people you meet this week not as opponents against whom you need to argue your case but, as Jesus did, "like sheep without a shepherd" (Matthew 9:36)? Then see yourself, not as someone who stands little chance of persuading others, but as a bearer of good news which is "the power of God that brings salvation to everyone who believes" (Romans 1:16).

- *Ask God to lead you this week to non-Christians who are not looking for an argument but are genuinely seeking what only Jesus can give, and to enable you to communicate the simplicity of the Gospel message.*
- *Pray for God to use the current uncertainty in the life of our nation to increase people's openness to the Gospel.*
- *Faced with the pressures of studying law or the demands of the legal profession, ask God for help to keep trusting Him in a child-like way.*

– Graham Whitworth (2019)

23 JUL Out of the office?

And God spoke all these words … 'Remember the Sabbath day by keeping it holy. Six days you shall labour and do all your work, but the seventh day is a Sabbath to the LORD your God. On it you shall not do any work, neither you, nor your son or daughter, nor your male or female servant, nor your animals, nor any foreigner residing in your towns. For in six days the LORD made the heavens and the earth, the sea, and all that is in them, but he rested on the seventh day. Therefore the LORD blessed the Sabbath day and made it holy.' Exodus 20:1, 8-11 (NIV)

Life as a lawyer can feel very busy. We all have peaks and troughs but, when the pressure is on, it can almost feel like you can't breathe under it. And if work's not enough, you may also have prayer meetings, homegroup or talks for church, friends or family, charitable work or a hundred thousand other things all clamouring for what little time you have left.

Nevertheless, God commands us to rest as we see in the passage above. It's not a guideline or a suggestion – we are required to build regular and genuine rest into our lives. It reminds us that we do not live to work, that we are not as indispensable as we like to think, and helps us not to idolise achievement. We can focus back on God, and actually be more fruitful for Him in the long run. I had pause to reflect on this recovering from a chest infection recently.

Hopefully you can find some time for holiday this summer, and your schedule is less full than usual. Why not try to enjoy some real and complete rest, perhaps even turning the mobile phone off for a time? Even God took a complete break, and we have no more that we have to do than Him.

- *Give thanks to God that there is nothing that we can do to make Him love us any more or any less, and that Jesus has already done everything necessary to reunite us to God. We can rest assured in the complete effectiveness of the cross to sanctify us.*

- Submit your diary to God afresh, and prayerfully consider how you might regularly build genuine Sabbath rest into it when you return to the office. You may be working for God, but (especially if you feel too busy) pray about whether you are doing the work that He has for you to do.

– Jon Hyde (2017)

24 JUL — Loving others via tracked changes and precedents

...The second is this: 'Love your neighbour as yourself' ...
Mark 12:31a (NIV)

Have you ever considered how doing your job as a lawyer can be a way of loving your neighbour?

The author Lester DeKoster once posed a thought experiment:

"[Look at that] chair you are lounging in … Could you have made it for yourself? … How [would you] get, say, the wood? Go and fell a tree? But only after first making the tools for that, and putting together some kind of vehicle to haul the wood, and constructing a mill to do the lumber, and roads to drive on …? In short, a lifetime or two to make one chair! … Imagine that everyone quits working right now! What happens? Civilised life quickly melts away." *

Some might joke that the world would be a better place without lawyers. But the reality is that, this side of eternity, it would be chaos. And even more so, if we lost all the lawyers who had their hearts set on God.

If we are to love our neighbour by doing our job as lawyers, our hearts must be set on God first of all (and thus be wary of blindly adopting the secular world's viewpoint about what good lawyering looks like). Remember that loving our neighbour as ourselves is the second greatest commandment. The first is in the verse beforehand and involves loving God with all our heart, soul, mind and strength. The more we love Him, the more we will see how best to love our neighbours in and through our work as lawyers.

*Taken from Work: The Meaning of your Life by Lester DeKoster. Copyright © (1982) by Lester DeKoster. Use by permission of Christian's Library Press.

- Pray that we would love the Lord our God more and more.
- Pray that, flowing from that love for Him, our work would love and serve our neighbours.

– Dominic Hughes (2017)

25 JUL — Imposter syndrome of cosmic proportions

The written notice of the charge against him read: **THE KING OF THE JEWS.** **Mark 15:26 (NIV)**

Do you feel like an imposter? Do you fear being found out, and ridiculed? If the statistics are to be believed, the legal profession is full of imposter syndrome.

The religious folks of Jesus' day thought they had found an imposter. Those who crucified him put a sarcastic, mocking sign above his dying body telling everyone so: "the King of the Jews". Of course, Jesus was no imposter. He is King of Kings, ruler of the entire universe.

Naturally, however, we cast ourselves in this role: we play by our own rules and act as if everyone else is there for our own convenience. Our sin makes us cosmic imposters – and yet, everything will be revealed on the last day. The King is enthroned on his holy hill; and he laughs (Psalm 2).

For those of us with a (relatively) comfortable lifestyle, it can be hard to identify with the physical pain Jesus endured on the cross. But what he took was much more than physical pain; he took the withering glare of the Father's white-hot anger and scorn. He was mocked so we need not be.

Do you feel like a spiritual imposter? Have you come to Jesus? If so, there is nothing to fear. Be secure in the knowledge that there is now no condemnation for those in Christ. Is that something that someone you know needs? Is it something you need?

- *Be thankful for the freedom from shame (and guilt) that Jesus offers.*
- *Be open with the Lord about the areas in which you might feel an imposter.*
- *Ask for opportunities to share this freeing news with others.*

– Robin Younghusband (2021)

26 JUL A world of opportunity

Go and preach the good news to everyone in the world.
Mark 16:15 (CEV)

As Jesus addressed his disciples with these words, I wonder what expectation he had that they would respond and act accordingly.

Do you see your office, chambers or other place of work – or, if you are a student, your student common room – as 'the world' where God has put you?

If so, have you tried fulfilling Jesus' command?

"How do I do it?" you may ask.

"You have the opportunity of a lifetime in the lifetime of the opportunity" was a favourite expression of Neville Knox, a former Chairman of The Lawyers' Christian Fellowship.

We need to be alert and open to God's prompting otherwise we may miss that opportunity to 'preach the good news'.

- Pray that we see our workplace as our mission field.
- Pray for opportunities to speak to our colleagues.
- Pray that we would always be ready to give an answer when someone asks about our hope.
- Pray that God would bring our colleagues from darkness to light, from death to life.

– John Head (2019)

27 JUL Bigger news than was first thought possible

Simeon took [Jesus] in his arms and praised God, saying: 'Sovereign Lord, as you have promised, you may now dismiss your servant in peace. For my eyes have seen your salvation, which you have prepared in the sight of all nations: a light for revelation to the Gentiles, and the glory of your people Israel.' Luke 2:28-32 (NIV)

Simeon had a vision of who Jesus was which was even news to Mary and Joseph. Simeon saw that Jesus was the salvation for all nations, that His mission and significance reached beyond Israel, and that the truth about Jesus would be revealed to the Gentiles.

May we discover more of the wonder of who Jesus is and what Jesus has done and may we be open to sharing the gospel even in the most surprising places and to the most unlikely people.

- Ask God to lead and direct you to share the gospel with those you meet and to be open to do so in even the most surprising of places.
- For your fellow Christian lawyers – that whatever their circumstances they may be able to praise God and give him the glory.

– Dr David McIlroy (2016)

28 JUL Dividing lines

The devil said to him, 'If you are the Son of God, tell this stone to become bread.' Jesus answered, 'It is written: "Man shall not live on bread alone."' Luke 4:3-4 (NIV)

As lawyers, we are often looking for dividing lines. Do the facts fall on this side of the law or the other? Is my client likely to be liable/convicted or not?

It is easy to think of sin in the same way. Am I on the right side of the line or not? Is this a 'sin' or isn't it? But here Satan turns even bread into a temptation. Good in itself, taken on Satan's terms it would have amounted to Christ distrusting his Father. As Paul writes, "… everything that does not come from faith is sin." (Rom 14:23)

Praise God that Jesus did not give in to Satan's offer. He lived solely by the word of God, and completely did his Father's will. We are inevitably on the wrong side of the line – he alone is our source of righteousness. Let us live by faith in him alone, and give up on our attempts at self-justification.

- *Give thanks for Christ's perfection and righteousness, and the fact that unlike Adam, he did not believe Satan's lies.*
- *Pray for opportunities to explain to colleagues and friends the offer of peace with God that can only be found in Christ.*

– Caroline Eade (2018)

29 JUL — What is heard through the everyday noise?

'The Spirit of the Lord is upon me,
because he has anointed me
to proclaim good news to the poor.
He has sent me to proclaim liberty to the captives
and recovering of sight to the blind,
to set at liberty those who are oppressed,
to proclaim the year of the Lord's favour.'
And he rolled up the scroll and gave it back to the attendant and sat down.
And the eyes of all in the synagogue were fixed on him. And he began to say to them, 'Today this Scripture has been fulfilled in your hearing.'

Luke 4:18-19 (ESV)

As I pen this thought from Edinburgh, the people of Scotland are selecting their representatives for Holyrood (the Scottish Parliament); indeed throughout the UK various elections are taking place. During this campaign season countless words have circulated – questions from voters and policies proclaimed by candidates. I wonder what gets heard through the noise of many words?

Jesus was always careful in what he said. Often, he delivered his message by using very few words, yet those words always penetrated. In this passage Jesus opens the scroll, reads from Isaiah and proclaims, "Today this Scripture has been fulfilled in your hearing".

His message is clear, concise and challenging. Jesus' call on our lives is to follow him. By the power of the Holy Spirit we follow and emulate not only what he said but also how he said it. You may have read this passage many times; do so now through the lens of your calling as a lawyer in the place or situation you are right now. If we are to answer Jesus' call to follow him, is there an obvious and unstrained application for you this day?

- *Pray that in our work we might see the obvious ways to follow him in deed and word.*
- *Pray that we would discern what it means to 'proclaim' in the context of our daily living, choosing our words with care.*
- *Pray for those in authority to govern transparently.*

– Brent Haywood (2016)

…he has anointed me to proclaim good news to the poor.
He has sent me to proclaim liberty to the captives and recovering of sight to the blind,

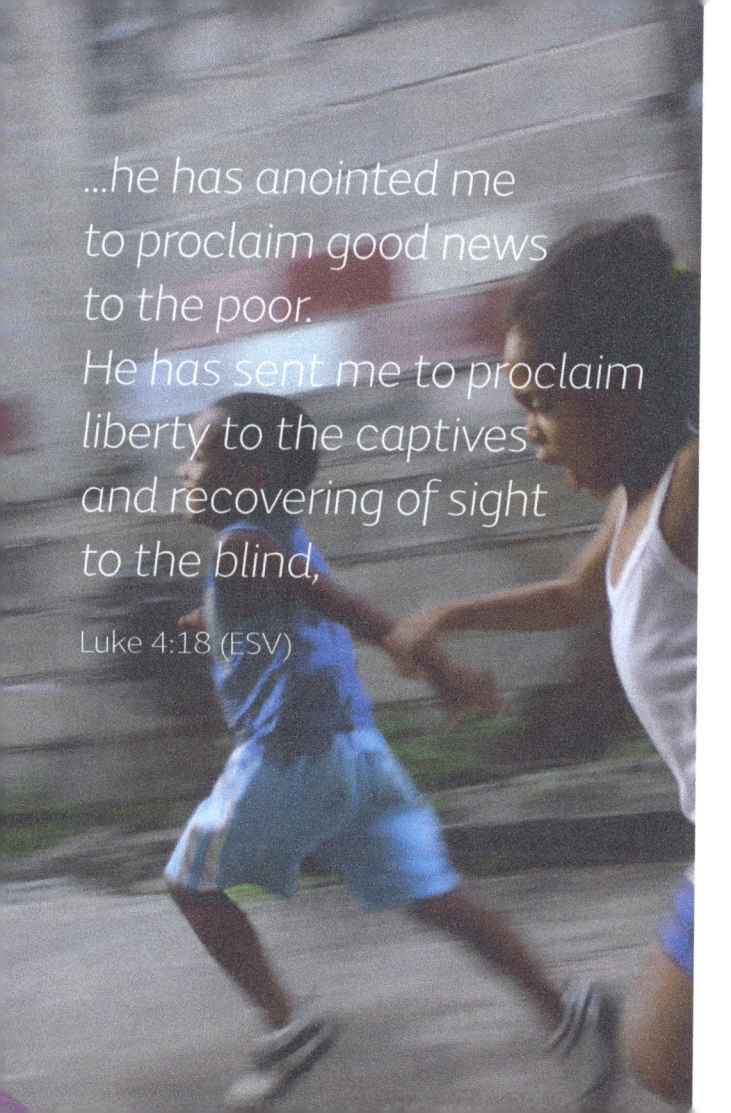

Luke 4:18 (ESV)

30 JUL New? No!

But new wine must be put into fresh wineskins. And no one after drinking old wine desires new, for he says, 'The old is good.' Luke 5:38-39 (ESV)

Christians worldwide are familiar with Jesus' metaphor of old and new wine. The gospel of the Kingdom of God is 'new wine'; neither the King nor His teaching can be made to fit within the religious traditions at the time of His coming.

Thank God for that! But how many of us remember the sharp observation Jesus made directly afterwards? "No one after drinking old wine desires new … he says, 'The old is good.'"

For us today, the image is of a person set in their ways, living the kind of life to which they are accustomed, saying, 'What I have is good enough thank you – I won't be trying anything new.'

I've been a Christian 20 years. Hearing those words of Jesus disturbs me. How much of my so-called Christian life is lived in complacency? How prejudiced am I about how God does and doesn't speak to me, what He does and doesn't say, how He does and doesn't use me? In my spheres of activity and influence as a lawyer, are there things which God wants to do with me, which I ignore because they seem too much like 'new wine'?

Let it not be so! Lord, help us to hear and keep hearing Your call, to find its confirmation in Scripture, and to walk in it, in boldness, in wisdom and in accountability to one another.

- *Re-read the final paragraph above, and spend some time praying the prayers contained within it for yourself.*

– Niazi Fetto KC (2021)

31 JUL No fear. Only faith.

And He said to her, 'Daughter, be of good cheer; your faith has made you well. Go in peace.' …
He answered him, saying, 'Do not be afraid; only believe …'
Luke 8:48, 50b (NKJV)

These are familiar words to many of us. The account of Jesus being touched by the woman who had the flow of blood for twelve years, healing her and then reassuring Jairus, who was anxious that the Saviour would reach his daughter in time to heal her too.

These are words of great encouragement, spoken by a sovereign God, who had the power to heal and raise the dead. But so often we fail to trust in them for ourselves. As lawyers, we work in a competitive world, where we are constantly under pressure to perform; to find the solution; to obtain the verdict. It can be terrifying, especially when we don't have the answer.

The wonderful lesson in all of this is that Jesus knows our fears. He is able to give us peace and meet our needs. He has met our greatest need, that of salvation through His death and resurrection. We need not fear. Have faith in God and know His peace today.

"For God has not given us a spirit of fear, but of power and of love and of a sound mind." 2 Tim 1:7 (NKJV)

- *Pray that members feeling the pressure of the competitive legal world would know God's peace today, and in the week ahead.*
- *Praise God that in Jesus, our greatest need has been met! Pray that we would not fear but trust in our Almighty Father, whose love and mercy have secured our salvation.*

– Esther Harrison (2019)

1 AUG Getting the answer right

Just then a lawyer stood up to test Jesus. 'Teacher', he said, 'what must I do to inherit eternal life?' He said to him, 'What is written in the law? What do you read there?' He answered, 'You shall love the Lord your God with all your heart, and with all your soul, and with all your strength, and with all your mind; and your neighbour as yourself.' And he said to him, 'You have given the right answer; do this, and you will live.' But wanting to justify himself, he asked Jesus, 'And who is my neighbour?'

Jesus replied, 'A man was going down from Jerusalem to Jericho, and fell into the hands of robbers, …'

Then Jesus told the Parable of the Good Samaritan, and asked:

'Which of these three, do you think, was a neighbour to the man who fell into the hands of the robbers?' He said, 'The one who showed him mercy.'

Luke 10:25-37 (NRSVA)

The lawyer in this passage does not get a good press. He thought he could cross-examine Jesus. And inevitably he received more than he bargained for when he stood up and asked his questions.

He was told the story of the good Samaritan, the man from a despised and rejected community, regarded by all good colleagues of the lawyer as unclean and uncouth, yet a man who rescued a badly injured Jew, when two supposedly upright men from the Jewish community had passed by on the other side of the road.

Note that this story was Jesus' answer to the question "… who is my neighbour?" The neighbour to be loved was the outcast who had come and shown God's mercy. Not the expected answer. And an answer we can sometimes miss.

If inheriting eternal life was conditional on loving such a neighbour, then the lawyer was going to be in difficulty. Neither he, nor we, of ourselves will satisfy the imperative of love, particularly when the neighbour, however merciful, is despised, rejected, unclean or uncouth.

In the end we need the mercy of the ultimate neighbour, Jesus himself, despised and rejected, dying as a criminal on a cross to save us.

And now we ourselves, in gratitude, must be prepared to be the instruments of God's kindness and thus a neighbour.

- *Give thanks for Jesus, who was despised and rejected in order that we might be rescued and receive the mercy of God.*
- *Pray for the insight to see and receive the mercy of God, the grace to love those through whom we receive His mercy and the power to be instruments of His mercy to others.*

– Janys Scott KC (2019)

2 AUG — Can't you see this needs to be done? … Now!

She had a sister called Mary, who sat at the Lord's feet listening to what he said. But Martha was distracted by all the preparations that had to be made. She came to him and asked, "Lord, don't you care that my sister has left me to do the work by myself? Tell her to help me!"

"Martha, Martha", the Lord answered, "you are worried and upset about many things, but few things are needed- or indeed only one. Mary has chosen what is better, and it will not be taken away from her."

Luke 10:39-42 (NIV)

I really empathise with Martha … always something to be getting on with and worry about, as frustration sets in because others seemingly prevaricate. "Can't you see this needs to be done? Now!"

Martha saw her chance for self-affirmation. The Lord will back me. He knows I am doing my bit whilst my sister sits. His response "Mary has chosen what is better …" may have surprised her, but his tender repetition of her name recognising Martha's anxiety called her to a deeper understanding that he is all-sufficient for her.

Life in the law means we constantly see things that need to be done, possibly more so as Christians. Preparing well for exams, client meetings, court hearings and giving judgments is good and right. Standing up for the poor and needy, whilst advocating for freedom of religion: really important. Evangelism, essential …

But nothing is better, or more necessary, than firstly sitting at the foot of the Master under His teaching, for this demonstrates who is our Lord, and where our trust lies.

When we next encounter Martha her brother is dead. Faced with this tragedy, in John 11:27 she expresses full trust in Jesus, "Yes, Lord; I believe that you are the Christ, the Son of God, who is coming into the world." * She had learnt well.

As you start this week, with many things to prepare and achieve, which Lord and Master will you trust?

- *Take time to bring yourself, as you are, and your worries, to the Lord Jesus Christ and commit everything, including your plans, into his hands, asking that He may through you bring glory to His name.*

– Mark Barrell (2019)

3 AUG Forgive as the Lord forgave you

Forgive us our sins, for we also forgive everyone who sins against us. Luke 11:4(a) (NIV)

Forgiveness isn't in fashion. High profile figures are frequently demoted or removed for things they did or said many years ago, and which they may well now regret or disavow. Forgiveness is pitted against 'justice', and 'justice' wins out. There is little public discourse on what repentance and restoration might look like for these people. In our workplaces, and perhaps even among non-Christian friends and family, a request for forgiveness – or an offer of forgiveness – may be met with bemusement or cynicism.

But as Christians we know that forgiveness and true justice need not be in conflict. Forgiveness is fundamental – as vital as daily bread. Without it we die. Jesus' death demonstrates that forgiveness is not a denial of justice but a fulfilment of it – he bears the punishment that we deserve. Forgiveness means absorbing the pain and cost of the offence, even if some of the consequences of it continue to be worked out. At a human level, the consequences may still involve a judicial process.

As those who have ourselves been forgiven, let us learn how to show forgiveness to others. Costly and counter-cultural though forgiveness may be, let's pray that it would also be life-transforming, both for us and for those we forgive.

- *Pray through the Lord's prayer, reflecting particularly on this sentence within it.*
- *Pray for someone who has hurt or offended you. Pray that God would soften your heart towards them so that you are able to reach out to them in a forgiving spirit, even if it takes time and repeated prayer before you can do so. Pray that they would know God's love and blessing, bringing them to repentance where that hasn't yet happened.*
- *Pray for any clients or colleagues who are trapped in a cycle of bitterness and revenge, that they would find the life-giving power of God's grace in their lives.*

– Caroline Eade (2021)

4 AUG Unfair advantage

When you are brought before synagogues, rulers and authorities, do not worry about how you will defend yourselves or what you will say, for the Holy Spirit will teach you at that time what you should say. Luke 12: 11-12 (NIV)

In the words of the late John W. Davis, the American politician, diplomat and lawyer:

True, we [lawyers] build no bridges. We raise no towers. We construct no engines. We paint no pictures – unless as amateurs for our own principal amusement. There is little of all that we do which the eye of man can see. But we smooth out difficulties; we relieve stress; we correct mistakes; we take up other men's burdens and by our efforts we make possible the peaceful life of men in a peaceful state.

John Davis was right: a lawyer does not rely on a toolbox full of spanners, screws and voltage indicators; our toolbox contains nothing more than words. But words are not nothing: in some contexts they are everything. We must therefore be intentional as Christian lawyers with our words. We must invoke the power of the Holy Spirit to tell us what we ought to say in that moment.

We must embrace the competitive advantage which the Holy Spirit avails to each of us and be conscious of his ever-present help when drafting agreements, pleadings or legal opinions; or when we are negotiating deals, writing arbitral awards, judgments or books.

When we season our words with his counsel and breathe his life into our work, we shall by his efforts "make possible the peaceful life of men in a peaceful state".

- *Give thanks for opportunities to speak into situations, which arise as a result of our role within the legal profession. Pray for God's wisdom, insight and words to speak into cases, conversations and situations you might face this week.*
- *Give thanks for Christian lawyers throughout the world and particularly for their 'access to justice' ministries, speaking up for those most vulnerable. May they be encouraged today.*
- *Pray for Christian lawyers practising within countries and regions where corruption or persecution is rife, that they may be able to speak 'hope and truth' with confidence.*

– Ashtiva Nelson (2021)

5 AUG Top judge declines to hear contested probate case

Someone in the crowd said to Jesus, "Teacher, tell my brother to divide the inheritance with me." Jesus replied, "Man, who appointed me a judge or an arbiter between you?" Then he said to them, "Watch out! Be on your guard against all kinds of greed; life does not consist in an abundance of possessions."
Luke 12: 13-15 (NIV)

The man in the crowd makes an entirely reasonable and fair request – some 1900 years' later, section 46 of the Administration of Estates Act 1925 imposed a similar requirement on an intestacy. Yet Jesus' reply is surprising. He declines jurisdiction – quite something for the One to whom the Father has entrusted all judgment (John 5:22).

So why won't Jesus deal with this man's request to get a share of the family's inheritance? It would appear that Jesus sees that the underlying problem which this man had was not that he was suffering from an injustice, but that he was suffering from greed. If this man wanted life, then he would not find it in an abundance of possessions – in stuff.

Jesus warns us to be on our guard against greed – in all the different ways it manifests itself. Greed is behind a lot of the injustices which we, as lawyers, have to deal with. Similarly, if we feel that we have been dealt an injustice at work, whether over what we are paid, say, or something else, we should consider carefully what the root problem is. I suggest that we should be "on our guard" against the possibility that, like the man in the crowd, our real problem is in fact greed.

- *Pray that we would be on our guard against greed, both at work and elsewhere, and that we would instead be generous and grateful for what we have.*

– Andrew M (2021)

6 AUG Lift up your hearts!

Be dressed ready for service and keep your lamps burning, like servants waiting for their master to return from a wedding banquet, so that when he comes and knocks they can immediately open the door for him. It will be good for those servants whose master finds them watching when he comes. Truly I tell you, he will dress himself to serve, will have them recline at the table and will come and wait on them. Luke 12:35-37 (NIV)

In the Communion liturgy at my church, before the bread and wine are taken, the vicar says, "Lift up your hearts", to which we respond, "We lift them to the Lord". What a wonderful affirmation of our love for God! In the weeks that follow the service, though, I find my heart may drop, my enthusiasm for serving God may wane.

Luke's watch-keeping example above recognises that waiting on 'high alert' for Jesus is not easy. As lawyers, we find our focus on Jesus may be distracted, and that our powers of concentration are completely expended on our work. The challenge is to seek the Lord in all we do, and to serve Him every day as if it were our last chance to do so before his second coming.

What are we to do when our hearts feel heavy, and difficult to 'lift up to the Lord'? We must redouble our practice of spiritual disciplines: remaining in close fellowship with Christian brothers and sisters; praying and reading the Bible daily; and regularly worshipping God.

Finally, be encouraged that hard work remaining 'alert for God' in this life will pay off. In the passage above, the master returns to find his servants awake, is delighted, and proceeds to serve his own servants – surely a reminder of the incredible rewards that await God's people when the Lord Jesus returns.

- *Pray that God may reveal to you opportunities to serve Him, especially when work seems to absorb all our efforts and attention.*
- *Pray for God's goodness to restore your soul, that you may live in joyful anticipation of His return.*

– Hugo Porter (2021)

7 AUG Have you been involved in an accident in the last 3 years which wasn't your fault?

'Or those eighteen who died when the tower in Siloam fell on them – do you think they were more guilty than all

the others living in Jerusalem? I tell you, no! But unless you repent, you too will all perish'. **Luke 13:4-5 (NIVUK)**

The secular legal world often loves to find fault: preferably in someone insured or with deep pockets. "After all", it says, "If no one is to blame, then there is no one to sue and no fees to be charged." What, however, was Jesus' approach to an accident in his time in which 18 people died? We find his response in Luke 13:4-5 (above).

Obviously, Jesus had compassion. But He also had realism and perspective. What is significant about Jesus' comment on this tragedy in his day is that he shifts the focus onto ourselves. The tragedy was not an opportunity for blame, or outrage, but for sober reflection. You, Jesus says, are no better or no worse than those unfortunate to have been underneath the tower when it collapsed.

The problem is that we are all guilty and we will all perish unless we repent. The blame is in fact inside us, and the tragic accident represents a timely warning for us all to repent whilst there is time to do so (Revelation 9:21).

- *Take this opportunity to reflect and bring to God those things you need to repent for.*
- *Give thanks for the love and grace of our heavenly Father who, if we confess our sins, is faithful and just and forgives us.*

– Andrew M (2015)

8 AUG — Which table to automatically look for at the professional dinner?

'For everyone who exalts himself will be humbled, and he who humbles himself will be exalted.' **Luke 14:11 (ESV)**

The legal profession is hierarchical and there is a certain comfort in it: we all know where we stand. There are the places of honour – there are those more distinguished and those who are less distinguished than us. The ranks are also reflected at our social occasions: you only need to think about the last drinks event you attended.

Jesus urges us against self-selecting the seats of honour. Is he concerned to protect us from the public humiliation of being moved aside for someone more distinguished? Yes; but there's also more.

This is a call to discipleship both at work and outside work. By choosing to be disciples of Jesus we are choosing a very lowly identity in the eyes of a prestige-oriented profession. And it calls us to associate with the humble, including in our offices: to love and serve the support staff too. But the encouragement is clear: one day Jesus' disciples will be visibly promoted and given honour when Jesus returns. With that future hope, how can we show ourselves his disciples by loving and serving the 'lower' ranks in our workplace today?

- *Ask God to show you those whom you have overlooked, and for opportunities to love and serve them this week.*

– Tim Laurence (2017)

9 AUG Unforgettable!

'Likewise, I say to you, there is joy in the presence of the angels of God over one sinner who repents.' Luke 15:10 (NKJV)

What will be really memorable – even unforgettable – in this week of 9th August? A successful trial? A big conveyancing deal? Cash flow now positive? Finished drafting that document – at last?

History can give us many memorable 9th August dates. The atomic bomb was dropped on Nagasaki in 1945. Colonel Gadhafi was married for the third time in 1987. O.J. Simpson's double murder trial began in 1994. Usain Bolt became the first person to win the 100m and 200m sprint in back-to-back Olympics.

But what could be the most significant thing that you and I could be part of during this coming week? Something that would set Heaven's angels alight with joy and 'ring the bells' there because of its everlasting and blessed effects?

In Luke 15 Jesus teaches about the lost sheep being sought, the lost coin being found, and the lost son repenting and coming home. One common theme is the genuine joy that accompanies each event. Jesus says, "Likewise, I say to you, there is joy in the presence of the angels of God over one sinner who repents."

If you have not yet trusted Christ as your Saviour your joy, if and when you do, will be shared in Heaven. If God enables you to help one other person to turn to Christ and be saved, the angels will share your joy at being used by God for something that lasts for eternity – the salvation of 'one sinner who repents'. As you go about your important tasks today, remember the one over which Heaven longs to rejoice and for which Christ shed His blood to enable it to happen.

- *Pray that my demeanour as I work will be a blessing to those with whom I work.*
- *Pray that I will see the deepest need of anyone I meet is to know Jesus Christ.*
- *Give thanks that Heaven's angels will rejoice over people I know coming to Christ.*

– Gerard Chrispin (2015)

10 AUG The tragedy of slavish obedience and the alternative

The elder brother became angry and refused to go in. So his father went out and pleaded with him. But he answered his father, 'Look! All these years I've been slaving for you and never disobeyed your orders. Yet you never gave me even a young goat so I could celebrate with my friends. But when this son of yours who has squandered your property with prostitutes comes home, you kill the fattened calf for him!' Luke 15:28-30 (NIV)

What matters most this week is our relationship with God and with our fellow men and women (colleagues, staff, clients, fellow students etc).

Tragically, the relationship between the father and the elder brother in the parable of the prodigal son was dead: it was nothing more than a dry legalistic life of obligation, slavish obedience and a sense of entitlement (v 29). In his view, his younger brother had not slavishly obeyed but had been disobedient and therefore should take the consequences. Unlike the father, the elder brother showed no mercy, no grace and no love.

The challenge for us is to come to our heavenly father recognising – like the younger brother – the hopelessness of our situation and our complete dependence on His grace, love and mercy. This should lead to joyful and obedient service of Him in our lives and to grace, love and mercy in our relationships with those around us – in our places of work and beyond.

- Praise to our gracious, loving and merciful heavenly Father.
- Pray that we would show grace, love and mercy to our colleagues, staff, clients and all those we encounter this week.

– Rev. Ian Miller (2017)

11 AUG Breach of fiduciary duty

'I tell you, use worldly wealth to gain friends for yourselves, so that when it is gone, you will be welcomed into eternal dwellings. Whoever can be trusted with very little can also be trusted with much, and whoever is dishonest with very little will also be dishonest with much. So if you have not been trustworthy in handling worldly wealth, who will trust you with true riches? And if you have not been trustworthy with someone else's property, who will give you property of your own?' Luke 16:9-12 (NIV)

The dishonest manager was commended for acting shrewdly. He had the foresight to use what he currently had for a short while (the ability to discount his (ex-)master's debts before it became apparent that he no longer had authority to do so) to gain goodwill in the future.

Jesus encourages his disciples to do the same. All our worldly wealth is God's. It is 'someone else's property', held by us. We are to have the foresight to use it for the short while we can 'to gain friends for ourselves', in other words to help those in need, and those who need to hear about Jesus. Not to buy our way to heaven (no price would ever be enough, and anyway Jesus has already paid on our behalf). But when we do get to our 'eternal dwellings' (by grace), those whom we have helped will thank us.

So let's use our worldly wealth in the way it's 'beneficial owner' in Heaven would want. The danger with this parable is that we focus so much on the dishonest steward's breach of his fiduciary duty to his master that we lose sight of our own breach to ours.

- *Recommit your 'wealth' to the Lord and ask Him to show you areas in your life where you have held back from properly using this for God.*
- *Pray for boldness that you may be open to helping others this week, especially in sharing the good news of the gospel.*

– Andrew M (2016)

12 AUG The secrets of our hearts

' ... when you have done all those things which you are commanded, say, 'We are unprofitable servants. We have done what was our duty to do.' Luke 17:10 (NKJV)

When we do something for God's Kingdom, whether in our daily work as lawyers or elsewhere, we may feel a glow of satisfaction, or even pride, that we have done something good. But there are reasons for humility in serving the Kingdom.

We have been given so much, and the opportunity and the grace to be part of God's Kingdom purposes is a privilege. And in our fallen nature, our motives for doing good can be mixed – a sentence from the Anglican Burial Service reminds us: 'Thou knowest, Lord, the secrets of our hearts.'

And, while we may be tempted to believe that we can always predict the outcomes of our actions (so that we achieve what we intend), those outcomes are under the sovereignty of God.

So, as we consider the tasks we have this week, we can pray that:
- *We will know what God requires of us and that selfish motives will not get in the way.*
- *We will want to do His will out of gratitude to Him.*
- *We will do so without the need for approval or applause from others.*

– John Scriven (2016)

13 AUG I'm not like them, am I?

The Pharisee stood up and prayed about himself ...
Luke 18:11 (NIV 1984)

I am not like that Pharisee. When I pray, I do not thank God that I am not like other men – like my work colleagues – constantly going after the money and status, always seeking to promote myself and my smart lawyering. I'm a Christian. Whooooops!

Here I go again, in the words of the song. It's insidious isn't it? We may not actually pray in those terms, but it is in our thinking, and our praying is so much about ourselves and what we think God ought to do for us.

We are so much more self-centred than we realise. Don't you pray most earnestly when praying about yourself? How much of your praying focusses on your needs, your aims, your plans, your desires – asking the Lord to do what you want Him to do? And how much is on His aims, plans and desires and what He wants not just you, but others to do? His kingdom, His righteousness?

It is often said that you can tell what a Christian really cares about – what you and I really care about – by asking three questions. First: what do I spend time on? Second: what do I spend money on? Third: what do I pray most about?

A spot of self-examination does not go amiss here.

"Wretched man that I am! Who will deliver me from this body of death?" Rom. 7:24 (ESV)

"God, have mercy on me, a sinner." Luke 18:13 (NIV 1984)

- *Seek forgiveness from the Lord for the times you have made your prayers more about you than about Him.*
- *Take time to offer afresh to God your time, money and prayers and ask Him to direct your heart and mind to His thoughts and ways.*

– Sir Jeremy Cooke (2016)

14 AUG Do we weep for peace?

As he approached Jerusalem and saw the city, he wept over it and said, 'If you, even you, had only known on this day what would bring you peace – but now it is hidden from your eyes.' Luke 19:41-42 (NIV)

I have always had a struggle as an imperfect Christian lawyer working in an imperfect legal system, helping imperfect clients to seek imperfect legal solutions. Human justice. Doesn't it sometimes make you weep?

As Jesus approached his death he wept for Jerusalem. The saviour of the universe wept when he saw that peace was hidden from that great city. He knew what was to come, he knew the price to be paid for peace. As we strive to love our neighbours as ourselves, as we strive to live out Jesus' teachings from the Sermon on the Mount, may we remember two things: only Jesus brings true peace – shalom (John 14:27) and only Jesus brings the fulfilment of the law (Romans 8:3-4). Oh, and there is a third thing: keep weeping, it is an opening to prayer.

- Pray, perhaps with weeping, that those around you and beyond may 'know on this day what would bring them peace'.
- Pray that opportunities might arise around you for conversations about peace and justice, and that you will take those opportunities.
- Pray that Christians might be fully equipped with the gospel when addressing issues of justice.
- Pray for what you might bring to the pursuit of peace and justice as a Christian lawyer.

– Brent Haywood (2020)

15 AUG Forfeiture for non-payment of rent

"… A man planted a vineyard, rented it to some farmers and went away for a long time. At harvest time he sent a servant to the tenants so they would give him some of the fruit of the vineyard. But the tenants beat him and sent him away empty-handed. He sent another servant, but that one also they beat and treated shamefully and sent away empty-handed. He sent still a third, and they wounded him and threw him out.

Then the owner of the vineyard said, 'What shall I do? I will send my son, whom I love; perhaps they will respect him.'

Luke 20:9b-13 (NIV)

Jesus addresses here a common problem faced by lawyers acting for landlords: tenant default. Rent (in the form of fruit from the demised vineyard) is demanded, but not paid. Three servants in turn come to collect the rent, but are sent away empty-handed, each having been more shamefully treated than the last. This abuse constitutes a great insult to the landlord.

"What shall I do?", this landlord asks himself. He is entitled to go in anger to sort the defaulting tenants out. But he doesn't do that. Instead, in total vulnerability he sends his own son, his beloved son, humbly, alone and unarmed. Perhaps the tenants will feel shame in his presence, the landlord thinks, and mend their ways.

Sadly, the tenants do not respect the son: they kill him, in an attempt to seize what was not theirs. So the landlord comes, and the tenants lose not just their lease, but their lives. The vineyard is re-let to others.

In total vulnerability the Landlord of the World sent his own son, his beloved son – the teller of this parable, in fact. He too was rejected by those to whom he was sent.

Just as in the parable, rejecting that son has consequences. One day that Son, Jesus, will come back. For those who rejected him, that re-entry will be anything but peaceable.

- *Lord, teach us to realise the seriousness of that day of your return.*

– Andrew M (2019)

16 AUG — Rash decisions made in haste

... and he [Jesus] touched the man's ear and healed him.
Luke 22:51 (NIVUK)

With the best of intentions, we so often get it wrong! Peter used a sword in what he believed was the defence of his Master. He only succeeded in slicing off the right ear of the High Priest's servant which perhaps suggests a lack of expertise or familiarity with the weapon. Jesus however is quick to put it right, touching the man's ear and healing him.

We too are bound to get things wrong from time to time. We should take it to the Lord who will not only forgive, but can help us retrieve the situation. We must not be too ready to rush in with our own solution as Peter did. Pause to consider what does Jesus want me to say and do?

In the busy week ahead, we are likely to be required to take many decisions, often with little opportunity to always give the fullest consideration to the point in question. At the beginning of each day, ask that the Lord Jesus will keep you in His will and guide your decisions. He knows what you will be facing even if you do not. May we all be conscious of His guiding presence this and every week.

- *Pause now and ask God to guide you in the decisions you face this week.*

– Michael Hawthorne (2015)

17 AUG — Suffered under Pontius Pilate

And he said unto them the third time, 'Why, what evil hath he done? I have found no cause of death in him: I will therefore chastise him, and let him go.'

And they were instant with loud voices, requiring that he might be crucified. And the voices of them and of the chief priests prevailed.

And Pilate gave sentence that it should be as they required.
Luke 23:22-24 (KJV)

When the Jewish leaders arrested Jesus, they charged him with offences which, according to Jewish law, merited the death penalty. Nevertheless, they had to convince the Roman authorities to impose that sentence, and that meant taking him before the Governor, Pilate.

However, Pilate committed four grave errors when 'trying' Jesus.

1. He saw that Jesus was innocent of the charges but did not release him. (John 18:38)

2. He tried to shift responsibility by sending Jesus to King Herod, who just sent him back to Pilate. (Luke 23:6-12)

3. He listened to the clamour of the crowd rather than considering the case calmly and quietly. (Luke 23:18-23)

4. Finally, he considered whether to release Jesus was consistent with his friendship with Caesar. (John 19:12-13)

The result was that Pilate chose between career and principle, and he abandoned principle in the face of expediency. He washed his hands of the matter and allowed injustice and suffering to follow – although, as Peter told the crowd on the day of Pentecost, God was in control and it was his plan of salvation (Acts 2:23-39).

Perhaps we can relate stories of how we and others have been treated unjustly by someone who did not act with integrity, or where our choices have been expedient rather than principled. Even so, God remains greater – so let us look afresh to the just and merciful Judge.

- *Pray that, as lawyers, we would seek to treat our clients justly and with integrity.*
- *Pray that justice systems around the world would reflect God's justice, and not man's corruption.*
- *Dwell on the words below, and praise God for Jesus' death on the cross.*

   Oh, the love that drew salvation's plan.
   Oh, the grace that brought it down to man.
   Oh, the mighty gulf that God did span, at Calvary.
   Mercy there was great, and grace was free;
   Pardon there was multiplied to me.
   There my burdened soul found liberty, at Calvary.

– HH Alan Taylor (2020)

18 AUG   Be witnesses to the light

There came a man who was sent from God; his name was John. He came as a witness to testify concerning that light, so that through him all men might believe. He himself was not the light. The true light that gives light to every man was coming into the world. John 1:6-7 (ESV)

"I want my day in court" – this is something we often hear on crime dramas. It might be something a client has said to you. People just want to tell their story. In Court, witness evidence is really important; sometimes it's the only evidence available. For those testifying, this is public affirmation of truth. There are criminal consequences for lying in the witness box.

In this passage we read that John was a man sent by God, a witness to testify concerning "that light". A man named John was given a holy commission. His testimony was not simply an assertion of truth or unfolding of events, it had a specific purpose: "so that through him all men might believe".

The light that John is to be a witness to is Jesus Christ, the Saviour of the world.

As we continue to live in uncertain times, we need to remember that Jesus is a light in the darkness. While the world feels shaken, remember that God did not send his son to condemn the world, but to save it (John 3:17). So, let's challenge ourselves this week to be witnesses to the light and point our colleagues and clients to the Saviour.

- *Particularly in uncertain times, pray we would remember that the light still shines in the darkness, and the darkness has not, and will not, overcome it (John 1:5).*
- *Pray that we would be faithful witnesses to the good news of Jesus Christ.*
- *Pray that we would be confident in the knowledge that Jesus is the same Saviour yesterday, today, and forever.*

– Esther Wade (2020)

19 AUG — Lawyers as children

Yet to all who did receive him, to those who believed in his name, he gave the right to become children of God …
John 1:12 (NIV)

The last few weeks have been a bit of a blur in our household – my wife and I were blessed by the birth of our first child, Lucy. Like all new parents, we find her indescribably wonderful and she is precious beyond imagining.

Which is exactly how God sees us: as his dearly beloved, precious children. Whatever challenges a day of legal practice or study might hold for you today, enter them secure in the knowledge that you are a dearly loved child

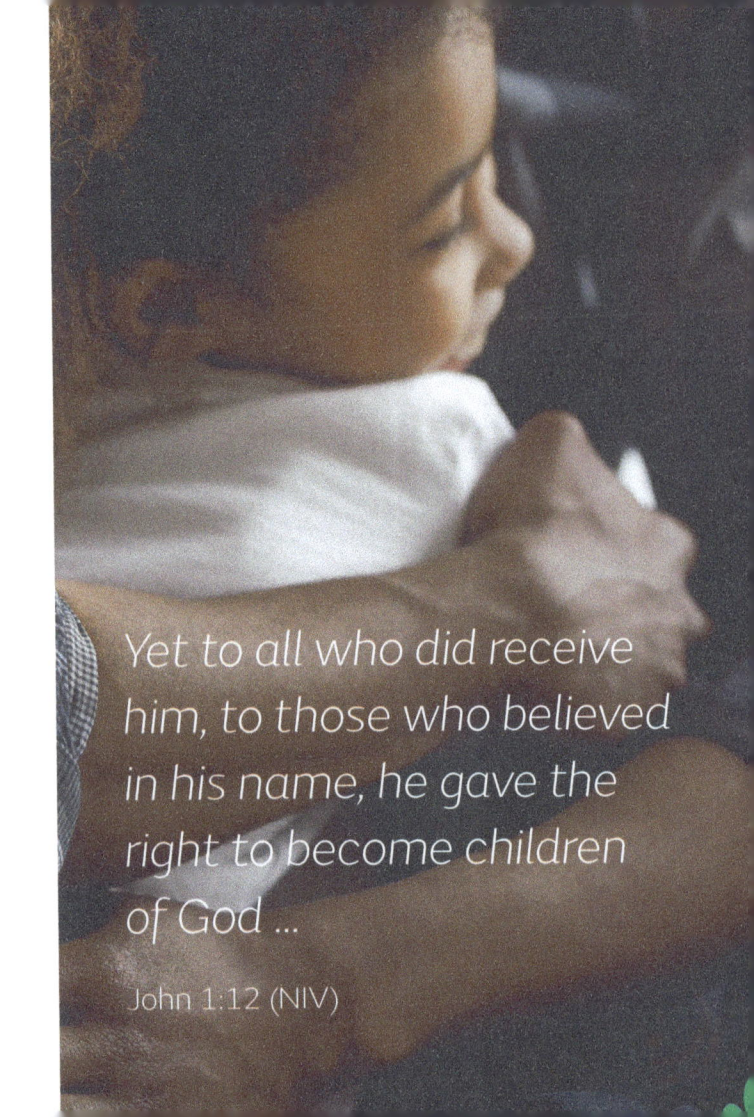

Yet to all who did receive him, to those who believed in his name, he gave the right to become children of God …

John 1:12 (NIV)

of the Creator of the Universe, who loved you so much he sent his Son to die for you.

But note too that this amazing gift is only for those who 'receive' him.

Have we received him? And how might we encourage friends and colleagues to receive him too?

- *Thank you, Father, for the wonderful privilege of being your dearly beloved children.*
- *We pray that in your mercy those around us who don't know you might receive Jesus and become your children too.*

– Adam McRae-Taylor (2020)

20 AUG Should your practice increase or decrease?

He must increase, but I must decrease. John 3:30 (ESV)

Lawyers are not usually known for being modest. The gift of advocacy on behalf of others frequently overlaps with the gift of advocacy on behalf of ourselves!

Even if we are more naturally the shy and retiring type, our firms and chambers constantly push us to achieve recognition in legal directories such as Chambers & Partners and Legal 500. The pressure to increase our 'personal brand' is continuous.

John the Baptist, however, chose a different approach. He was a hugely successful preacher with a large and committed following. Yet, when he met Jesus, he chose to step out of the limelight and point his followers to someone far greater. Like the friend of the bridegroom at a wedding (3:29), he knew that his role was to step back and delight in the one who should be centre stage: Jesus.

So as another week begins, let's pause and consider this question: how might we 'decrease' in our practice or study of law, so that Jesus might 'increase'?

- *Pray that we might humbly and joyfully make Jesus and his glory the focus of our legal study and practice.*

– Adam McRae-Taylor (2018)

21 AUG You can't do that – trust me, I'm a lawyer!

Then Jesus said to him, 'Get up! Pick up your mat and walk.' At once the man was cured; he picked up his mat and walked. The day on which this took place was a Sabbath, and so the Jewish leaders said to the man who had been healed, 'It is the Sabbath; the law forbids you to carry your mat.' But he replied, 'The man who made me well said to me, "Pick up your mat and walk."'
John 5:8-11 (NIV)

As Christian lawyers, we have two obvious distinctives. In the legal world, we are Christians. We can make a positive contribution, having access to God's power and wisdom, knowing He loves righteousness and justice.

In the Church, we are the lawyers. Sadly, we can so easily make a negative contribution, with a tendency to think of reasons why something cannot be done.

A man disabled for 38 years had just been healed and was carrying his mat as instructed by Jesus. Yet all the Jewish leaders could think of was a legal prohibition. In fact, as Don Carson comments,

> "By Old Testament standards, it is not clear the healed man was contravening the law. He broke the law only according to the 'tradition of the elders'." *

Among other Christians, away from our office or chambers, do we express legal opinions less carefully than we would when advising clients, erring on the side of caution to protect ourselves? Do we assume an air of authority as lawyers that may not be justified, when claiming that the law does not allow something? According to *Speak Up*, first published in 2016** by the LCF and the Evangelical Alliance, based on careful research, the law is less restrictive of our Christian witness than we might have assumed.

Let us not fall into the same trap as the Jewish leaders, but rather use our expertise to find ways in which the Kingdom of God can be advanced.

*From 'The Gospel According to John', D.A. Carson. © D. A. Carson. All rights reserved. No part of this publication may be reproduced, stored in a retrieval system, or transmitted, in any form or by any means, electronic, mechanical, photocopying, recording or otherwise, without the prior permission of the publishers, or the Copyright Licensing Agency. Reproduced with permission of the Licensor through PLSclear.

**Speak Up has since been revised and updated.

- *Pray for power, wisdom and an awareness of God's love of righteousness and justice in all you do.*
- *Pray for God's help to offer constructive advice, rather than careless opinions on what the law permits Christians to do.*
- *Pray for the freedoms the law currently allows to continue.*

– Graham Whitworth (2022)

22 AUG Nothing false

'Whoever speaks on their own does so to gain personal glory, but he who seeks the glory of the one who sent him is a man of truth; there is nothing false about him.' John 7:18 (NIV)

Jesus tells it like it is – there is a strange relationship between trustworthiness and personal ambition. The more we promote ourselves, the less we are trusted. As lawyers, our professional reputation stands on this fault-line. We build our own legal practice by establishing trust in the eyes of senior colleagues and clients. But it is only when we serve their interests, rather than our own reputation, that we really establish that trust.

Are we tempted to act independently today in order to advance our own name? Let's refrain from such selfish autonomy, and we will ultimately prosper all the more.

Jesus' words speak to a deeper level too, of course. If we seek first of all to honour Christ and apply his standards and share his name through our profession, then we may fear the cost to our personal reputation. But ultimately such a truly Christian lawyer – like Daniel – is recognised for incorruptible integrity, and Christ will share his glory with us (John 17:20-26).

- *Pray for a spirit of integrity to honour the King of Kings first and foremost in all you do and serve him and others in truth.*
- *Pray for those in Government – that they will have wisdom and be led to uphold biblical values.*

– Tim Laurence (2015)

23 AUG Even now…

When Jesus arrived at Bethany, he was told that Lazarus had already been in his grave for four days. Bethany was only a few miles down the road from Jerusalem, and many of the people had come to console Martha and Mary in their loss. When Martha got word that Jesus was coming, she went to meet him. But Mary stayed in the house. Martha said to Jesus, 'Lord, if you had been here, my brother would not have died. But even now I know that God will give you whatever you ask'. Jesus told her, 'Your brother will rise again'. John 11:17-23 (NLT)

In difficult times, it is easy to wonder what God is doing and why things have not changed. We may experience human consolation but, like Martha, we long for God to move.

In John 11, Martha's brother Lazarus has died. Jesus, who was his close friend and who, as Martha knows, has miracle working power, was down the road. He could have come to Bethany sooner. The passage tells us others did. Jesus did not.

Today's challenge from this passage comes in two words. Even now. Martha is distressed and disappointed. However, she knows who Jesus is and declares that "even now", even after Lazarus has been dead four days, God has the power to raise Lazarus from death.

Martha looks at the present situation, speaks out her disappointment and confusion and yet declares that even now, even when it seems hopeless, God can move.

What encouragement for our own situations! For those of us tired of working and studying from home, may we declare that 'even now' God is at work. For those seeking employment at this time, might we be assured that 'even now' God is Jehovah Jirah and will provide. For those of us who are frazzled and exhausted, might we know that 'even now' his grace is sufficient.

- *For those who feel disengaged from their colleagues and places of work, we pray for fresh encouragement. That God would open our eyes to see the way he is always at work in us and through us so that we might be agents of change, sharing the light and resurrection hope of Jesus in our workplaces.*
- *For those grieving professional dreams or ambitions which seem completely out of reach or even dead and for those feeling hopeless as they search for work. Praise God that in Him all things are possible, and He is the God of resurrection power.*

– Beki Muinde (2020)

24 AUG An unbeatable invitation

Peace I leave with you; my peace I give you. I do not give to you as the world gives. Do not let your hearts be troubled and do not be afraid. John 14:27 (NIV)

In one of the last conversations Jesus has with His disciples before he goes to the cross, the disciples are anxious and full of questions. Understandably, they ask: 'What's the plan, Lord?'

Life is full of uncertainty and things we can't control – including (or especially) for lawyers. Whilst our clients expect clear direction, it is easy for us too to find ourselves asking God: 'WHAT'S THE PLAN, LORD?'

As many of us will have experienced, God does not always share His plan with us. Instead, like the disciples, He invites us to choose obedience and to trust that He knows what He is doing even when we can't see what is next.

As we walk this road of trust, God promises us peace. Not peace "as the world gives" – God's promise is not peace based on external circumstances. It is a richer, deeper and qualitatively different 'peace'. God invites us into what the Jews call *Shalom* – a Hebrew word which can be translated as 'peace' but really means wholeness/wellbeing/completeness – made possible because the sacrifice of Jesus on the cross has made a way for us to live wholly and at peace with God. Daily, God invites us into this peace. Will you accept the invitation?

- *For those who are anxious or fearful today. Pray that they would know the deep Shalom that only God offers.*
- *For those who are in a season of waiting and feel restless for God to show what is next. Pray that they would trust God in the journey, knowing that He is faithful and is working all things together.*

– Beki Muinde (2019)

25 AUG — Need a trim?

[God] cuts away every branch of mine that doesn't produce fruit. But he trims clean every branch that does produce fruit, so that it will produce even more fruit.
John 15:2 (CEV)

The gardeners among us will know the importance of pruning – cutting off the dead branches and cutting back others.

Cutting off the dead branches is a salutary reminder that if we decide to go it alone we lose our intimate relationship with God and 'wither and die'. We are disconnected from God.

Cutting back is a reminder that in order to retain or restore our fruitfulness in serving God we may need to feel his pruning shears. In pruning us God might remove opportunities and cut down cherished projects. These may have been hindering our effectiveness in God's service even though we might not have realised this.

We need to trust that God knows what he is doing and stick with him.

Then when the fruit of the Spirit comes – love, joy, peace, patience, kindness, goodness, faithfulness, gentleness and self-control – it will bring a new lease of life to enrich our walk with God.

Are you ready for pruning?

- *Ask the Lord for the strength to trust completely in Him as He works to make us more like Christ.*
- *Pray for those who you know are struggling with difficult situations, that they may know the peace of God that passes all understanding.*

– John Head (2017)

26 AUG — Are you abiding?

'Abide in me, and I in you. As the branch cannot bear fruit of itself, except it abide in the vine; no more can ye, except ye abide in me.' **John 15:4 (KJV)**

The picture which Jesus paints of the vine and the branches indicates more than the need for the believer to be close to him. It indicates a need to share and grow in him – in practice being part of him.

This comes about through the empowerment of the Holy Spirit. The Holy Spirit can carry us throughout our Christian lives (see, e.g. John 16:12-15, Romans 8:5-11). In all aspects of our lives: professional, family, social, spiritual, Christians are called upon to remain faithful to their Lord, to abide in him, to consider what is the Christian answer to any situation that may arise in all walks of life. That answer should not be that of the natural mind, but of the mind being renewed (see Romans 12:2), as we share our lives with Jesus. The longer we go on with the Lord, the more we should develop our ability to hear from Him through His word and His Spirit, because we abide in him – forever.

*"Abide with me, fast falls the eventide,
the darkness deepens: Lord with me abide:
when other helpers fail and comforts flee,
help of the helpless, O abide with me."* *

*From 'Abide with me', by Henry Francis Lyte

- *Praise God that we are empowered through the Holy Spirit to abide in our Lord! Give thanks that we have renewed minds to be guided into all the truth.*
- *Pray that as God's words abide in us, we would bear fruit for his glory.*

– HH Alan Taylor (2018)

27 AUG Remember, remember

'This is my commandment, that you love one another as I have loved you. Greater love has no one than this, that someone lay down his life for his friends.' **John 15:12-13 (ESV)**

… the Lord Jesus on the night when he was betrayed took bread, and when he had given thanks, he broke it, and said, 'This is my body which is for you. Do this in remembrance of me'. **1 Corinthians 11:23b-24 (ESV)**

2022 marked the one hundredth anniversary of the end of a period which saw numerous historic events for the people of both parts of Ireland at home and overseas. Their ripples can still be felt today, sometimes in subtle ways – my own firm would undoubtedly have been a very different place in 2016 had the heir apparent, then a 31-year-old apprentice solicitor, not succumbed almost 100 years ago to the wounds he suffered earlier at the Battle of the Somme in 1916.

His gravestone (*see link below) like many others is inscribed with a biblical reference and there have been many religious services in recent weeks, especially here in Northern Ireland, to remember the sacrifice of the 3,500 soldiers from the island of Ireland who were killed in the Battle of the Somme (between July and November 1916).

The Bible talks about remembering numerous times and arguably the most referred to is the Last Supper where Jesus reminded his followers to continue to do this in remembrance of Him. What we should be remembering is that Jesus was the ultimate demonstration of sacrificial love, through which we have peace with the Father. Those brave young men who never returned from the First World War, whose gravestones so often quote

Jesus speaking about His own death, are a reminder of that greatest love: laying down one's life for one's friends.

Next time we all partake in the Lord's table, we should not forget that every Sunday is Remembrance Sunday.

- *Give thanks and praise this morning as you remember the wonderful gift of life we have through the sacrificial death and glorious resurrection of Jesus Christ our Lord who gave everything he had to reconcile us to the Father.*
- *Give thanks for all those who have given their lives for our freedom.*
- *Pray for those who today suffer for their faith in Christ – even to the point of death – as they witness to his saving grace and offer true hope in Him.*

*http://www.northirishhorse.com.au/NIH/Images/In memoriam/Full pictures/Greer.htm

– Peter Brown (2016)

28 AUG What Sunday school never taught me about the arrest of Jesus!

When Jesus said 'I am He' they drew back and fell to the ground. John 18:6 (NIV)

Imagine the scene as a member of chapter 18:3's "detachment of soldiers and some officials from the chief priests and Pharisees. They were carrying torches, lanterns and weapons". "Officials" – very likely to be the lawyers of the Temple! You would expect them to be on hand wouldn't you! You have gone at night – mob handed and armed to the teeth – against just one unarmed man. YET – all he has to say is "I am he" (God's very name) … and you are blown off your feet! Torches, shields, swords, spears, legal papers, all in a heap! He waits – you pick yourself up and sort yourself out from a defenceless pile – and still he allows himself to be arrested! HE was the one in control, not the mob. He allowed His plan, the plan He came to fulfil, to work out!

THAT is the power of the creator Son of God, my Saviour, with whom we are offered and can enjoy a living relationship. He is recorded in Matthew 26:53 saying to Peter at the time of his arrest: "Do you think I cannot call on my Father, and he will at once put at my disposal more than twelve legions of angels?" That is 72,000 ANGELS against a pathetic mob in the garden!

REJOICE as you face your day: YOUR Saviour has not lost control – HE Reigns supreme!

- *Lord we fall at your feet – empower us please to play our part in your plan today. Your will be done!*

– Richard Borgonon (2021)

29 AUG — Don't stop me now…

So they called them and charged them not to speak or teach at all in the name of Jesus. But Peter and John answered them, 'Whether it is right in the sight of God to listen to you rather than to God, you must judge, for we cannot but speak of what we have seen and heard.' Acts 4:18-20 (ESV)

On occasions I have returned to the office from court or arrived in the morning to an email simply amazed at the turnaround of events. What previously looked hopeless had resolved against the odds. Inevitably my first reaction was to announce to my colleagues: "you won't believe it but …"!

You may have also experienced such joys, but maybe not to the same level as the man at the 'Beautiful Gate', whose life was transformed by his encounter with Peter and John. Hoping for alms, he was healed of his crippling illness.

His joy attracted the interest of the ruling authorities who asked the apostles how they had performed such a miracle. They declared that this was nothing to do with them, but only to do with Jesus. Outraged, but unable to deny the evidence, these leaders banned them from speaking further of Jesus. The apostles' reaction was clear – you won't and can't stop us!

It is right that we should celebrate (and commiserate) with colleagues about work – but it is also right that we should celebrate Jesus, in whom we have put our trust and to whom all the glory should be given. If meeting Jesus is the most wonderful life changing event, have you told everyone your story, or do you feel that there is an unwritten rule in your place of work that you don't do that here? Be inspired by the apostles, and never be put off speaking about Jesus and testifying about his everlasting faithfulness.

- *Praise and give thanks to our Father for the wonderful gift of knowing Christ and the transforming work of the Holy Spirit dwelling in us.*
- *Ask for opportunities to share your testimony with others this week.*

– Mark Barrell (2015)

30 AUG — Right to say 'No'

Peter and the other apostles replied: "We must obey God rather than human beings! The God of our ancestors raised Jesus from the dead – whom you killed by hanging him on a cross. God exalted him to his own right hand as Prince and Saviour that he might bring Israel to repentance and forgive their sins. We are witnesses of these things, and so is the Holy Spirit, whom God has given to those who obey him." Acts 5:29-32 (NIV)

A 2015 half day conference hosted by The Lawyers' Christian Fellowship and the Christian Medical Fellowship was entitled "The Right to say "No"!". It had been planned as a successor to a previous event on 'assisted dying' in the context of the conscience clause in the 1967 Abortion Act. The day subsequently took on greater significance with the proposal of a 'conscience clause' defence to the equality legislation here in Northern Ireland. This was a response to the Ashers Bakery 'gay marriage cake' case where later, overturning the Appeal Court ruling, the Supreme Court upheld the right of the bakery not to promote a belief with which they disagreed, holding that this did not amount to discrimination.

A striking analogy to the freedom of conscience issue was drawn by Stephen Shaw KC, referring to the painting of 'St Ambrose barring Theodosius from the Milan Cathedral' by Anthony Van Dyck, portraying the Roman Emperor and his entourage being excluded as punishment for the Massacre of Thessalonica. He emphasised the significance and importance of the church entering the public square and expressed the concern that, if it were to be painted today, it might instead portray the emperor trying to prevent the archbishop leaving the church.

Christians, and arguably especially Christian lawyers, should always be acutely aware of our responsibility to leave the church building when appropriate and go into the public square, even when we are likely to meet resistance. Perhaps, more importantly, we should equally be cognisant of when it is not appropriate to do so, and we should intercede through prayer.

- *Pray that God would guide you to know when to make a stand for Him, and for the grace and confidence to do this with gentleness and respect.*
- *Pray for all those who do contend for the Christian faith on various legal issues in the public square.*

– Peter Brown (2015)

31 AUG Let justice roll

But let justice roll on like a river, righteousness like a never-failing stream! **Amos 5:24 (NIV)**

The Israel of Amos' time was prosperous and successful. Under the King of the time, Jeroboam II, Israel was a stable and politically strong country, even expanding its territory to the same boundaries as during its heyday under King Solomon. The temples built at the sites of some of the most significant places in Israel's history were packed out with worshippers. Everything was going wonderfully.

But it is into these seemingly great times that Amos speaks a word of judgment. And the charge that Amos laid against the people was at its heart their failure to do justice. The poor were trampled, the needy oppressed and justice was only available to those who were able to pay the bribes demanded of them.

The message of Amos is that God cares about justice and he longs for his people to be people of justice. Indeed, seeking justice is, for Amos, a mark of authentic Christian discipleship. As Christian lawyers we are ideally placed to be expressing God's concern for justice – whatever area of law we spend our days practising. Whether it is ensuring contracts are certain for both parties or making sure court proceedings are conducted in a fair way – and everything else that we might be involved in – let's commit ourselves again to seek justice in all we do this week!

- *Pray that Christian students and young lawyers will be encouraged that they can serve God in the law.*
- *Pray that all Christian lawyers would be authentic Christian disciples, seeking justice in whatever area of law they are practising in.*

– Rev. Matthew Price (2018)

1 SEP — Yet I will rejoice

Though the fig tree does not bud and there are no grapes on the vines,
though the olive crop fails and the fields produce no food,
though there are no sheep in the sheepfold and no cattle in the stalls,
yet will I rejoice in the LORD, I will be joyful in God my Saviour.

Habakkuk 3: 17-18 (NIV)

At around the end of the sixth century BC, the prophet Habakkuk understood from God that tough times were ahead. He saw that things would get worse before they improved. At the end of his oracle, he ponders the situation where all seems to be gloomy and uncertain and ends by declaring his steadfast confidence in God and his determination to rejoice despite all that occurs.

Whatever challenges we face, let us follow Habakkuk's example and rejoice and be joyful, mindful of all the blessings that we enjoy. May we encourage others by our example, and may our trust in God shine through, as we bear witness day by day to the inner peace which only Christ can give.

- *Pray for our confidence and joy in the Lord to be apparent in our lives.*
- *Pray for opportunities to encourage and spur on others.*

- Ask the Holy Spirit to guide what we say in our phone calls and emails, and in phone and video conferences.

– Michael Hawthorne (2020)

2 SEP Litigator peacemakers?

Blessed are the peacemakers, for they will be called children of God. **Matthew 5:9 (NIV)**

The case of *G.D. Searle & Co Ltd v Celltech Ltd* [1982] FSR 92 concerned an interim injunction to restrain use of hi-tech information. At the end of his judgment, Templeman LJ poignantly highlighted the lack of shalom in the case:

> It is a great pity that ... eminent scientists ... sit at the back of the court glowering at one another instead of devoting their energies to their craft.

There was a judgment on the issues in front of the court, but there were wider issues that needed healing.

Jesus is the ultimate peacemaker. He is the One who brings peace and healing for the whole world. When we long to help bring peace in the environment where He has placed us, we are, in a small sense, 'chips off the old block'.

Litigation done well can be a way of enabling parties (or the court) to justly resolve a dispute that the parties can't resolve themselves. There are, however, ways of litigating that help to foster peacemaking, and there are ways of litigating that unhelpfully stoke the fires. This isn't always easy, because some parts of the litigation process need us to push people robustly in order to uncover falsehoods and get at the truth.

Wherever we serve in the law, how much do we have a heart to see peace – not just in the case before us but also in the issues underlying the dispute?

- *Lord Jesus, Prince of Peace, thank You that You bring peace to the world.*
- *Lord Jesus, please guide us to know what peacemaking looks like in our context and help us to be better at it.*
- *Lord Jesus, may those around us know the real peace that is only found in You.*

– Dominic Hughes (2022)

3 SEP Thinking about power

For thine is the kingdom, and the power, and the glory. **Matthew 6:13 (KJV)**

The Lord's Prayer is said innumerable times; the words may trip off our lips easily whether we think of them or not. One of the words I believe we fail to think about sufficiently is the word 'power'. Lawyers exercise power ever day of their professional lives when they advise clients. When I was appointed to the bench a senior judge said to me "you are going to have great power". Such was his tone of voice and body language that he really meant "you mind how you use your power".

Christians should remind themselves constantly that, however blessed (and powerful) they are in this world, they are to trust in the Lord Jesus Christ whom the Apostle Paul describes as "the power of God, and the wisdom of God" (1 Cor 1:24 KJV).

Perhaps the one text lawyers should keep in mind is Ephesians 6:10, where Paul encourages believers to be "strong in the Lord and in his mighty power" (NIV) i.e. in all our advising and decision-making to have a deep faith in God, the Father of our Lord Jesus Christ and giver of the Holy Spirit and in his power to help us and guide us throughout life. In all we say and do for God, we must rely upon his power rather than our own. He chooses us to work for him and promises the power to do it. Obedience is accompanied by power.

- *Pray the Lord's Prayer and dwell on the power of the one to whom we pray.*
- *Pray for humility and a recognition that all power comes from the most powerful one.*

– HH Alan Taylor (2019)

4 SEP What's your field?

The kingdom of heaven is like treasure hidden in a field. When a man found it, he hid it again, and then in his joy went and sold all he had and bought that field.
Matthew 13:44 (NIV)

If you tell someone at a dinner party that you are a lawyer, a question that often follows is "What's your field?" Having a specialism is how we define ourselves against other lawyers (you know – the boring ones!). It's also, often, how we try to progress in our careers, developing expertise and contacts. There is, of course, nothing wrong with this, but every so often (and perhaps particularly at the start of a new year) it's worth asking: am I digging in the right field?

This is because there is only one field which is worth everything you have, and that's the field that Jesus speaks about in this parable: the field containing the treasure, which is the kingdom of heaven. This is, as Jesus says elsewhere (Matt 6:19-21), the only treasure that lasts.

So, as we think about our priorities this year, let us think first and foremost about how we are going to glorify God by using the gifts, the privileges and the expertise that we have to advance His kingdom and we should do so with joy – just like the man in the parable.

- *Thank God that, as believers, we can look forward to eternity in His kingdom – a treasure worth more than anything we can imagine, bought for us by His precious son Jesus Christ.*
- *Ask God for wisdom to know how you can best use your work to glorify Him.*

– Ben Fullbrook (2022)

5 SEP God's rest

**There remains therefore a rest for the people of God.
Hebrews 4:9 (NKJV)**

I am sharing this thought from a place in the (admittedly intermittent) sun! Each morning starts with a swim in the local bay's glacial waters! Then I need the sun!

Here on holiday, lawyers and labourers, politicians and postmen, teachers and taxi drivers basically seek the same thing. In one word, 'Rest'. The form of that rest will differ from person to person. For some that rest is found in inactivity and for others in a change of activity.

What a privilege God has given us with regard to rest. I don't mean solely putting the lights out and going to bed at night, though that is good too! Jesus gives us His rest that lasts through eternity: 'Come to Me, all you who labour and are heavy laden, and I will give you rest', are His words recorded in Matthew 11:28. Those who turn from their sins to the One who died as the sinner's substitute on the cross know that rest which will never end.

Then in the trials and problems of every day's work and living, we are aided by His Holy Spirit and through His word to know the rest of God's peace. We can say with Isaiah, 'You will keep him in perfect peace, Whose mind is stayed on You, Because he trusts in You.' (Isaiah 26:3).

And to prepare for each week's work, He gives us a whole day of special rest each Lord's day. Those who keep His day from the heart know that wonderful rest of spirit that Isaiah again speaks of, in chapter 58:13-14, and which enables us to delight in Him who uplifts us, feeds us spiritually, and gives us the great assurance of trusting His word.

May you know His rest in your life – even when its going crazy around you!

Let us
- *Enter into each type of rest the Lord has for me by coming to Jesus in every situation.*
- *Bless others by showing them God's rest in a stormy world around and to help others by my words and my life to seek that rest in Christ.*

– Gerard Chrispin (2015)

6 SEP — Abiding in Christ

'Abide in me, and I in you. As the branch cannot bear fruit of itself, except it abide in the vine; no more can ye, except ye abide in me.' **John 15:4 (KJV)**

As we return from the summer holidays, we will probably quickly forget that we have had a holiday at all. Yet there is a rest, or an abiding, that the believer is to maintain at all times. Sometimes as lawyers we are weighed down by the complexity and time pressure of some of our cases. We can be squeezed to the limit of our endurance. When oranges are squeezed, juice comes out. When we are under pressure what comes out of us? That will depend in whom we are abiding.

The Christian is to abide in Christ: that is to rely upon the Lord: that means letting his word abide in us (v 7). It is a wonderful thing to be able to ask the Lord for wisdom and be confident of an answer (James 1:5) when we are faced with an intractable problem. When we are worried, we are to present our requests to God (Philippians 4:6). And, when it is our client who is worried and without hope in this world, to hold out to them the word of life (Philippians 2:16).

Let us take this new quarter as an opportunity actively to maintain our rest in the Lord Jesus day by day, and to look forward to the fruit this will produce.

- *Let us give thanks for the holidays and in particular time spent in Christian fellowship.*
- *Let us pray that we would learn to abide in Christ; asking for wisdom and praying in place of worrying.*
- *Let us pray for Gospel opportunities.*

– Mark Mullins (2019)

7 SEP — Netflix or the gospel?

For I am not ashamed of the gospel, because it is the power of God that brings salvation to everyone who believes: first to the Jew, then to the Gentile. **Romans 1:16 (NIV)**

It's Monday morning. You're in the office kitchen making a coffee and scrolling through The Lawyers' Christian Fellowship's *Word For The Week* on your phone. Then someone enters the kitchen, breaking your reverie.

"Hello! What did you get up to this weekend?"

You have two options: Netflix or your church away day. What do you choose?

This is a trite example, and of course saying, "I binge-watched Squid Game", doesn't necessarily mean you're ashamed of the gospel. But perhaps there are other areas of life where you have been ashamed of Christ.

As the Apostle Paul knew all too well, holding out the genuine gospel is often terrifying and costly. But hear in these verses the urgent, compelling reason Paul gives to count the cost anyway: don't be ashamed of the gospel, because it is the power of God to save everyone who believes.

What would it look like to live unashamed of the gospel today? Maybe you've been asked to work on a matter that undermines gospel truth. Maybe you're putting off inviting your colleagues to the church quiz. Maybe you'd rather pretend the church away day never happened and talk about Netflix instead.

By God's grace and with Paul's reasoning ringing in our ears, let's hold out the gospel today, unashamed, because it is the power of God to save.

- *Praise God for His patience and kindness towards us even when we fail to speak of the gospel as we should.*
- *Let's repent of when we have been ashamed of the gospel, and pray that we would grow in our confidence that it truly is the power of God to save.*

– Claire Thompson (2021)

8 SEP The bridge of faith

Therefore, since we have been justified through faith, we have peace with God through our Lord Jesus Christ, through whom we have gained access by faith into this grace in which we stand. **Romans 5:1-2a (NIV)**

For through him we both have access to the Father by one Spirit. **Ephesians 2:18 (NIV)**

For Christ suffered for sins once for all, the righteous for the unrighteous, to bring you to God. **1 Peter 3:18 (NIV)***

It is a surprising fact that the common English word 'bridge' does not appear anywhere in the Authorized Version of the Bible nor in the New International Version and maybe other modern translations. Yet the picture of a bridge between God and mankind is so powerful. Further, it is important to note that it is God who provides the bridge, mankind does not.

A bridge makes it possible to reach the other side of a gap. The gap in our case is our sin. Sin separates us from God (Isaiah 59:2), but God has made it possible for that gap to be closed by giving us the Lord Jesus Christ to die for our sins and for us to be forgiven. So, the Lord Jesus Christ is the bridge who makes it possible for us to be united in faith to God the Father.

There is a sense in which lawyers act as bridges. They reach across and help their clients to have access to courts and their opponents in a professional manner. As we reach across to other members of our profession, we should do well to remember how God uses his bridge when we interact with courts and colleagues, thereby acting not only in a professional manner but in a Christlike manner also.

> For we know that our old self was crucified with Him so that the body ruled by sin might be done away with, that we should no longer be slaves to sin
>
> Romans 6:6 (NIV)

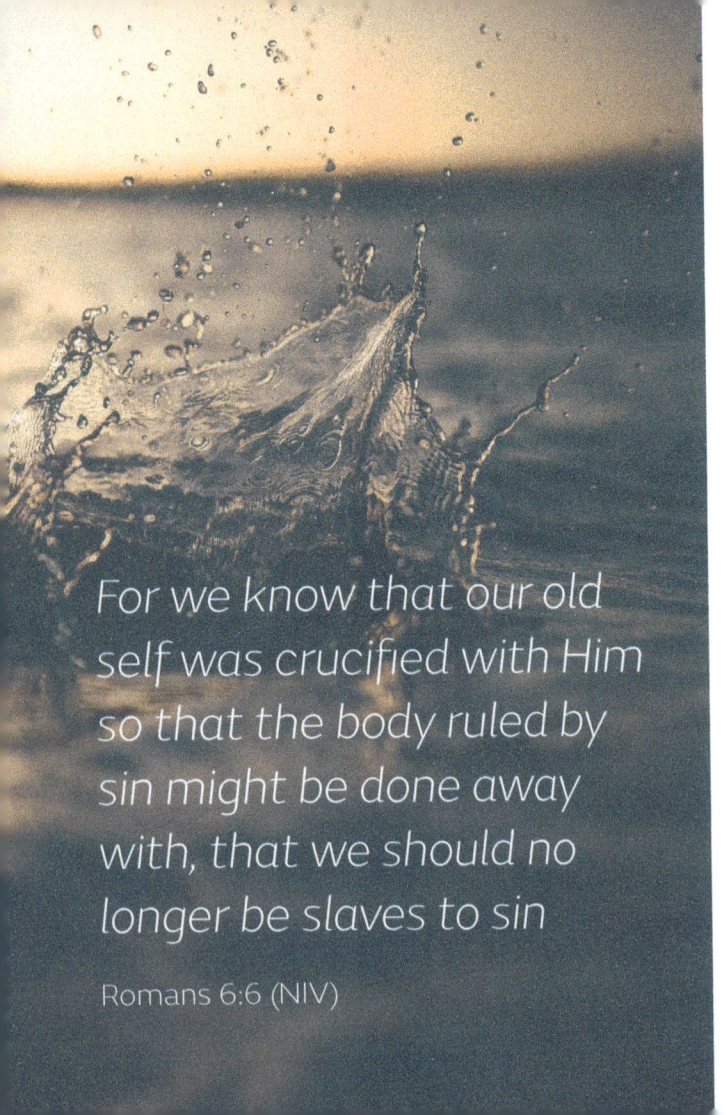

A final word. An even better word picture is to think of God lowering a drawbridge in the form of the Lord Jesus Christ, enabling us to have access to him.

- As we go about our daily tasks, let us commit to the Lord all those to whom we reach across whether they be our clients or our opponents or the courts so that the gap between us is covered in a Christlike way.
- Let us pray for all those we meet today, that our relationship with them will be Christlike, remembering what God has done for us in Christ.

– HH Alan Taylor (2022)

9 SEP — Dying for Christ, living for Christ

For we know that our old self was crucified with Him [Christ] so that the body ruled by sin might be done away with, that we should no longer be slaves to sin – because anyone who has died has been set free from sin.

Now if we died with Christ, we believe that we will also live with him. For we know that since Christ was raised from the dead, he cannot die again; death no longer has mastery over him. The death he died, he died to sin once for all; but the life he lives, he lives to God.

In the same way, count yourselves dead to sin but alive to God in Christ Jesus. Therefore do not let sin reign in your mortal body so that you obey its evil desires.

Romans 6:6-12 (NIV)

On 26 July 2016, Jacques Hamel, an 85 year old Catholic priest, was brutally murdered by two 19-year-old Islamic State terrorists while leading a church service in France. It was a shocking event. His sister, Roseline Hamel, has lived on through the pain ever since.*

In stark contrast to the suspicion and condemnation of the terrorists' families, Roseline reached out to their mothers, whose sons had been shot dead by police within minutes of their crime. She knew they might deal with their pain and grief together.

Roseline might so easily have let anger 'reign' within her, prompting 'evil desires' in her heart (v 12). Instead, she responded with grace and love.

As lawyers, we are tempted to sin all the time. For example, by provocation to angry email exchanges; being dishonest about delays; or joining in with workplace gossip. And so, whilst our work will not require us to die for our faith, we must not be ruled by sinful behaviours and habits. Instead, we must count ourselves 'alive to God in Christ Jesus'!

*Roseline Hamel's story was reported in The Times on 11 Feb 2022.

- Ask God for forgiveness for any sin that we have allowed to reign in our lives. Know that Jesus' sacrifice on the cross suffices to cover all and any sin.
- Ask the Holy Spirit to guide, inspire and strengthen our resolve in rejecting sin, especially where to do so is countercultural.
- Thank God for the freedom and joy – new life – we find when we die to sin, made possible by Jesus' sacrifice for us on the cross.
- Pray for the families, friends and churches of all those who have died because of their faith in Jesus.

– Hugo Porter (2022)

10 SEP Something better than the law

For God has done what the law, weakened by the flesh, could not do. By sending his own Son in the likeness of sinful flesh and for sin, he condemned sin in the flesh, in order that the righteous requirement of the law might be fulfilled in us, who walk not according to the flesh but according to the Spirit. **Romans 8:3-4 (ESV UK)**

When I was studying law, a friend gave me a birthday card in which was written (I assumed light-heartedly) "Luke 11:52", which commences, "Woe to you lawyers!" Jesus was berating teachers of the Mosaic Law and the regulations they had added to it. He accused them in verse 46 of loading people with hard burdens, without giving them any help.

Although the law we practise is different, our training can give us a tendency to set a high standard and condemn those who fail to attain it. The New Testament is clear that any kind of law has its limitations: it cannot actually change people and free them from sin. As Paul put it, regulations "are of no value in stopping the indulgence of the flesh" (Colossians 2:23).

But, praise God, there is a way people can be changed! Through Jesus' death in our place, not only are we counted by God as righteous the moment we believe, but we can walk "according to the Spirit" and thus avoid gratifying the desires of the flesh (Galatians 5:16). Learning to walk this way is a gradual process during which God's grace covers our failures. For those who do not know Christ, no amount of moralising will change them – only the Gospel.

- *Ask God for the ability to live in the good of His grace, to reject the accusations of Satan and to make allowance for the failures of fellow believers (without condoning any sinful behaviour).*
- *Pray for opportunities to share the good news of Jesus with colleagues, clients and others, and for help to avoid coming across as a morally superior person who looks down on them.*

– Graham Whitworth (2017)

11 SEP "TMI" and getting to the truth

For as many as are led by the Spirit of God, they are the sons of God. Romans 8:14 KJV

"However, when He, the Spirit of truth has come, He will guide you into all truth." John 16:13 NKJV

The word for the guiding of the Holy Spirit in John's gospel (above) has been likened to that used for a tour guide who is familiar with the territory. He can take us to places to which we would not, or could not, go ourselves. And, in the process, He can change us, so that we become a little more like Jesus in the sometimes complex situations in which we find ourselves.

We are imperfect in our reason as well as in our will. We live in an uncertain world and there is a seeming overload of information available to us. 'TMI' (too much information) is a watchword in many a meeting. Personal feelings or prejudices can also get in the way of getting to the truth. When faced with an unfamiliar or unwelcome point of view, we may find ourselves only asking: "Do I agree?" and not also asking: "Is it true?". We may need guidance by the Spirit and from God's Word to get to the truth.

Just as we need the Spirit to understand God's word because we can be naturally blind to truth, let us use our Spirit-led Christian insights to show us truth in our legal practice. We can ask God to show us fresh perspectives on legal issues, great and small. And, when faced with new or challenging situations, we can pray that we will be guided by Him who is all truth and, when we ask, can give us wisdom.

So let us pray

- *That we will be guided into the truth by the Spirit and the Word.*
- *For humility to be open to what this teaches us.*
- *In our individual circumstances, for His wisdom and for the courage to act upon it.*

– John Scriven (2015)

12 SEP Waiting for freedom

For the creation waits in eager expectation for the children of God to be revealed. **Romans 8:19 (NIV)**

As those who work in the legal profession, our job is usually about getting things done. We have clients who want a contract finalised, or a dispute resolved, or a company formed. Or we have colleagues who are relying on us to help with moving a project forward in some way.

Our training and experience may mean we have never really learnt to wait. In the pandemic we waited for the lockdown to end. We waited to be reunited with loved ones. Perhaps some of us waited for waves of grief to subside.

But waiting is what all of creation is doing – and has been doing since the fall. It is waiting "to be brought into the freedom and glory of the children of God" – to be liberated from death and decay, and to be renewed under the rule of Christ and his people.

Let's turn this experience of waiting into a deeper longing for that day when all waiting will be over, for ever.

- *Pray for those we know whose lives are not only frustrating, but uncertain and difficult – perhaps because of grief or illness or financial pressure. Pray for the ability to trust God's loving purposes and find hope in his promises.*
- *Pray for opportunities to speak to those who don't know Christ about the hope of eternal life in him, especially when the decay and devastation of a fallen world are so evident.*

– Caroline Eade (2020)

13 SEP Cherish your discontentment

For we know that all creation has been groaning as in the pains of childbirth right up to the present time. And we believers also groan, even though we have the Holy Spirit within us as a foretaste of future glory, for we long for our bodies to be released from sin and suffering. We, too, wait with eager hope for the day when God will give us our full rights as his adopted children, including the new bodies he has promised us. **Romans 8:22-23 (NLT)**

When last did you let discontentment at the way things are bubble up inside you?

It's not often you hear a message on the value of cherishing discontentment. If anything, we are enjoined to do just the opposite – to fix our eyes on Jesus, to soar in our spirits above the chaos of the world.

This is, of course, both right and good to do. We need to live with an eternal perspective, aware of the majestic presence of the Spirit of God in us as a foretaste of glorious things to come. This should bring us comfort, and for this we should rejoice.

At the very same time, however, a consciousness of eternal realities should strike in us a deep-seated dissatisfaction with the sin, brokenness and misery which permeate our current experience – and which we observe and participate in uniquely through our work in the law. This leads us to hunger for the heavenly city, and to await the King with expectation and hope.

So, cherish your discontentment. Praise God for the daily (even hourly!) reminders that this world is not your home. Use them as springboards to thank God for your confident hope in Christ, and attend to the frustrations of the day, both in your work and in other areas of life, with the assurance that they have an expiration date.

- *Spend time thanking God for the confident hope we have in Jesus.*
- *Reflect on the current frustrations and pressures you are experiencing at work and elsewhere. Acknowledge the dissatisfaction within you, and bring these issues and your role in them before the cross.*
- *Invite the Spirit of God to lead you into inhabiting the life of Jesus amidst the trials of Jesus.*

– Damilola Makinde (2021)

14 SEP He justified what…?

… those he called, he also justified; those he justified, he also glorified. **Romans 8:30 (NIV)**

Justification is a good lawyer word. We can be pretty good at it: he threw the punch, but it was self-defence; the documents are late, but it was another agency; they told the reputation-damaging anecdote, but it's true.

How often do we try the same in our dealings with God? Attempts that start: "my family …", "my work …", "my upbringing …"? When we look deeply, is our conscience satisfied? Where do we turn when our self-justifications fall short?

Unlike a lawyer, God does not offer a justification for our actions – there is none. Instead, he justified his people. When he comes in glory, it will not be those with an ingenious defence who join in, but those who are justified in Jesus. If that is me, I have nothing to prove; or to fear. The question is not "Are my deeds justified?" but "am I?"

- Acknowledge any "lawyerly" justifications we have put forward.
- Give thanks and praise for the freedom of true justification.
- Pray for those you know who need to hear the good news of the call of Jesus.

– Robin Younghusband (2021)

15 SEP Counter-cultural humility

For by the grace given to me I say to everyone among you not to think of himself more highly than he ought to think, but to think with sober judgment, each according to the measure of faith that God has assigned.
Romans 12:3 (ESV)

Recently in Scotland, the categories have been announced for one of the annual legal awards. There is of course nothing wrong with celebrating excellence in the professions, but it seems that lawyers have become increasingly adept at self-promotion in the online age. I have yet to view any profile on a firm or chambers website that does not describe any given lawyer as generally outstanding. In recognising the risk of over-promoting ourselves, we must equally avoid the trap of unnecessarily doing ourselves down. We can dishonestly present ourselves in more than one way.

But Paul's admonition to the Christians in Rome is an apt reminder for any lawyer. Not that we are to do ourselves down and hide our light under a bushel, but we should avoid the danger of simply following the way of the world in ways that can ultimately be ungodly. Instead, I think that one practical implication of this verse for us as Christian lawyers is that we should seek, under God, to live this week in the profession counter-culturally, in how we present ourselves to our colleagues and clients. Let's delight in the gifts God has given us, but be realistic about our limitations too.

Let's make a point this week of living out this text.

- *Give thanks for the gifts you have been given by God, and commit your use of them this week into His care and for His glory.*
- *Pray for those fleeing persecution because of their faith this week, and don't have the same opportunities as us to use their skills at work.*

– Gavin Callaghan (2015)

203

16 SEP — On which grounds do we compete?

Love one another with brotherly affection. Outdo one another in showing honour. **Romans 12:10 (ESV)**

As lawyers, we seek to excel in our work. Are we as committed to outdoing one another in showing honour?

While this call to show honour is given in the context of relating to other Christians, Paul also extends this duty to people outside of the church family (Romans 13:7), encouraging us that "as we have opportunity, let us do good to everyone" (Galatians 6:10). So how do we honour those around us?

Contrary to worldly views, which could often be mistaken for public flattery, Paul clearly links showing honour with loving one another deeply. If we sincerely care for our colleagues, our clients, our staff, then we will be more willing to listen to them, to serve them and to build them up. This is not about empty platitudes, but intentional encouragement and valuing their uniqueness. Jesus models this through his servant leadership, giving honour and dignity to those he met – regardless of profession, age or societal status.

How can we honour our colleagues, clients, those who oversee us and those whom we manage? Whom do we need to honour today in our law firms or places of study?

- May we seek to be intentional in honouring others in our places of work and study today.
- Please pray for Christian Lawyers working for justice, as we honour them for their service and faithful commitment to serving God.

– Mhairi Hamilton (2018)

17 SEP — Father, take this cup from me?

Everyone must submit himself to the governing authorities, for there is no authority except that which God has established… he who rebels against the authority is rebelling against what God has instituted… **Romans 13:1-2 (NIV 1984)**

Then they called them in again and commanded them not to speak or teach at all in the name of Jesus. But Peter and John replied, 'Judge for yourselves whether it is right in God's sight to obey you rather than God. For we cannot help speaking about what we have seen and heard.' **Acts 4:18-20 (NIV 1984)**

If you are anything like me, I suspect that you try to obey the law as much as possible, and dislike the idea of breaking it. But what about where the requirements of the laws of the land and the requirements of God's law are different, and you can't obey both? As the UK moves away from its Christian heritage, this may become a growing issue. Perhaps there are already issues arising in your practice area or context?

Acts 4 would suggest that we need to obey God's law. But what if we are not clear on exactly what God's law requires? Daniel objected to his diet under the Babylonian regime, but not his new name or education (Daniel 1). The newly converted Naaman promised never to make burnt offerings or sacrifices to any god other than the LORD, but sought forgiveness for when his master bowed in the temple of Rimmon causing him to bow too (2 Kings 5:17-18). Jesus paid the temple tax so as not to offend (Matthew 17:24-27), but Peter and John do not seem to have been so concerned about offending when declaring their primary allegiance to God (Acts 4:18-20). It may be that different approaches are required in different situations. May God give us the wisdom (James 1:5) to know what honouring him looks like in our context.

Further listening: Mike Ovey: Keeping a clear conscience as a lawyer; workplace ethics: where should we draw the line? www.lawcf.org/resources/christianity-in-the-workplace/app/resource/32/title/Keeping-a-clear-conscience-as-a-lawyer

- *Pray for the wisdom to know what to do, and the courage to do it.*
- *Pray for those facing a cost for obeying God, wherever they are in the world.*
- *Pray for robust and clear biblical teaching to equip the church in this generation.*

– Nat Johnson (2019)

18 SEP Demonstrating

The commandments, 'You shall not commit adultery', 'You shall not murder', 'You shall not steal', 'You shall not covet', and whatever other command there may be, are summed up in this one command: 'Love your neighbour as yourself'. Love does no harm to a neighbour. Therefore love is the fulfilment of the law. **Romans 13:9-10 (NIV)**

Love, as Jesus demonstrated, and Paul reminds us here, goes beyond law. Love changes lives and transforms societies in deeper ways than law ever can. But love, as Paul points out in verse 9, sums up and fulfils law, it does not replace it.

God's good commands as set out and summarized in the Ten Commandments remain indispensable to Christian living just as good laws are needed to provide order, to ensure peace, and to deliver a measure of justice in society.

Paul's message presents a number of challenges for us as Christian lawyers:

Are we, in our lifestyle, disobeying any of God's commands?

Who are 'our neighbours' in the work that we do?
Are we demonstrating love in the way we practise law?

- *Ask God to reveal the areas in your lifestyle where a change has to take place and, if there is a need to repent, do so.*
- *Give thanks for the work you are about to embark on this week and ask for the Lord's guidance to help you demonstrate Christ's love in the way you do this.*

– Dr David McIlroy (2015)

19 SEP To judge or not to judge?

Who are you to judge another man's servant? To his own master he stands or falls. Indeed, he will be made to stand, for God is able to make him stand. Romans 14:4 (NKJV)

As Christians and lawyers, we are sometimes called upon to give advice to fellow believers in challenging situations. They may have been going down the wrong path and we may be tempted to judge them, rather than their actions.

We are responsible for our own actions and, where we have been given authority over others, we may need to exercise this responsibility with courage as well as grace.

But, to others who come to us for our help in making difficult decisions, we should offer our thoughts with humility. While we should be clear in what we say about their situation, it is not our place to judge them as people. We should pray for them that they will seek the Lord for the right course of action.

- *Pray for all believers known to us facing difficult decisions: for God's guidance and that they will find the support that they need.*
- *Pray that we will be available to those who ask for our help, and that God will give us wisdom in offering our advice.*

– John Scriven (2017)

20 SEP More fool me

For the message of the cross is foolishness to those who are perishing, but to us who are being saved it is the power of God. For it is written:

'I will destroy the wisdom of the wise; the intelligence of the intelligent I will frustrate.' 1 Corinthians 1:18–19 (NIV)

Most lawyers spend an awful lot of time trying not to sound foolish. Our trade is the sale of knowledge and of good judgment. If we are at risk of sounding like fools, it is often a sign we should stop talking.

As these verses make clear, though, the gospel message is foolishness to those who do not accept it. It does not matter how eloquently, logically and sympathetically we present the cross of Christ – to some it will always seem foolish. And we will seem fools for believing and sharing it.

Normally we avoid saying or doing things that would appear to be foolishness. As people see the Christian message as foolishness, we may be put off from living and speaking for Jesus. But this foolishness is not an accident or an oversight by God – it is entirely deliberate that his salvation plan appears so weak, when it is in fact his unstoppable power. A power that can only be seen by those who have the joy of being saved. Trusting in God's plan and power means accepting that God is pleased when we keep speaking his message – even though we may well make ourselves appear fools in the process.

- Pray that our hope would be in the saving power of God, no matter how the world might see it.
- Pray that Christian lawyers would trust God enough to make ourselves fools for the sake of his gospel.

– Elsa Glauert (2022)

21 SEP The hazard of haughtiness

Brothers and sisters, think of what you were when you were called. Not many of you were wise by human standards; not many were influential; not many were of noble birth. But God chose the foolish things of the world to shame the wise; God chose the weak things of the world to shame the strong. God chose the lowly things of this world and the despised things – and the things that are not – to nullify the things that are, so that no one may boast before him. It is because of him that you are in Christ Jesus, who has become for us wisdom from God – that is, our righteousness, holiness and redemption. Therefore, as it is written: 'Let the one who boasts boast in the Lord.' **1 Corinthians 1:26-31 (NIV)**

'Haughtiness' – it is a word that has gone out of fashion somewhat. I'm campaigning for its return to popular use, mainly because there seems to be a lot of it around just now.

Clients and colleagues like to see self-confidence in their lawyers: it provides a sense of assurance. After a few years in the law I have, however, observed many instances of self-confidence flipping into haughtiness. I've seen it in others, and I've seen it in myself. It is both ugly and blinding. Many able lawyers become foolish in their own wisdom. We ought not to be surprised by this for, left to our own devices, our inclination to self-sufficiency knows no bounds. Haughtiness is a particular occupational hazard.

Lawyers would do well to keep some passages of scripture particularly close and I think this is one of them. Experience tells me that as soon as I think I am in control of a situation the rot begins to set in. Oswald Chambers said it with much more elegance:

> "God's friendship is with people who know their poverty. He can accomplish nothing with the person who thinks that he is of use to God." *

*From 'My Utmost for His Highest', by Oswald Chambers.

Only in Christ Jesus is there wisdom from God – "that is, our righteousness, holiness and redemption". Maybe it is as simple as this: strive to be wise, not right?

- *We are all drawn to haughtiness. Do some examination and pray that you seek the wisdom from God.*
- *Pray for wisdom to discern the haughtiness in your own heart and seek forgiveness.*
- *Pray for the wisdom to read haughtiness in others and then for the grace to pray how God might "choose the foolish things of the world to shame the wise; the weak things to shame the strong".*
- *Pray that we all might react to haughtiness with grace and love and not, as is tempting, with disdain.*

– Brent Haywood (2019)

22 SEP Gospel gardening

What, after all, is Apollos? And what is Paul? Only servants, through whom you came to believe – as the Lord has assigned to each his task. I planted the seed, Apollos watered it, but God has been making it grow. So neither the one who plants nor the one who waters is anything, but only God, who makes things grow. The one who plants and the one who waters have one purpose, and they will each be rewarded according to their own labour. For we are co-workers in God's service; you are God's field, God's building. **1 Corinthians 3:5-9 (NIV)**

As lawyers, the prospect of sharing the gospel with our friends and colleagues can seem very intimidating. What if our submissions fall on deaf or apathetic ears? What if our advocacy is unpersuasive?

Paul's horticultural metaphor helps to put things into perspective for us: Paul and Apollos had each played his role with the avowed purpose of growing and maturing the 'crop' of Christians in Corinth. But farmers don't actually make anything grow – they merely create the conditions to facilitate growth by planting and watering. Hence those important words in verse 7: "but only God". Only God makes things grow.

The planter and irrigator have their own complementary function, co-operating with the same result in view. So one Christian may tell you the good news in the first place. Another may provide you with real encouragement when life gets tough. Yet another may open your eyes to new areas of Christian service. But at every stage it is the Holy Spirit working through imperfect humans who is really responsible for the growth, for the maturity. And that should be a great relief for us as lawyers. Evangelism is not about our advocacy skills. We're not labouring in our own strength; we are not even labouring in our own field. It's God's field and we are co-workers in His service.

- *Give thanks for the work of the Holy Spirit, bringing Christians to maturity.*
- *Pray for the unity and cohesion of God's people in a divided nation and a divided world.*

– Phil Roberts KC (2019)

23 SEP Serious fishing

… if I preach the gospel, I have nothing to boast of, for necessity is laid upon me; yes, woe is me if I do not preach the gospel! **1 Corinthians 9:16 (NKJV)**

I share this thought as two days of my holiday remain. Each morning before breakfast, Sunday excluded, I have swum across the beautiful bay just 3 minutes' walk from my hotel. The Menorcan sea is warm in early autumn. I have repeated this swim later in the day, as I did on Friday. I find it helpful to pray and sing some hymns to myself and the many fishes in the bay!

Imagine my sadness to learn that an hour before my Friday afternoon swim a holidaymaker, twenty-one years my junior, had a heart attack in that same bay, drowned and died. As a recent recipient of a pacemaker that sad news came to me with added meaning.

Although failing too often, I seek to speak to at least one person each day about the Lord Jesus Christ. Low-cost package holidays provide 'fish' in this sea of opportunity. Many people are willing to engage happily in conversation and often to then discuss the gospel.

Friday's tragedy reminded me that each day of my life is the last day of life for someone else. Maybe the person I meet every day perhaps in the office or at court or at lunchtime, or on the train, or at the bus stop, or when filling up the car, or at home – the list could go on – has much less time to live than he or she thinks. And maybe I have much less time left to share wisely with others that Christ has died for our sins, risen again, and will forgive and bless eternally anyone who will turn from sin and trust Him.

- *Every person is either a missionary or a mission field. Which are you?*
- *How many times in the last week have you shared an appropriate word with someone about Jesus?*
- *Pray now for boldness to speak of and share the good news of the Lord Jesus Christ to someone you meet this week.*

– Gerard Chrispin (2017)

24 SEP — What is your future aspiration?

Everyone who competes in the games goes into strict training. They do it to get a crown that will not last, but we do it to get a crown that will last forever.
1 Corinthians 9:25 (NIV)

In our work as lawyers, it is so easy to be driven by ambition. We see everyone chasing after the job as partner and aim to do just the same. But this verse tells us that amazingly, if we're following Jesus, we will receive something that will last forever and truly satisfy us, an everlasting crown!

In following Jesus, we can trust in an eternal inheritance for us in heaven, as we rule as co-heirs with Christ. But we cannot take that for granted – Paul urges us to be strict with ourselves and guard our own walk with Jesus. So beware if your focus is unwittingly becoming the next promotion or pay rise, and keep trusting in the future inheritance we will have in Jesus, living in a way that honours Him.

Furthermore, we have the incredible chance to tell our colleagues about this hope that we have, that they might share in this everlasting crown for themselves.

- Pray that we might have a right perspective on our work and careers, and to remember the everlasting crown that awaits us.
- Pray for opportunities to speak of this hope of a future inheritance, that we may seek to live distinctively.

– Peter Thompson (2016)

25 SEP — Love for lawyers

But the greatest of these is love. **1 Corinthians 13:13 (NIV)**

This great chapter of the Bible is probably best known as a classic wedding reading, but bear with me as it also has something important for lawyers. You may wish to read the whole chapter (which won't take long!) before continuing.

In the first three verses, Paul mentions four wonderful and very valuable things – speaking in tongues, prophesying, having great faith and being extremely generous. All of these things are good and to be desired. However, Paul notes that if they are exercised without love then the result is "nothing" (vs 2-3).

In the next four verses, Paul goes on to describe the love that he means, which God shows to us and which we should show in turn. This love was so amazing, and so different from the love that people show each other, that Paul used a new word for it – *agape*. This is love so radical that it needs a brand new name.

There are many things that we may strive for as lawyers, such as clear analysis, thorough advice, persuasive advocacy, excellent drafting. But like the examples Paul uses, if we do so without love then they are "nothing". They have eternal value when *agape* drives them all.

- *Thank God for the great love that He shows each one of us every day.*
- *Pray that all that we do as lawyers this week is grounded in, and filled by, that same love.*

– Jon Hyde (2017)

26 SEP Oh my, how you've grown!

But whenever anyone turns to the Lord, the veil is taken away. Now the Lord is the Spirit, and where the Spirit of the Lord is, there is freedom. And we, who with unveiled faces all reflect the Lord's glory, are being transformed into his likeness with ever-increasing glory, which comes from the Lord, who is the Spirit. **2 Corinthians 3:16-19 (NIV)**

The legal profession is so often about hard facts. Evidence. Proof. Documentation. Yet as Christians, we believe in the transformational power of God working in us through the Holy Spirit. Our evidence is much more akin to a witness statement, a testimony sometimes rebutted in a 'your word against mine' way.

Some might be sceptical about the work of the Spirit. Nonetheless, each Christian encounters the Holy Spirit, transforming the way we live our lives as in:

- the sticky situation where God gives us exactly the right words and we know the power of the Holy Spirit speaking through us;
- intensely worshipping God, and feeling the 'heart-rush' of the Holy Spirit in us;
- 'co-incidences' that really can't be just co-incidences;
- the very definite prompting by the Holy Spirit to make a decision; or
- simply the way we live our lives, resolutely trusting God through the most difficult (or ordinary) of times.

"Oh my, how you've grown" says the relative to a child they haven't seen for several months. And perhaps it can be the same with us too. As Jesus shines through us, we don't notice incremental differences ourselves. Our prayer could be that someone who hasn't seen us for a while might see a step-change, as we are "transformed into his likeness with ever-increasing glory, which comes from the Lord, who is the Spirit".

- *Let's thank God for the Holy Spirit, and welcome His presence into our lives, homes and workplaces.*
- *In the words of a 2011 song by Brian & Katie Torwalt:*

    Holy Spirit, You are welcome here
    Come flood this place and fill the atmosphere
    Your glory, God, is what our hearts long for
    To be overcome by Your presence, Lord.

– Janet Cole (2022)

27 SEP — Treasure found in our weaknesses

But we have this treasure in jars of clay to show that this all-surpassing power is from God and not from us.
2 Corinthians 4:7 (NIV)

As we sit at our respective desks this morning, I wonder how many of us might be feeling rather weak? Summer is long gone and the chance to rest with family and friends is still several weeks away. So much to do and so little time!

Paul knew what it was to feel weak. In this famous passage from 2 Corinthians 4 he variously describes himself as feeling "hard pressed", "perplexed", "persecuted" and "struck down". Facing harsh opposition to his preaching of the gospel, he had experienced such troubles that he felt as though he was "outwardly … wasting away". But despite external appearances, he knew that he was being "inwardly … renewed day by day" because these "light and momentary troubles [were] achieving an eternal glory that far outweighs them all".

This morning we might feel weak from the challenge of speaking about Jesus in our offices and lecture halls, or simply from the ordinary pressures of work (quite probably both!). But let's have confidence that, however much like jars of clay we might feel, we have the treasure of the hope of heaven to keep us going and to share with others.

- Pray that we will be sustained through experiences of feeling weak by finding great joy in the treasure of the gospel.
- Pray for those you work with for opportunities for them to hear about and respond to the hope found in the Lord Jesus Christ.

– Adam McRae-Taylor (2017)

28 SEP — Entrusted with the message of reconciliation

All this is from God, who through Christ reconciled us to himself and gave us the ministry of reconciliation; that is, in Christ God was reconciling the world to himself, not counting their trespasses against them, and entrusting to us the message of reconciliation. Therefore, we are ambassadors for Christ, God making his appeal through us. We implore you on behalf of Christ, be reconciled to God. For our sake he made him to be sin who knew no sin, so that in him we might become the righteousness of God. **2 Corinthians 5:18- 21 (ESV)**

Someone recently said to me, 'It seems to me that things have gotten a whole lot more rancorous.' They were referring to how social and mainstream media seemed to be adversely affecting how people were communicating. I think that they were right; it feels as though people are finding it harder to be civil to one another.

I see this spilling over into the practice of law. I am a litigator and, more often than not, clients and colleagues assume they will get a nasty and aggressive operator to do their bidding. In stark contrast, how countercultural is the message of the Cross?

We are reconciled to God through Christ and, awesome though that fact is, things don't stop there. We are in turn entrusted with this message of reconciliation and as such we are appointed ambassadors for Christ. There can be no rancour in the message of reconciliation and if we are Christ's living sacrifices (Romans 12) there can be no rancour in how we operate as his ambassadors. Avoid being infected by the disease of rancour by reflecting on, and living, the message of reconciliation.

- *It may be very challenging for you not to be drawn into practising law in a way which follows the spirit of the age. Ask the Lord to give insight into how you practice the law and pray for the grace to change.*
- *It may be that you live out the counter-cultural message of reconciliation; this will come at a cost. Pray for courage, wisdom and perseverance.*
- *Pray for those around us caught up in the rancour we have been considering; ask the Lord for opportunities to use your awareness of this to 'speak the truth in love'.*
- *Give thanks that we have been reconciled to God and are entrusted to share that fact with others.*

– Brent Haywood (2017)

29 SEP Too late!

… now is the accepted time; behold, now is the day of salvation. 2 Corinthians 6:2 (NKJV)

Don't we feel stupid or guilty when we have been too late to meet an important deadline, or when we arrived at an important meeting too late?

The Bible says the best time to turn to Christ for forgiveness is always 'now'. The offer of Christ is open now to save those who turn from wrong and trust in Him. Indeed, 'now is the day of salvation'. Only Jesus saves those trusting Him from the penalty, the power and, one day, the presence of sin. His saving work on the cross means He bore our wrongdoings and their punishment in our place. The penalty has been paid for all who turn and trust Him. The saving life of the risen Christ becomes ours as He indwells us by the Holy Spirit. Eternal life is promised to all who come to Him as Saviour and Lord. But it will be 'too late', either when Christ returns, or when we die, if earlier.

What an urgent reminder to pray for others to trust Him, and to share the wonders of our Saviour with them. As a former criminal lawyer, the need of many I dealt with was obvious. But all people are dying sinners, including lawyers and clients, and the offer is open to all. 'Now is the accepted time.'

- *Praise God that He sent His son to bear our wrongdoings and take our punishment.*
- *Pray that we would not delay in sharing the wonders of our Saviour with those around us.*

– Gerard Chrispin (2019)

30 SEP Who knows your name?

Thanks be to God, who put into the heart of Titus the same concern I have for you. For Titus not only welcomed our appeal, but he is coming to you with much enthusiasm and on his own initiative. And we are sending along with him the brother who is praised by all the churches for his service to the gospel. What is more, he was chosen by the churches to accompany us as we carry the offering, which we administer in order to honour the Lord himself and to show our eagerness to help. We want to avoid any criticism of the way we administer this liberal gift. For we are taking pains to do what is right, not only in the eyes of the Lord but also in the eyes of man. In addition, we are sending with them our brother who has often proved to us in many ways that he is zealous, and now even more so because of his great confidence in you. 2 Corinthians 8:16-22 (NIV)

The apostle Paul was arranging a collection for poor believers and wanted total integrity in its administration. Titus, known to have a close connection with Paul, had volunteered (v 17) to collect the contribution from Corinth. To avoid any suggestion of impropriety, two others were chosen to accompany him, one by the churches (v 19) and the other apparently (v 22) by Paul and Timothy (1:1). Unlike Titus, neither is named, yet their service was of vital importance.

There are many well-known names in our profession. They may represent celebrity clients, hold high judicial office or be active in politics. They may feature as 'Lawyer of the Week' in the law section of *The Times*. Their cases may appear in the Law Reports. Most of us will have avoided such fame.

What about your name? It will be known to your clients and professional colleagues now, but they may forget it in years to come. As a retired lawyer, I must confess that I have forgotten the names of many lawyers I encountered when in practice. Yet, like that of these two unnamed men, your service is of great significance, as you demonstrate faithfulness and integrity, doing "what is right, not only in the eyes of the Lord but also in the eyes of man" (v 21). Rejoice that your name is written in heaven (Luke 10:20)!

- *Give thanks that, as a believer in Jesus, your name is written in heaven.*
- *Ask for God's help to be a faithful and trustworthy servant of the Gospel as you go about your work.*
- *Pray for the name of Jesus to be made famous in your sphere of influence as you represent Him to others.*

– Graham Whitworth (2021)

1 OCT — The ultimate commendation

We do not dare to classify or compare ourselves with some who commend themselves. When they measure themselves by themselves and compare themselves with themselves, they are not wise. … But, 'Let the one who boasts boast in the Lord.' For it is not the one who commends himself who is approved, but the one whom the Lord commends. 2 Cor 10:12, 17-18 (NIV)

Commendation counts for lawyers. The profession has developed sophisticated ways of commending itself and individuals within it. But it's as dangerous as it is easy to become drawn into an economy of mutual self-congratulation.

Our professional responsibility is to serve our client well, not to pursue the congratulation offered by the profession. And ultimately, our duty is to serve the Lord Christ whose servants we are.

Let's ask ourselves which future commendation is really driving our actions today, and perhaps reprioritise accordingly. If that leaves us missing out on some chance for boasting, we can remember that, as servants of Christ, we have more than enough to boast about already!

- Ask God to show you where you might need to reprioritise your thoughts and actions today, and seek His guidance as to how to do this.

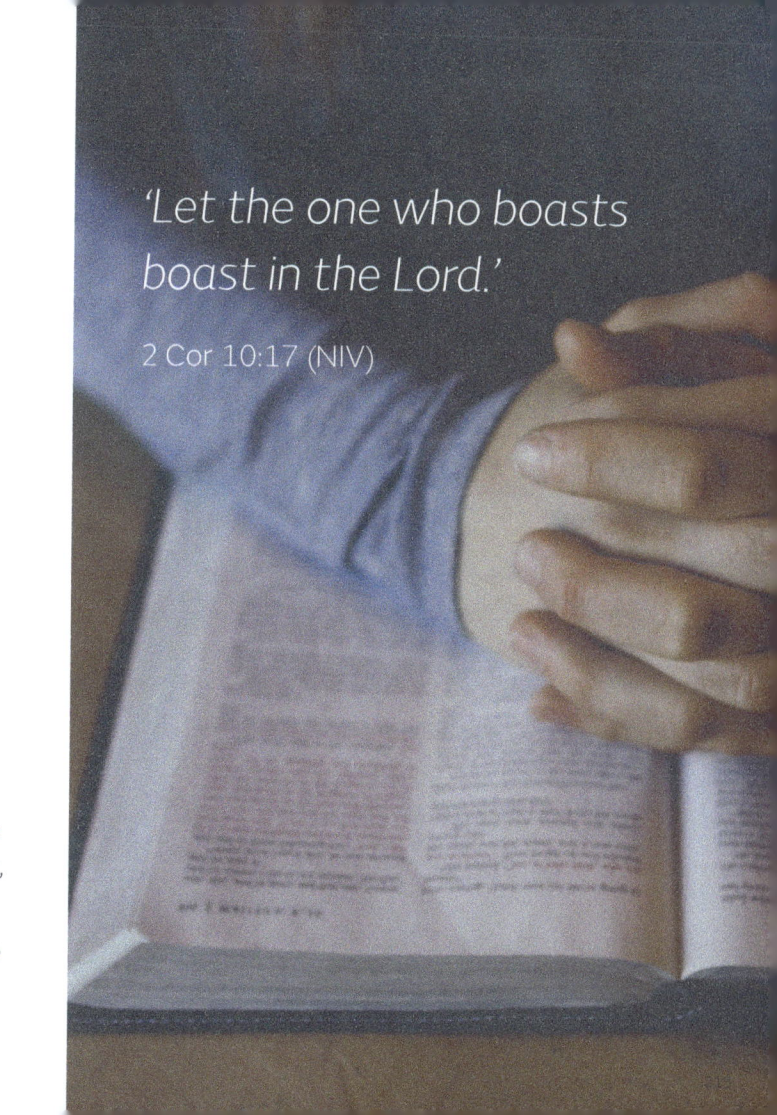

'Let the one who boasts boast in the Lord.'

2 Cor 10:17 (NIV)

- *Give thanks for those you work with or study alongside and ask for opportunities to encourage them as you serve others for Christ.*

– Tim Laurence (2015)

2 OCT Working with the Trinity

May the grace of the Lord Jesus Christ, and the love of God, and the fellowship of the Holy Spirit be with you all.
2 Corinthians 13:14 (NIV 1984)

It is good to consider God's nature. He is Father, Son and Holy Spirit: One God in three persons – the triune God. Some Christians find it difficult to understand the concept of the Trinity but it is wrong to ignore it. Someone has said, "It is a mystery beyond our comprehension", but in the gospel we see God revealed as Trinity.

Paul's description in his letter depicts a perfect relationship between three distinct persons. God, the Father, is the originator – the creator and sustainer, the loving planner of salvation. We see God the Son, by his grace, as revealer and redeemer. We experience God the Holy Spirit as our sanctifier and empowerer. The Father is above us, his Son is with us and His Spirit is within us.

As lawyers, we are dealing with relationships each day between clients and colleagues, and these are often imperfect. We can rejoice in the fact that the Trinity gives us the best example of harmonious relationship – and that should encourage us in on our work each day.

Most Christian services include a reference to the Trinity at least once. Let us be mindful of whom we are worshipping as we work for Him this week.

- *Give thanks and praise for the fact that as a Christian you have this wonderful relationship with the Father, Son and Holy Spirit.*
- *Pray for those you will be encountering this week whose relationships are strained, and ask how you may help bring reconciliation.*

– HH Alan Taylor (2015)

3 OCT The bubble

All they asked was that we should continue to remember the poor, the very thing I had been eager to do all along.
Galatians 2:10 (NIV)

The whole book of Galatians completely demolishes the argument that we are saved by what we do. Paul repeatedly shows us that it's through faith in Christ – and not our own works – that we are saved.

Yet in the context of that demolition job on a philosophy of works, it's interesting to note the works that Paul is eager to do (not as a way to be saved, but as a natural response in the life of someone who is saved). He is eager – in the words of 2:10 – "to remember the poor".

In some areas of law (mine included), it's easy to live in a sort of artificial bubble where your clients are comparatively wealthy, your colleagues are wealthy and your friends have had all the benefits of a university education. And even if we give money to ministries for the poor, we might do so at arms-length and not actually understand the lives of the poor and the oppressed.

Wherever we're at, let's remember how the Lord Jesus – resplendent in power and riches in Heaven – chose to live whilst He was on earth. He hung out with the poor and the oppressed. He touched lepers. He befriended social outcasts and the downtrodden. True, He also spent time with the rich and powerful too. But if we want to be like Him we need to understand not just the perspective of the rich but also that of the poor.

- *Thank God that all power and authority is vested in the One who understands and loves even the poorest and weakest in society.*
- *Pray that, if our lives are sheltered in an artificial bubble, we would be better at reaching out to the poor and the oppressed and understanding their pressures.*

– Dominic Hughes (2016)

4 OCT Freedom for lawyers

It is for freedom that Christ has set us free. Stand firm, then, and do not let yourselves be burdened again by a yoke of slavery. **Galatians 5:1 (NIV)**

Chapter 5 of Paul's letter to the Galatians is about Christian freedom. Christians have been set free through the cross of Christ (vs 1, 11) and are therefore freed from the requirement to have to comply with all the minutiae of the law of Moses in order to be justified before God (vs 2-4). Instead, through the Spirit we hope for justice, waiting by faith, and acting in love (vs 5-6). In Jesus' example and teaching, the shape of justice and the other moral virtues has been clarified and demonstrated. Through the Holy Spirit, Christians recognise wrongful actions as contrary to God's will (vs 19-21) and grow in love, joy, peace, forbearance, kindness, goodness, faithfulness, gentleness and self-control (vs 22-23), things against which there is no law.

Here, in Galatians, we have the heart of Paul's understanding of the Gospel, how the law has been displaced by Jesus Christ and the Holy Spirit as the way we are made right with God and the means by which we become righteous.

These Gospel truths, the theology of law and justice, have profound implications for Christians who study and practice law. Can I encourage you to meet with other Christian lawyers to work them out together?

- *Please pray for God's help to live and walk by the Spirit;*
- *Pray for Christian lawyers that you know, and for opportunities to encourage them with God's word for the work that they do.*

– Dr David McIlroy (2020)

5 OCT — Don't give up – keep going!

Let us not become weary in doing good, for at the proper time we will reap a harvest if we do not give up. **Galatians 6:9 (NIV)**

Have you been praying for someone for a long time, but not seeing any apparent answer to your prayer? It is so easy to get discouraged and give up. But as believers and disciples of the Lord Jesus we know that the path is not going to be easy. Jesus gave many warnings to those who would follow him to expect problems and difficulties as we carry our cross from day to day. May this verse encourage us today and throughout this week.

Let us approach every problem in our legal work and in life in general with a positive attitude that God is going to use us. We may never see in this life the results of our prayers and witness but, if we remain faithful, then one day we will be amazed at what God has done.

- *Is there someone you used to pray for but have not done so for some time? Why not intercede for them once again.*
- *Is there a task you have been putting off? Perhaps this week is the time to tackle it.*
- *We are here to witness for the long term. Ask God to rekindle your desire to serve.*

– Michael Hawthorne (2019)

6 OCT — Burnout or resilience?

Then, because so many people were coming and going that they did not even have a chance to eat, he said to them, 'Come with me by yourselves to a quiet place and get some rest'. **Mark 6:31 (NIV)**

It's that time of year again when supermarkets are already supplementing their pumpkins, sparklers and masks with selection boxes, crackers and cards – yes its early autumn! Schoolchildren are over half-way to Half Term, the nights are already closing in (especially if you live as far north as I do!) and the legal and church year are already back up to full speed after the relative calm of the long vacation and summer break respectively.

We as Christians have to not only strike the traditional balance between our work and family lives, but understand that our spiritual life intersects with both. Even Jesus needed times of solitude and time alone with his heavenly Father during his ministry and especially prior to significant events.

So at the start of (yet) another busy day at the start of (yet) another busy week at the start of (yet) another busy month at the start of (yet) another busy year at work, at home and at church let's not forget that in order to meet, defy and exceed expectations even Jesus needed to recharge his physical, professional and spiritual batteries to avoid burnout and demonstrate resilience.

- *Take time to commit your next minutes, hours and days into the Lord's hands. Then ask yourself if you need to build in some extra time this week to recharge yourself with the Lord.*
- *Pray for those who are feeling or are under pressure and need to know the Lord's rest.*

– Peter Brown (2017)

7 OCT He holds the future

[God] made known to us the mystery of his will according to his good pleasure, which he purposed in Christ, to be put into effect when the times reach their fulfilment-to bring unity to all things in heaven and on earth under Christ. **Ephesians 1:9-10 (NIV)**

The law and its challenges are constantly changing. Perhaps you take these things in your stride. Perhaps you are a worrier.

In Ephesians Paul tells us: "God has purposed … [planned]… to bring unity to all things in heaven and on earth under Christ". He is in control. He is working His purposes out and His plans will not be thwarted.

We may not have the answers we seek to the detail of our futures, but we know that the whole universe will one day be united in Christ and that should give us fortitude, strength, confidence and hope to cope with whatever lies before us.

- *Pray that we will have hope and confidence in God's sovereignty and His good plan for us.*
- *Pray that we will serve Him, in obedience to His Word, with our work and our lives, whatever the future holds.*

– Debbie Woods (2016)

8 OCT An audience with One beyond compare

In him and through faith in him we may approach God with freedom and confidence. **Ephesians 3:12 (NIV)**

Many will remember the sense of trepidation that accompanied the first time they exercised rights of audience in court, whether before Magistrates, a District Judge, or someone higher up the judicial ladder. It's a feeling that those more senior still recognise on certain cases or before certain judges.

However we may feel before earthly judges, this verse reminds us of the wonderful truth that, through faith in Jesus, we can approach the living God, the final tribunal, with both freedom and confidence.

Freedom: We can approach God anytime, anywhere, for anything. He has no hours of sitting. We do not have to wait for a space in the list. There is no time constraint on how long we can linger. There is nothing too great or too trivial to bring before Him. We have complete freedom to enter the courts of the living God.

Confidence: And we can do so with confidence. Our rights of audience are not based on our own qualification, eloquence or worth. They have been achieved and secured for us by Christ's death in our place. Even our persistent sin and failure need not deter or delay us from coming humbly before Him.

- *Whatever rights of audience you do or don't have as a lawyer, through faith in Christ you have rights of audience beyond compare. Take a moment to exercise them now:*
- *Thank God for the freedom and confidence to approach Him through Christ.*
- *Address Him as to what is on your heart today, however trivial or great.*
- *What a privilege to carry everything to God in prayer!*
- *"O what peace we often forfeit, O what needless pain we bear,*
- *All because we do not carry everything to God in prayer."*
- *('What Friend we Have in Jesus' by Joseph M. Scriven)*

– Rob Horner (2020)

9 OCT An exceedingly abundantly powerful God

Now to Him who is able to do exceedingly abundantly above all that we ask or think, according to the power that works in us, to Him be glory in the church by Christ Jesus to all generations, forever and ever. Amen.
Ephesians 3:20-21 (NKJV)

Lawyer Paul covers all possibilities when he extols the omnipotence of God's ability to act on our behalf. Nothing is impossible with God. Our imaginations are too small to comprehend His measureless greatness and power. Yet often we feel afraid, powerless, useless and doubtful.

As we face this week, we need to remind ourselves of all that God is and all that He has done. Starting with us! If we are Christians, His power has worked in us to bring us from death to life; from slavery to freedom; from unbelief to faith; from sin to righteousness. We have nothing to boast about. Ultimately, His work in us will last forever and bring Him eternal glory.

Over the last few days, these words have been both a song of praise and a challenge for me. Whatever the joys and pressures of legal practice today, bring Him glory through your faith in His power – not yours.

- *Give praise to God in your heart this morning for all that He has done, is doing and will do in your life, because of His great love for you.*
- *Offer to God any fears and doubts that you have as you start this week and trust in His word and His promises, knowing that His power is at work in you for His Glory and purpose.*

– Esther Harrison (2016)

10 OCT Walking in unity together

I, therefore, a prisoner for the Lord, urge you to walk in a manner worthy of the calling to which you have been called, with all humility and gentleness, with patience, bearing with one another in love, eager to maintain the unity of the Spirit in the bond of peace. **There is one body and one Spirit – just as you were called to the one hope that belongs to your call – one Lord, one faith, one baptism, one God and Father of all, who is over all and through all and in all. Ephesians 4:1-6 (ESV)**

While spending time first with our justice mission teams, who will travel to East Africa later this year to fellowship with our 'CLEAR' partners working for justice in Africa, and then preparing to travel to Germany with an Lawyers' Christian Fellowship team to engage Christian lawyers from across Europe, these verses have led me to reflect on how we encourage each other within the body of Christ. It is easy to focus on the differences, especially with our legal minds, trained to distinguish facts and to spot the detail, but Paul exhorts us to bear with one another in love as we are one body through Christ.

As a fellowship, the LCF membership represents a range of church traditions, expressions, and diversity. To help us keep Christ at its core, and with a commitment to the supreme authority of Scripture, we have a doctrinal basis which enables us to navigate well amongst the different views and human traditions. But how do we practically bear with each other in love, being eager to maintain the unity of the Spirit, in our law firms, chambers and colleges? At the end of chapter 3, Paul prays for the Ephesians to have spiritual strength and encouragement.

Are we praying for one another? Are we, with humility, gentleness and patience, encouraging our Christian colleagues in their spiritual walk and witness, and allowing them to do the same with us?

- Give thanks for Christians we know in our workplaces, and for opportunities to meet, read the Bible and pray together. May we be an encouragement to each other today.
- Please pray for our partners in Africa and the LCF teams working with them – that relationships would be strengthened, and for Christian lawyers across Europe to be salt and light within their legal systems.

– Mhairi Hamilton (2016)

11 OCT Handling money God's way

Anyone who has been stealing must steal no longer, but must work, doing something useful with their own hands, that they may have something to share with those in need. **Ephesians 4:28 (NIV)**

Having moved house and engaged the services of two firms of solicitors, one for the sale and the other for the purchase about 350 miles away, as well as dealing with a third firm concerning a deceased's estate I was reminded that, whilst some lawyers undoubtably face issues (especially with legal aid cuts), most do pretty well financially and some do very well!

The Apostle Paul was keen to urge everyone, including past criminals, to earn their living. But not only so; he encouraged his readers to earn more than enough in order to be able to give to those in need. It is important not to be a burden on others if we can maintain ourselves, and in the modern day most lawyers are able to do that, but Paul highlights the Christian duty to give to others when we can too.

The other day I heard a local preacher, Paul Barton, say words to the following effect: "It is not a question of holding onto and not wasting your money; it is a question of not letting your money hold you."

Let us thank God, our Father that we are able to earn our living and pray that we will receive enough to give to others, and to do so prayerfully and wisely.

- Pray that out of that which we receive from our work we will respond to the biblical call to give to others, and to do so with Godly wisdom.
- Pray for those who are struggling to find work, for those looking for training contracts, pupillages, and for those looking for new work after redundancies – that they may be aware of the Lord's peace and sovereignty in the process.

– HH Alan Taylor (2015)

12 OCT — Prayer is where a lawyer does their best work

I thank my God in all my remembrance of you, always in every prayer of mine for you all making my prayer with joy, because of your partnership in the gospel from the first day until now. And I am sure of this, that he who began a good work in you will bring it to completion at the day of Jesus Christ. **Philippians 1:3-6 (ESV)**

How does prayer impact our approach to our legal practice and studies? How do our circumstances shape our prayers?

Bound in chains and under house arrest, Paul experienced the joy of knowing that everything counts for Christ. His opening prayer is therefore full of thankfulness to God, joy and encouragement to continue pressing on in Christ.

Despite his circumstances, Paul knew to whom he prayed, and this knowledge gave him comfort and confidence. With love, compassion, and joy, Paul encouraged his readers to go deeper in their relationship with Christ, knowing this would similarly enrich and strengthen them for their circumstances, and for their gospel witness.

We are encouraged to bring our own needs before the Lord – see Philippians 4:6 – but let us not forget that He also cares deeply about our clients, our colleagues and fair and just practices within our legal system. Because we are confident of God's love and compassion for us, how much more so can we ask the Creator to intercede on their behalf, both in the immediate and in the eternal?

- *Paul's deep joy was rooted in his personal relationship with God. Let us pray today for one another that we might grow in love and knowledge of our Lord, and experience His joy regardless of our circumstances.*
- *Let us pray for those among our fellowship who find themselves in difficult circumstances and are struggling to find the words to pray. May the Lord hear their cry and may they know His love and peace in the midst of this time.*
- *Let us pray for colleagues and clients – that they may come to a deeper realisation of the good news of Jesus Christ and choose to way in His ways.*
- *Let us pray for those involved in our legal system, that they may act with integrity and fairness.*

– Mhairi Hamilton (2021)

13 OCT — This is my prayer

And this is my prayer: that your love may abound more and more in knowledge and depth of insight, so that you may be able to discern what is best and may be pure and blameless for the day of Christ … **Philippians 1:9-10 (NIV)**

A good Christian friend and colleague once told me: "I'm really grateful when people tell me they pray for me, but I am especially grateful when I know what they are praying for". Now I don't necessarily know why that is really helpful, but perhaps it's because it's a specific prayer with a specific purpose.

In this verse from Philippians, Paul seems to be of that mind set. Paul's prayer is that "your love may abound more and more in knowledge and depth of insight". Paul is saying that he hopes the Philippians' love would multiply (the meaning of abound). But why does Paul pray this? The specific purpose for the Philippians is that they would "discern what is best and may be pure and blameless for the day of Christ." Paul's hope is that love which multiplies in knowledge would lead people to discern what will make them pure and blameless for the day of Christ – eternity.

This applies to lawyers and law students and reminds us that as we grow in love, knowledge, and depth of insight, the purpose of this is eternity.

Take a moment to think about the needs of a particular colleague or client and pray about that specifically – you may the only person praying for them. Also, pray that we would:
- *be lawyers or law students who act with love towards God, our clients, and colleagues and who have depth of insight*
- *act with good discernment in our day to day lives*
- *be pure and blameless for the day of Christ.*

– Esther Wade (2022)

14 OCT In chains, but in progress

Now I want you to know, brothers and sisters, that what has happened to me has actually served to advance the gospel. As a result, it has become clear throughout the whole palace guard and to everyone else that I am in chains for Christ. And because of my chains, most of the brothers and sisters have become confident in the Lord and dare all the more to proclaim the gospel without fear. **Philippians 1:12-14 (NIV)**

The Apostle Paul had a strong desire to preach in Rome, as a strategic city to spread the gospel. He went there eventually, not as a free man able to go to the streets and synagogues, but as a prisoner, precisely for preaching the message of salvation in Christ.

During his time in prison, he wrote the letter to the Philippians, which shows a unique and distinctive reaction to suffering. He looks to the difficult circumstances and acknowledges that the Gospel has spread. Paul's primary concern is not his own well-being, wealth or comfort, but with the advancement of the Kingdom, in whatever circumstances God places him. He was in chains, but the Gospel was not – and is not.

Some who are reading this may be tied to a difficult case where injustice seems to prevail; many feel trapped in a secular and anti-God university environment or alone in a workplace where no one else is Christian. Paul's message encourages us to see the adverse circumstances as opportunities to bear witness for Christ, to be a source of motivation for fellow believers (v 14) and a lighthouse that guides non-believers to the message of endless hope and joy.

Further reading: *Philippians for You*, Steven J. Lawson (2017), The Good Book Company.

- *Pray for wisdom to navigate the challenges we have in the legal profession in a way that will motivate other believers to progress in the faith.*
- *Pray for Christian lawyers who are feeling weak or weary due to difficult circumstances; that they would find comfort and joy in God's presence.*

– Felipe Carvalho (2021)

15 OCT Transformed thinking: transformed lives

Have this mind among yourselves, which is yours in Christ Jesus, who, though he was in the form of God, did not count equality with God a thing to be grasped, but emptied himself, by taking the form of a servant, being born in the likeness of men. And being found in human form, he humbled himself by becoming obedient to the point of death, even death on a cross. Therefore God has highly exalted him and bestowed on him the name that is above every name ... Philippians 2: 5-8 (ESV)

Thinking right is perhaps our greatest challenge. For Christian lawyers, Godly ambition and assertion of legal rights are important but, in these verses, Paul is clear that the way we think about both needs to be transformed through fellowship with Christ (v 5); this is how Christ thought, therefore this is how I am to think.

How did Jesus think? As God, he refused to stand on his rights as God but, in obedience to his Father and for our salvation, he set them aside. As God, Christ made himself nothing by becoming a man, taking the form of a servant or slave, a nobody-in-law. As a man he humbled himself further, becoming obedient to the point of death, the death of a condemned criminal on the cross.

When Jesus humbled himself to the Cross, people wrote him off, but (v 9) God saw it differently: Obedience led to the Cross, and our salvation! And the Cross led to the Crown, Christ's exaltation.

In East Africa, the transformed Christian thinking of our CLEAR partners has led them to serve in prisons, homes, schools and communities. Their Gospel thinking has seen lives transformed. In your legal workplaces this week, where might such transformed thinking lead you?

- *Pray for opportunities this week to serve those you work or study with Christian humility.*
- *Ask God to help you explain to others how you think differently about life as a Christian and why.*
- *Pray for strength, wisdom and grace for The Lawyers' Christian Fellowship's CLEAR partners in East Africa, that they might share the whole Good News about Jesus Christ known through law.*

– Mark Bainbridge (2019)

16 OCT Star quality

Do everything without grumbling or arguing, so that you may become blameless and pure, 'children of God without fault in a warped and crooked generation'. Then you will shine among them like stars in the sky as you hold firmly to the word of life. **Philippians 2:14-16a (NIV)**

If we asked a member of the public to describe characteristics of a lawyer, it is doubtful that the words 'blameless and pure' would feature high up the list. It is more likely that 'warped and crooked' might get a mention, however flawed (or not!) that perspective may be.

In Philippians 2, Paul reminds us that we should "have the same mindset as Christ Jesus" (v 5) and gives us some practical examples in these verses, encouraging us not to grumble or argue. This phrase is reminiscent of the Israelites' complaining to God in the wilderness and is a prompt not to follow in their grumbly footsteps.

As we work and study, we may be tempted to complain about the challenges we come across – about our difficult clients, inconsiderate colleagues or classmates, and trying situations and opponents. We may find ourselves less than pure as we seek to thrive in an adversarial system and an adversarial world.

In that context, we may seek 'star quality' as we construct arguments to advance our case or aim to stand out from the crowd in our applications. More significantly, Paul tells us that as we hold onto the word of life, we can expect to shine like stars, distinctive lights for Jesus as his glory reflects through us into the darkness of our surroundings.

- *Praise God for Jesus' humility and sacrifice for us.*
- *Pray for opportunities to be a shining light to those you work with and for.*

– Naomi Cooke (2021)

17 OCT How would you describe yourself in five words?

I think it is necessary to send back to you Epaphroditus, my brother, fellow-worker and fellow-soldier, who is also your messenger, whom you sent to take care of my needs. **Philippians 2:25 (NIV)**

Have you ever thought about Epaphroditus? The Christians at Philippi sent him to Paul while he was in prison with a gift (4:18), and it is clear how grateful Paul was for his help which nearly cost him his life (2:26-30).

Paul describes him in five ways: "brother, fellow-worker, fellow-soldier, messenger, servant" ('minister' in AV and RSV). What a tremendous Christian example he must have been to Paul, other prisoners and their guards – in other words, to people in great need and to people who had positions of responsibility and power over others. We Christian lawyers can do well to think about this description of Epaphroditus and see how our lives compare with his.

What a blessing he was to Paul! Let us, too, try to be a blessing to all whom we know who are in need. Let us pray each day for God's help in the tasks which lie ahead and in the opportunities for service for the Lord which our professional life can bring.

- *Ask the Lord to show you ways in which you can serve Him and your fellow-workers in the gospel this week, and to be open to His leading.*
- *Give thanks to God for The Lawyers' Christian Fellowship partners, especially in East Africa, for their example of service and blessing to others, often in difficult circumstances.*

– HH Alan Taylor (2016)

18 OCT Eyes on the prize!

Not that I have already obtained this or am already perfect, but I press on to make it my own, because Christ Jesus has made me his own. Brothers, I do not consider that I have made it my own. But one thing I do: forgetting what lies behind and straining forward to what lies ahead, I press on toward the goal for the prize of the upward call of God in Christ Jesus. **Philippians 3:12-14 (ESV)**

When I was younger, I ran the 100m sprint at a local club. Foregoing longer distances out of laziness, a straight sprint is simple: you keep your eyes on the finish line and run as fast as you can. But is the Christian life a straight sprint? Often it feels more like an ultra-marathon, with the end never in sight: we despair over injustice rather than grow in joy; we are weary of difficult clients or colleagues; we may even stumble over losing loved ones (spiritually or physically).

Paul urges the Philippians to ground their battle for progressive sanctification in the certain truth of their definitive sanctification. Paul's remedy is to remember who has definitively saved him, and pursue Jesus, the eternal prize. He writes, Christ has made me his own (v 12, literally: I was laid hold of), so the prize at the end of the race is secure. Brothers and sisters, we are his prize and he is ours.

Yet, Paul is humble and pragmatic. He writes acknowledging the weight of his sin, yet urges us to follow his example and press on*, looking straight ahead, because God's people are fully forgiven at the Cross. And remember, we press on corporately: if there is something particularly impeding your progress, speak to a Christian friend and pray together about it.

* Specifically, Paul uses the Greek verb for 'press on' that can also mean persecution, e.g. his prior zeal to persecute the church (Philippians 3:6) and how Jesus confronted Paul in Acts 9:4-5.

- *Praise Jesus for what he won at the Cross: we are a people saved by grace, with eternal life and riches in Christ ahead of us, and a life to get to know him more and to become more like him by the Spirit.*
- *Satan loves to 'guilt' Christians by their past sins, to keep us in despair, and tempts us to look to ourselves and not to Christ. Pray for God's help in today's daily battle, to say no to Satan but look to Jesus.*
- *Pray for the perseverance of brothers and sisters who are persecuted globally: that they will keep looking forward to the prize of Christ, their ultimate, unique, and eternal glorification in Jesus.*

– Jane Allen (2022)

19 OCT Never quite fitting in

For, as I have often told you before and now tell you again even with tears, many live as enemies of the cross of Christ. Their destiny is destruction, their god is their stomach, and the glory is in their shame. Their mind is set on earthly things. But our citizenship is in heaven. And we eagerly await a Saviour from there, the Lord Jesus Christ, who, by the power that enables him to bring everything under his control, will transform our lowly bodies so that they will be like his glorious body. Philippians 3:8-21 (NIV)

Do we feel at home in our office or workplace? Do we feel like we really belong there? Well, if the answer is no, then that could be a sign of health for our spiritual state. Paul explains here that our citizenship is in heaven, meaning we are just passing through this world, on our way to our true home. This means that we shouldn't feel like we really belong in our earthly context. We should feel that there is something different about us from our non-Christian colleagues and friends.

This heavenly citizenship is in contrast with the fate of non-believers that Paul mentions. They are opposed to God and so will face judgment. How we might long to have the same attitude as Paul as he grieves at the thought that these people will be judged by God.

And part of our citizenship in heaven means we will be given new resurrection bodies. Gone will be all their current failings, the signs of too many coffees or late nights in the office. We will be given perfect bodies, like Jesus' resurrection body.

Our citizenship in heaven means that we should not hold too tightly to the things of this world but should seek God's glory now as we live for Jesus. How might we strive to do so this week in our work, in our actions and in our words, looking ahead to our eternal home?

- *Praise God that, if we are trusting in Jesus, we know that our citizenship is secure in heaven.*
- *Pray that we would grieve for how our colleagues in our workplaces and fellow students face God's judgment and that this would spur us on to share the gospel with them;*
- *Pray that we would long for the day when we would be given perfect resurrection bodies.*

– Peter Thompson (2019)

20 OCT Do not be anxious – the Lord is at hand

The Lord is at hand; do not be anxious about anything, but in everything by prayer and supplication with thanksgiving let your requests be made known to God. And the peace of God, which surpasses all understanding, will guard your hearts and your minds in Christ Jesus. **Philippians 4:5b-7 (ESV)**

We are living through anxious times – at the time of publication, the Covid-19 crisis has partially lifted, but there is war in Europe, a healthcare crisis, a continuing energy crisis, high inflation and a cost of living crisis, not to mention strikes. As a result of the pandemic, there are long delays in court hearings.

However, this passage reminds us that we are not to be anxious about anything. The reason for this is that the Lord is at hand. The present crisis brings into sharp focus the frailty of humanity, but also the sovereignty of God, and his wonderful assurance that through prayer, and by placing our trust in God, we have a Saviour in Jesus Christ. A Saviour through whom we can eternally enjoy the peace of God.

- *We pray for those in our legal community who are bereaved, or who are sick.*
- *We pray for those who are anxious about their practices, and about the continuing impact of the pandemic on the justice system. We pray that they might be relieved from their anxiety in the knowledge that the Lord is at hand.*
- *We pray that these uncertain times might provide the impetus for those who have yet to place their trust in Jesus to reflect upon the priorities in their own lives, and turn to him as Saviour.*

– HHJ Mark Cawson KC (2020)

21 OCT — The contented lawyer

I rejoiced in the Lord greatly that now at length you have revived your concern for me. You were indeed concerned for me, but you had no opportunity. Not that I am speaking of being in need, for I have learned in whatever situation I am to be content. I know how to be brought low, and I know how to abound. In any and every circumstance, I have learned the secret of facing plenty and hunger, abundance and need. I can do all things through him who strengthens me. Philippians 4:10–13 (ESV)

Every day we are bombarded by advertisements telling us that if only we bought or had this particular thing, our lives would be complete, whether that be a new car, a new house or even ordering a take-out meal using one of the many apps or delivery companies. In our culture, everything is instant. Patience is generally at a premium and contentment and peace are not the currency of our culture.

The Apostle Paul knew what it was to have his plans suddenly changed, to face opposition and deal with adversity, as is documented particularly clearly in the second half of the book of Acts. He knew that material things are fading and passing, and as such he focused on the lasting and eternal.

As lawyers, we can be tempted to want 'the next thing', whatever that may be. Perhaps something material

I can do all things through him who strengthens me

Philippians 4:13 (ESV)

or even that promotion at work. As we are reminded in Matthew 6:21, "where your treasure is, there your heart will be also". As we start this new working week let's remember where our treasure is, where our hope is and as such to learn to be content in all circumstances, knowing that our hope and strength is in Jesus and our home is in Heaven.

- *Pray that God will open our eyes to any 'blind spots' that are stopping us from finding contentment in Him.*
- *Pray that the hope and contentment that we have will be an example to our colleagues, friends and family who will want to know more about the hope and contentment we have.*

– Tim Grainger (2021)

22 OCT What is your engine running on?

To them God chose to make known how great among the Gentiles are the riches of the glory of this mystery, which is Christ in you, the hope of glory. Him we proclaim, warning everyone and teaching everyone with all wisdom, that we may present everyone mature in Christ. For this I toil, struggling with all his energy that he powerfully works within me. **Colossians 1:27-29 (ESV)**

As lawyers, we will all be familiar with the dreaded feeling of facing up to a heavy workload that seems insurmountable. Not only can it impact on our productivity, but it can also affect our relationships both in and out of the workplace.

When we start to feel as though we are running out of steam, it is incredibly encouraging to reflect on Paul's letter to the Colossians. We must never forget that through our work, we have a unique opportunity to proclaim Christ to our colleagues and our clients, however much strain we might be under. This can be through our words, our actions, and even our attitude.

Paul makes clear that through his exhausting efforts in proclaiming Jesus, his power-source is Christ's energy. What a privilege it is to know that we don't have to rely on our own strength – it's the equivalent of having rocket fuel available to us!

As this week begins, perhaps take a moment to reflect on the things ahead that you know are going to be an uphill struggle. Commit them to Christ, and ask for His energy to sustain you through them.

- *Praise God for his boundless energy that works so powerfully in us.*
- *Pray for opportunities to proclaim Christ even through times of difficulty and stress.*

– Laurence Wilkinson (2018)

23 OCT — Be who you already are

If then you have been raised with Christ, seek the things that are above, where Christ is, seated at the right hand of God. Set your minds on things that are above, not on things that are on earth. For you have died, and your life is hidden with Christ in God. When Christ who is your life appears, then you also will appear with him in glory. **Colossians 3:1-4 (ESV)**

What are you like under pressure? Impatient? Snappy? Quick to blame-shift?

As lawyers, we so easily yield to our circumstances – deadlines, difficult colleagues, fatigue – and forget ourselves. But if what Paul writes here is true, then right now we are – spiritually – where Christ is: at God's right hand! Because of what Jesus did on the cross, we have already attained the same sinless status as Christ in God's eyes.

After establishing this extraordinary truth, Paul sets us an incredibly challenging task: to set our minds on things that are above, not on things that are on earth. That is, to deny our earthly desires, and be like Christ in our thoughts, words and deeds.

In His kindness, there is grace for when we fail, but let's seek to be Christ to those around us in our colleges, firms and chambers today, because that is who our Heavenly Father sees, when He sees us. In the midst of our hectic schedules, let's set our minds on the perfection of Christ, and obey Him above all else.

Let's be who we already are.

- *Praise God that our lives are now hidden in Christ because of what He accomplished on the cross.*
- *Pray that we would live as those who are raised with Christ, reflecting His character in our thoughts, words and deeds this week.*

– Claire Thompson (2018)

24 OCT — Audience of one

Whatever you do, work at it with all your heart as working for the Lord, not for men, since you know that you will receive an inheritance from the Lord as a reward. It is the Lord Christ you are serving. **Colossians 3:23-24 (NIV 1984)**

God sees everything, and our motivation should be to honour him. No work done for God's glory is insignificant. Even the most mundane task. It means giving our best – not only for the big name corporate clients which pay large amounts for legal services, but also for the pro bono clients, and not only in our work but also in our unpaid service too. It means holding praise lightly – a 'nice to have' but not our primary motivation.

Jesus gives us an anchor – the culture around us may change, clients and colleagues may come and go, we may graduate or change jobs or be out of work for a period, but through it all our ultimate boss remains the same. He is the same yesterday, today and forever. And he is loving and good and just. Whether life/work feels easy or hard, whether we are well-paid now or struggling to get by, those of us who know Jesus as Lord and Saviour can look forward to an eternal inheritance with him which will never perish, spoil or fade (1 Peter 1:4). It is guaranteed by the creator and sustainer of the universe – that is some guarantee!

- *Pray that we would really grasp the inheritance that is ours in Christ.*
- *Pray that we would honour God in the work we do – paid and unpaid.*
- *Pray for those who are struggling at the moment – those who are out of work or on furlough, those who are finding work hard, those who feel that their work is insignificant, and those who may be struggling to work for an audience of one.*

– Nat Johnson (2021)

25 OCT What are you totally devoted to?

Devote yourselves to prayer, being watchful and thankful.
Colossians 4:2 (NIV)

How is your prayer life? Your quiet times may be an easy everyday occurrence; however, it is remarkable how quickly time spent alone reading God's Word and in prayer can be squeezed by the pressing task list and immediacy of competing demands in the legal profession. Yet it is core to our walk with Jesus.

Paul encourages the Colossians to adopt three attitudes towards prayer:

1. "Devotion", also translated as "continue steadfastly" in ESV. Devotion speaks of love and care, a commitment to continue over time to invest and persevere. Are we devoted to prayer, driven by a desire to know and understand God more?

2. "Watchfulness". While it can be tempting to bring a wish-list to God for fixing, Paul encourages an intentional listening ear, to see where and how God is at work, and how we engage; and

3. "Thankfulness". Even when life's challenges seem overwhelming, we need to lift our eyes to God Himself, who gives us so many reasons to be thankful.

May I encourage you today to pause for a few moments, to focus on God, with a thankful heart and a desire to know Him even more deeply.

- *Give praise to God for who he is and thanks for his faithfulness. Be specific in your thanks.*

– Mhairi Hamilton (2017)

26 OCT — What seasoning do you use?

Let your conversation be always full of grace, seasoned with salt so that you may know how to answer everyone. **Colossians 4:6 (NIV)**

Words are the stock-in-trade of the lawyer, whether written or oral. Paul urges that we are to be gracious in our speech (and writing).

We may have to disagree fundamentally with an opponent or even with our client, but we should always do it graciously. We should give due consideration to all we write and say. It is so easy to speak thoughtlessly or to send off that e-mail without too much thought. We know all too well that our tongues are hard to govern so all the greater need for care.

Paul also suggests that our conversation be seasoned with salt. There needs to be some seasoning to our speech which will awaken in those who hear us an interest in the things of Christ.

- *Pray that God will guard your tongue and thoughts today.*
- *Pray that you will be gracious in your speech and writing in both work and leisure.*
- *Ask the Holy Spirit to season your words that others may be drawn to Christ.*

– Michael Hawthorne (2016)

27 OCT — Passionate concern

We always thank God for all of you, mentioning you in our prayers. We continually remember before our God and Father your work produced by faith, your labour prompted by love, and your endurance inspired by hope in our Lord Jesus Christ. **1 Thessalonians 1:2-3 (NIV 1984)**

Acts 17 tells us that Paul and Silas' preaching in Thessalonica led to the conversion of some Jews and Greeks, but also such vehement opposition from others that they had to be smuggled out by night. Subsequently, Paul had been desperate to find out how the new Thessalonian converts had been doing and so he sent Timothy. Had their fledgling faith been stamped out by persecution? How were they doing? Paul was passionately concerned.

The report came back in glowing terms. Timothy found remarkable faith, hope and love: a faith which meant the Thessalonians had stuck to the gospel in spite of terrible pressure and they lived to please God, a love for one another which had struck Timothy forcibly and a tremendous hope in salvation through Jesus.

What would a Timothy find if he visited you in your workplace? With his focus on Jesus' return Paul encouraged the Thessalonians and prayed that their faith, love and hope would increase. It would be good to be doing that for our fellow Christian lawyers.

- Pray for the Christian lawyers whom you know, that they would know an increase this week in their faith, hope and love in Christ.
- Pray for Christians in public life, that they would stand for biblical values.

– Rev. Ian Miller (2015)

28 OCT What are you waiting for?

… and to wait for his Son from heaven, whom he raised from the dead, Jesus who delivers us from the wrath to come. **1 Thessalonians 1:10 (ESV)**

Basildon Crown Court is not an especially impressive building, but its corridors are forever etched on my memory. Every pupil's first jury trial is nerve wracking, but I found waiting for the verdict the most gut-wrenching few hours of my life. As I paced up and down outside Courtroom 2, I played every question, and every piece of evidence, back and forward in my mind. The consequences of my contributions in court weighed heavy: if convicted, my client would likely face a custodial sentence.

We might not be facing criminal charges this morning, but we know that a day is coming when every piece of our sinful lives will be laid out before the ultimate judge: Jesus Christ. When we reflect on our thoughts, words and actions this week, that may seem like a scary prospect, where the just consequences would drive us to pace up and down worrying.

But as Christians, we know that, for those who repent and believe, Jesus has taken another role: he has served our sentence, and borne our punishment at the cross. We have been rescued from the wrath to come, and can wait for Jesus' return with a certain confidence, an assured security, and a glorious hope.

- Confess your sins and ask for Jesus' forgiveness.
- Praise God that He has delivered us from the wrath to come.

– Jen McKelvin (2020)

29 OCT Manual work

… and to make it your ambition to lead a quiet life: you should mind your own business and work with your hands, just as we told you, so that your daily life may win the respect of outsiders and so that you will not be dependent on anybody. **1 Thessalonians 4:11-12 (NIV)**

This verse gives us a radical view of ambition. Our ambition is not to seek what will fade one day, but instead to live calmly, quietly, as we walk with God in our daily lives.

Paul told the church in Thessalonica to "work with [their] hands". That doesn't mean that Christian lawyers must type their letters, as opposed to dictating them. After all, both Jeremiah (Jer. 36:4) and Paul (Rom. 16:22, 2 Thess. 3:17) dictated. What it does mean is that Christians should not be afraid of the unglamorous, lowly, or menial work. For that is how "working with one's hands" would have been understood in a Greek, 1st century port.

All honest work – document checking as well as dreaming up that killer legal point that wins the case – is dignified because God made us to be workers like him. So no work is beneath us. And all work, if done to please God, can result in a daily life that will not only earn respect but which will commend the gospel of Christ – whose unglamorous work for his Father on the cross achieved more than anyone could have imagined.

- Praise God for Christ's lowliness in working for our salvation.
- Pray for a Christian ambition at work today especially for the lowly bits.
- Pray that our work will prompt both the respect and gospel interest of those around us.

– Andrew M (2017)

30 OCT Rejoice today

Rejoice always, pray without ceasing, give thanks in all circumstances; for this is the will of God in Christ Jesus for you. 1 Thessalonians 5:16-18 (ESV)

Lawyers, some would say, are not always the most joyful bunch of people.

Rejoicing always is not the flippant command of a life coach trying to convince us that we can wish away our troubles with the power of positive thinking. Life before Jesus' return will for most people contain times of genuine and deep sadness and hardship, and the writer of these verses experienced many such situations. Instead, the command to "rejoice always" points the Christian to adopt a conscious attitude of not being ruled by those circumstances; to remember that we can find real joy in Jesus, and the incomparable hope and treasure we have in him even when times are hard.

Christians in the legal profession will often encounter difficulties in our workplaces, in the lives of our clients/colleagues and in our personal lives. Those difficulties are not be minimised or ignored, but even as we acknowledge and engage with them, as Christians, we must also deliberately remind ourselves and each other of the unchanging blessings we have in Jesus, which enable us to remain joyful and thankful always.

So take time today to rejoice and give thanks in Jesus for all that he is and all that he has done for us.

- *Give thanks to God for the unchanging hope and assurance we have in Jesus.*
- *Pray that we would be a fellowship marked by a deep joy in Jesus and in the hope he brings, no matter what our individual circumstances.*

– Elsa Glauert (2020)

31 OCT Choosing the best

Now it happened as they went that He entered a certain village; and a certain woman named Martha welcomed Him into her house. And she had a sister called Mary, who also sat at Jesus' feet and heard His word. But Martha was distracted with much serving, and she approached Him and said, "Lord, do You not care that my sister has left me to serve alone? Therefore tell her to help me."

And Jesus answered and said to her, "Martha, Martha, you are worried and troubled about many things. But one thing is needed, and Mary has chosen that good part, which will not be taken away from her."

Luke 10:38-42 (NKJV)

It's the time of year when many have moved on to a new stage in life: beginning a degree; starting at law school; undertaking pupillage or a training contract. For some, we have reached the stage where we are delivering the training. Until recent times at the bar, we used the title 'Pupil Master' or 'Pupil Mistress' for those who supervised the pupil barristers. A title given to Jesus, more often in days gone by, was 'The Master'.

Whatever phase of life we are in as lawyers or Christians, we need to learn from Jesus. We need to choose "that good part" and sit at his feet. This takes effort and hard work, discipline and habit. It may mean getting up early on Monday morning to prepare a case so that we have time to rest and worship on Sunday, drinking in his word, fellowshipping with his people. Perhaps keeping a Bible in our desk or on our phone so we may "redeem the time" when it arises. We may have to set the alarm clock earlier so we can rise and pray (Mark 1:35).

Mary and Martha were to face a great test of faith when their brother Lazarus died (John 11). We face daily challenges in our careers and studies, and we live in a world hostile to our Saviour. We need to spend time at his feet – pierced and bloodied for us, yet beautiful in bringing the good news of salvation to all who repent in faith.

- *Pray for those who are facing new challenges in their study or practice of the law; that they might be a living witness to the reality of Jesus to all around them.*

- *Seek wisdom from God as to how you can "choose the best", prioritising godly habits that bring you closer to The Master.*

– Esther Harrison (2019)

1 NOV — The secret to saying 'No'

For the grace of God has appeared that offers salvation to all people. It teaches us to say "No" to ungodliness and worldly passions, and to live self-controlled, upright and godly lives in this present age, while we wait for the blessed hope – the appearing of the glory of our great God and Saviour, Jesus Christ … Titus 2:11-13 (NIV)

In private practice, the culture is to be at the beck and call of those calling the shots. To the client's instruction, the partner says "Yes". The trainee does the same to their supervisor. But when that instruction contradicts God's Word, or when we feel tempted to fall into sin, how will we say "No"?

According to Paul, the answer is found in God's grace, his undeserved kindness to us in sending Jesus. It is as we look back at God sending Jesus to save us and forward to meeting him in the New Creation that we realise all we owe to him and want to live godly lives.

So when we are feeling the pressure to compromise our faith, let's turn back to God's grace.

- *Praise God for his grace shown to us in sending Jesus to save us.*
- *Pray for members to be reminded of that grace and so to live distinctive lives.*

– Peter Thompson (2018)

2 NOV — The voice that really matters

In the past God spoke to our ancestors through the prophets at many times and in various ways, but in these last days he has spoken to us by his Son, whom he appointed heir of all things, and through whom also he made the universe. The Son is the radiance of God's glory and the exact representation of his being, sustaining all things by his powerful word. After he had provided purification for sins, he sat down at the right hand of the Majesty in heaven. Hebrews 1:1-3 (NIV)

As lawyers, there are so many voices which claim to have the last word, and to be the one we should listen to – be that the partner at work, the client on the end of the phone, or our law tutor.

But the writer of Hebrews makes it clear that God's word through His son Jesus is truly the final word. His Jewish listeners were tempted to turn back to the prophets, to Moses and Elijah and so on, but they were only a patchwork, pointing forward to Jesus and the message that He held out that He came to save us from our sins.

But we might think, why should we listen to Jesus? Why His, over all the other voices? Well, the writer seems to pre-empt that question and goes onto look at His qualifications. Let's take a couple – He made the universe. He was there in the beginning with God in creation. And He is the radiance of God's glory. When we look to Jesus, we see God's love and character. Nothing can be found of God that is not found of Jesus.

So let's make sure we take time to listen to Jesus' voice, to prioritise listening to His words each day.

- *Pray to be rooted in God's word and feeding on it.*
- *Pray that as we see His amazing qualifications, we would all want to continue to make Jesus king of our lives.*

– Peter Thompson (2022)

3 NOV Rest at the top of the to-do list

So then, there remains a Sabbath rest for the people of God, for whoever has entered God's rest has also rested from his works as God did from his. Hebrews 4:9-10 (ESV)

How do you feel about 'rest'? Perhaps you are envious of the exciting travel of colleagues? Perhaps you are approaching a family holiday with nervousness? Or perhaps you have just come back from a holiday but wish it could have been longer!

As lawyers who bill their time, judges who have little control over their court time, and students who notoriously always run out of time, the idea of just stopping to take rest may seem strange when not in the context of 'holiday'. However, rest is a good gift from our good God who Himself rested on the seventh day (Genesis 2:2)!

The true rest promised in Hebrews is for any who believe in Jesus for salvation. It is a rest from relying on your works but trusting that His crucifixion won eternal rest for His people. It fulfils the promises of rest in the Old Testament* Promised Land and points us to the eternal rest to come in the New Jerusalem.

When (and not if) you take rest today, how can you remind yourself to rest in Him and not your own works? How can you prioritise physical, mental, and spiritual rest in God this week?

* See Joshua 1:13, 15; Exodus 33:14; Deuteronomy 3:20

- *Praise God that He has won eternal rest for His people on the Cross. Ask for forgiveness for how we deprioritise resting in God and don't set our hearts on the eternal rest of the New Creation.*
- *Pray for how you can take time to stop and rest in God, meditating on the Cross and Heaven this week. In what way can Christian brothers and sisters hold you*

accountable to rest? How can you encourage them to take rest?

- Pray for your rest to provide a witness to colleagues and friends.

– Jane Allen (2021)

4 NOV Promises. Turned to dust or delivered?

When God made his promise to Abraham, since there was no one greater for him to swear by, he swore by himself, saying, 'I will surely bless you and give you many descendants.' And so after waiting patiently, Abraham received what was promised. Hebrews 6:13-15 (NIV)

As lawyers, we know that a promise is a firm agreement, either orally or in writing, to perform or refrain from an act or action, and the performance of which can at times be conditional. The law teaches us too that as humans we are frail and often forget or fail to fulfil our promises.

In Old Testament Hebrew there is no specific word for 'promise'. Abraham had to take God on his own oath, trusting that he had both the ability (sovereignty) and integrity (faithfulness) to deliver. In the new covenant, we have the benefit of knowing that God has already kept his promise in Jesus Christ, alongside the confident expectation of the promise of eternity which we, like Abraham, wait for with patience.

In the meantime, as we live as children of the promise, do we care that we are surrounded by others in our profession who don't?

David Ferguson, a former Lawyers' Christian Fellowship member serving alongside his wife Lorna (a former solicitor too) with OMF in Japan, died of cancer in 2017. In their last prayer letter before his death they wrote, "… we know that this life is not all there is. We have a certain hope. Yet we are surrounded by Japanese people who know nothing of that hope."

Will the testimony of David and Lorna and your assurance give you an urgency to make the promises of God known to others this week?

- *Give thanks and praise to God for his promises to you and ask that you will have the courage to share them with others.*

– Mark Barrell (2017)

5 NOV Whom are you going to call?

[And] let us consider how we may spur one another on towards love and good deeds … Hebrews 10:24 (NIV)

Christians are meant to live in company with others not alone. We need fellowship with other Christians to encourage us and to enable us to grow in our faith, and we need to be alert to opportunities to spur others on in their walk with the Lord.

Time is precious and we have to prioritise but fellowship is too important and necessary to be side-lined. Is our church attendance suffering? Are we making an effort to get to LCF events or local group meetings?

In the very next verse, Hebrews 10:25, the writer challenges "… not giving up meeting together, as some are in the habit of doing, but encouraging one another …"

- *For the spirit of discipline as we follow our Lord.*
- *For opportunities to encourage and spur on another believers.*
- *That we may seek to do good as we have opportunity.*
- *Is there a call we need to make or a letter to write to thank someone for the help we have received recently?*

– Michael Hawthorne (2017)

6 NOV I do not have time

By faith the prostitute Rahab, because she welcomed the spies, was not killed with those who were disobedient. And what more shall I say? I do not have time to tell about Gideon, Barak, Samson and Jephthah, about David and Samuel and the prophets. **Hebrews 11:31-32 (NIV)**

We know nothing about the anonymous writer to the Hebrews, but he managed to produce a weighty letter full of rich theology. His detailed account of people commended for their faith ends with a Gentile prostitute, and is followed by only a brief summary of the exploits of some of Israel's most significant leaders. Why is that? Because the writer did not have time! Yet this chapter tells us all we need to know about the "cloud of witnesses" spurring us on to run the race set before us (12:1); or at least we have some more names to look up in the Old Testament.

Such pressure of time will be familiar to practising lawyers. There are deadlines to meet, set by statute, the Court, clients and other parties to transactions. Time recorded in excess of the fee estimate may need to be written off. Other clients' business competes for our attention. Will we have time to get everything done?

Our doctrine of Scripture tells us that this writer was inspired by God. He demonstrates that it is possible to do everything God wants us to do within the available time. If we seek His guidance, we may find that some things we would like to achieve are not so important after all, and that what we can actually achieve is sufficient for His purposes.

- *Pray for the ability to make the best use of the time available to complete each piece of work, concentrating on what will be sufficient to achieve its purpose, rather than our own standard of perfection.*

- *Pray for self-discipline in managing our time and priorities, not only in the conduct of professional business, but in all areas of our lives, including work, family, church and leisure.*
- *Pray for help to invest sufficient time in our relationship with God, including personal worship, prayer for ourselves and for others and allowing Him to speak into our lives about His priorities for us.*

– Graham Whitworth (2020)

7 NOV Don't give up!

Therefore, since we are surrounded by so great a cloud of witnesses, let us also lay aside every weight, and sin which clings so closely, and let us run with endurance the race that is set before us, looking to Jesus, the founder and perfecter of our faith, who for the joy that was set before him endured the cross, despising the shame, and is seated at the right hand of the throne of God. Consider him who endured from sinners such hostility against himself, so that you may not grow weary or fainthearted. **Hebrews 12:1-3 (ESV UK)**

If you are a lawyer, you will have discovered that practising law is not for the faint-hearted, and if you are a law student, you have now been warned! The persistence of your opponent can tempt you to take the easy way out, such as recommending a 'drop hands' settlement when perseverance would achieve a better outcome, or agreeing those ill-conceived amendments to your draft lease. The temptation might even be to take one of those short-cuts that you know is not quite right, just to keep your impatient client happy.

Then there is weariness – with clients, colleagues, opponents, Court staff, even some judges, whose aim in life seems to be to make things difficult for us. How easy it can be to vent our frustration and say or even write things we later regret!

We could just try being thick-skinned and gritting our teeth, relying on our own strength to avoid reacting wrongly. However, as Christians we have the advantage that Jesus lives in us (Galatians 2:20). He experienced far worse opposition, enduring to the point of death on the Cross, yet looked forward in faith to His resurrection and ascension. Have you asked for His help with your work today?

- *Thank God that, because Jesus believed He would be raised from the dead and ascend to the right hand of the Father, He was able to endure the Cross and now empowers us to endure as we fix our eyes on Him.*
- *Ask Him to enable you to see beyond that Court hearing, complex completion, difficult meeting or whatever else looms large on your horizon and to persevere in doing what is right.*

– Graham Whitworth (2018)

8 NOV — A simple truth with no 'ifs' or 'buts'!

My dear brothers and sisters, take note of this: Everyone should be quick to listen, slow to speak and slow to become angry, because human anger does not produce the righteousness that God desires. James 1:19-20 (NIV)

Have you had a real rant at someone recently? Shouted down the phone at the hapless lawyer on the other side? Or publicly upbraided a junior colleague in the office when they messed up a simple task despite your painfully clear instructions? Did it make you feel better? Did you reassure yourself that you were acting in your client's best interests by being firm? Or by reflecting that a trainee just won't learn unless they know how costly and irritating their mistake was? And besides, there's nothing unchristian about showing a bit of backbone, right?

We can all give into the temptation to let assertiveness slip into anger and to let robustness tip into aggression. Especially when some in our workplaces will celebrate belligerence. It is easy to lose our cool with an opponent or to get wrapped up in our seniority and self-importance and pick on the peer who is deserving of criticism.

But James reminds us of a simple truth which sounds a direct challenge to us as Christian lawyers. Man's anger does not produce the righteousness that God desires.

No 'ifs' or 'buts'. Man's anger does not produce the righteousness that God desires.

Have we made excuses for becoming angry this week? Is it time to kneel before God, ask for forgiveness and ask his Spirit to inspire in us a new way to act at work?

- *Seek forgiveness from the Lord and reconciliation with those you need to on any anger issues that the Lord has laid on your heart as you have read this.*

– Thomas Cordrey (2016)

9 NOV — Thinking we are good when even our thoughts make us guilty

For whoever shall keep the whole law, and yet stumble in one point, he is guilty of all. For He who said, 'Do not commit adultery,' also said, 'Do not murder.' Now if you do not commit adultery, but you do murder, you have become a transgressor of the law. So speak and so do as those who will be judged by the law of liberty. James 2:10-12 (NJKV)

It has been my privilege over the past 18 years to preach the gospel in prisons. I am struck by the relative honesty of many prisoners on a one-to-one basis when considering that we are all guilty sinners before God and need to be saved through personal faith in Jesus, who shed His blood for us.

On the negative side, I am at times flabbergasted by how men guilty of terrible crimes will look down in judgment on others whose crimes have been of a different kind. A triple killer could not believe that God could forgive certain sex offenders.

But are we not at times guilty of similar thinking? James makes it clear that either committing murder or committing adultery, which is not even a crime in the UK, make me equally guilty of breaking God's law. Jesus went further and taught that to hate or to lust in the heart – the *mens rea* without the *actus reus* – renders me guilty and deserving God's eternal punishment.

May we never settle for 'little sins'. Why? Because there are none. And may we always be grateful and surrendered to the only One "who Himself bore our sins in His own body on the tree" (the cross) 1 Peter 2:24 (NJKV).

- *Ask the Lord to be led away from temptation and delivered from the evil that displeases God and offends His holiness.*
- *Be grateful and give thanks to the Lord that the Christian message is one of mercy and grace.*
- *Ask for eyes to see and the strength to be diligent in using our privileged position as lawyers to do people the maximum good that we can!*

– Gerard Chrispin (2016)

10 NOV Two kinds of wisdom

Who is wise and understanding among you? Let them show it by their good life, by deeds done in the humility that comes from wisdom. But if you harbour bitter envy and selfish ambition in your hearts, do not boast about it or deny the truth. Such 'wisdom' does not come down from heaven but is earthly, unspiritual, demonic. For where you have envy and selfish ambition, there you find disorder and every evil practice. But the wisdom that comes from heaven is first of all pure; then peace-loving, considerate, submissive, full of mercy and good fruit, impartial and sincere. Peacemakers who sow in peace reap a harvest of righteousness. **James 3:13-18 (NIV)**

Although it is not part of scripture, the heading that the NIV gives to this portion of James is a useful one. There are two kinds of wisdom.

Clients come to lawyers for 'wise counsel', but have you ever mused on what that phrase means? In this passage James suggests that it is vital to recognise where professed 'wisdom' and 'understanding' come from. James teaches that a 'wisdom' derived from "envy and selfish ambition" manifests in "disorder and every evil practice". Now, pause for a moment to reflect on how much "envy and selfish ambition" exists in that part of the law that you inhabit!

In contrast, wisdom from heaven is "'pure, peace loving, considerate, submissive, full of mercy and good fruit, impartial and sincere". Could anything be more starkly different? Interestingly, those who display such hallmarks seem to be called 'peacemakers'. When your clients and colleagues look to you, is that what they see, a 'peacemaker'? Now, I am sure that the word 'peacemaker' is not a regular synonym for 'lawyer', but if you are to raise a "harvest of righteousness" then that is the kind of wisdom that is to be to be demonstrated.

Above I used the word 'mused' deliberately. Before you delete this email and move on with the day, stop and muse on the words of the passage again. If there are two kinds of wisdom, which do you employ?

- Lord, as I examine my heart before you, test me so that I can consider truthfully which kind of wisdom I draw on.
- I've never seen myself as a peacemaker; please help me to see what that means for me right now in the place I am.
- Thank you for your mercies to me, be patient with me and may your grace let me resolve to be a peacemaker, sowing in peace, that a harvest of righteousness might be reaped. Amen.

– Brent Haywood (2018)

11 NOV How to plan ahead

Come now, you who say, 'Today or tomorrow we will go into such and such a town and spend a year there and trade and make a profit – yet you do not know what tomorrow will bring. What is your life? For you are a mist that appears for a little time and then vanishes. Instead you ought to say, 'If the Lord wills, we will live and do this or that.' **James 4:13-15 (ESV)**

Lawyers tend to be highly organised people: client deadlines are carefully noted in the work diary and even social calendars are frequently planned many months in advance. Yet perhaps we are not always as in control as we like to think we are. In just this last week, I have had two friends come to me in a personal capacity for employment law advice as they face losing their job – a stark reminder that we cannot control the future. As James says in the passage above, we "do not know what tomorrow will bring".

Those around us may look outwardly secure and confident, but the reality is that both our lives and legal careers are extraordinarily transient – like "mist that appears for a little time and vanishes".

Instead, let us remember afresh that every decision we make in this next week is dependent purely on God's grace and humbly trust the future to Him.

...he has given us new birth into a living hope

1 Peter 1:3 (NIV)

- Pray for the humility to know that God is sovereign over all our plans and the confidence to entrust ourselves to His good and loving purposes.
- Give thanks for the good news of the Gospel and that whatever may pass, those who have believed and trusted in Christ can rest in the knowledge that our future is secure in Him.

– Adam McRae-Taylor (2017)

12 NOV The riches you cannot earn

Praise be to the God and Father of our Lord Jesus Christ! In his great mercy he has given us new birth into a living hope through the resurrection of Jesus Christ from the dead, and into an inheritance that can never perish, spoil or fade. 1 Peter 1:3-4a (NIV)

The legal profession is renowned for its work ethic and rigorous billing regime; but these verses remind us that there are some riches we simply cannot earn. According to Peter, these are gifts given to us by God in His great mercy, and we are to praise Him for them.

First, we praise Him for the 'living hope' that we have been born into. We are told that this hope was made available to us through Christ's resurrection from the dead. What better assurance that our hope is 'living', than that Christ conquered death itself?

Secondly, we praise Him for the inheritance we have been born into. Peter tells us that, unlike earthly estates and legacies, the inheritance we have from God is immune to the eroding effects of time or taxation. The God who held back the damning consequences of death is more than able to guard perfectly that which He promised His people.

If we are tempted as lawyers to think that we can earn the mercy of God, the same way we bill clients for time spent on their matters, we are wrong: God has given us riches we cannot earn, and thankfully, these are riches we cannot lose.

- *Praise God for the living hope you have in Christ! This is hope that transcends earthly struggles, even death itself.*
- *Praise God for the inheritance you have been born again into that will never perish, spoil or fade!*
- *Pray for the people around you who don't yet know this great mercy of God, that they would turn and receive these riches themselves.*

– Claire Thompson (2018)

13 NOV The rareness of joy

Though you have not seen him, you love him; and even though you do not see him now, you believe in him and are filled with an inexpressible and glorious joy, for you are receiving the end result of your faith, the salvation of your souls. **1 Peter 1:8-9 (NIV)**

How do we respond when we suffer for our faith? When we're passed over for a promotion, scorned by our friends or given the silent treatment, it's so easy to despair. The believers that Peter was writing to here, however, show a completely different attitude. He speaks of the amazing joy that these Christians show.

When my fellow law student raised their eyebrows at me when I told them I was a Christian, I found it so easy to turn inward – to say, "Poor me". This verse was a great one to turn to. It reminds us that despite our salvation being something which we only completely enjoy in the future, we have joy in our faith now! A joy of knowing Jesus personally, as we trust in Him and get to know Him better. This joy comes through faith, of trusting in Jesus even though we have not seen Him and don't see Him now.

How rare it can be that we take the time to dwell on this joy of being in a relationship with Jesus, or of speaking about it with our fellow believers at church or with our colleagues at work. And what perspective this joy can bring to us now, amidst suffering for our faith.

- *Pray for members to be struck anew by the joy we have in knowing Christ personally, and for that joy to shine out of the lives of Christian lawyers, pointing others to Christ.*

– Peter Thompson (2017)

14 NOV — Remember you are God's precious possession

But you are a chosen people, a royal priesthood, a holy nation, a people belonging to God, that you may declare the praises of him who called you out of darkness into his wonderful light. **1 Peter 2:9 (NIV 1984)**

It is very unhealthy to think either that the world revolves around us or that we are worthless specks of matter in a vast and pitiless universe. Yet those are the options our secular culture offers.

The wonderful truth is that the world does not revolve around us; in this vast universe we are unimaginably small. But neither are our lives meaningless. The awesome God who created this breathtaking cosmos sees us as His precious possession. The images in 1 Peter 2:9 come from Exodus 19, when God demonstrated His holiness and power to the people with fearsome fire and thunder. But the same God who shook the earth in unapproachable majesty also told His people that they were His treasured possession, set apart for Him.

The Apostle Peter applies these descriptions to those who trust in Jesus. If we depend on Christ for our righteousness, God sees us as His people. Special, holy, royal priests. What a tremendous thought as you sit this morning at your desk, run for the train on your way to court, or slave away at a photocopier! And why has God made us His special people? So that we may declare His praises to those around us. Our friends and colleagues need to hear about the amazing God who calls His people out of darkness into light.

- *Pray that God would give you a confidence and assurance today, whatever lies in store for you, that you are his precious possession.*
- *Pray that you might have an opportunity today to declare God's praises to a colleague, friend or family member.*

– Alasdair Henderson (2017)

15 NOV — Respectfulness in a secular world

Show proper respect to everyone, love the family of believers, fear God, honour the emperor. **1 Peter 2:17 (NIV)**

It is a great privilege for the practising lawyer to deal and work with many people in the course of the working week. It is a particular joy to encounter other Christians, but many who cross our paths will not be, and their values and attitudes may be challenging to us. At times it may seem easier not to engage with some people and the secular and hostile world they often represent.

We must be careful to ensure that we honour God in all our professional dealings. That may be easiest when dealing with Christians, with whom our faith can be expressed freely, and we should experience similar joy when able to discuss our faith with those who do not presently share it. When we deal with trying or disrespectful individuals, however, Peter reminds us that it is for God's sake that we should act respectfully at all times. In doing so, we may silence the ignorant talk of those who would criticise us (see 1 Peter 2:15) and thus enable ourselves better to witness to Jesus.

- *Give thanks for all the people with whom we deal professionally, and pray that we may see our interactions with them as an opportunity to live out our faith.*

– James Brightwell (2015)

16 NOV Plead 'Guilty' and be acquitted!

He himself bore our sins in his body on the tree, that we might die to sin and live to righteousness. By his wounds you have been healed. **1 Peter 2:24 (ESV)**

But he was pierced for our transgressions; he was crushed for our iniquities; upon him was the chastisement that brought us peace, and with his wounds we are healed. **Isaiah 53:5 (ESV)**

Plead 'Guilty' and be acquitted!

Never! How can that be?

The simple definition of a 'crime' which I heard many years ago as a first year Law undergraduate was: "A crime is an offence against the state punishable at the instigation of the state". The concepts of crime and punishment are intertwined.

The prisoners I preach to each week say, "You do the crime – you do the time", and are shocked to hear that the Highest Judge of all can acquit if there is a guilty plea blended with appropriate sorrow for the wrongs committed and a determination to turn from such wrongs.

But when I tell them that the same Judge has stepped down from the Bench, into the dock, and has taken the penalty such offenders deserved, in their place, they are amazed.

How can this possibly be?

There is only one answer. The Bible teaches that the Lord Jesus Christ willingly "bore our sins in his body" when He died as our substitute on the cross. Though innocent of any sin, the incarnate Son of God accepted being "smitten by God and afflicted" when "He was pierced for our transgressions" and "crushed for our iniquities" by His heavenly Father.

Now risen and ascended, He is willing to pardon, indwell by the Holy Spirit and give eternal life to all who call on Him for mercy and forgiveness.

Many prisoners seem to 'get it'. Do you?

For further reading 1 Peter 2:21-25 (ESV) and Isaiah 53:3-6 (ESV).

- *Thank God for our wonderful salvation in Christ.*
- *Share the message with others – lawyers or not.*
- *Please pray for the preaching of the gospel in our troubled and needy prisons.*

– Gerard Chrispin (2017)

17 NOV A lion stalking the office

Be sober-minded; be watchful. Your adversary the devil prowls around like a roaring lion, seeking someone to devour. Resist him, firm in your faith, knowing that the same kinds of suffering are being experienced by your brotherhood throughout the world. And after you have suffered a little while, the God of all grace, who has called you to his eternal glory in Christ, will himself restore, confirm, strengthen, and establish you.
1 Peter 5:8-10 (ESV)

On a Monday morning, we often do not know what the week will bring. We may be anxious about tight deadlines, difficult clients or long hours. But Peter warns us that there is a much greater danger lurking as we go about our week. Our offices and libraries are actually a savannah: the devil stalks the corridors and conference rooms like a lion, looking for someone to devour. Peter tells us to be alert to the spiritual dangers which threaten us day-to-day.

When facing a lion, the natural reaction might be to run as fast as we can in the opposite direction, but this isn't what Peter tells us to do when we face the devil. Rather than fleeing, we are to stand firm, immovable in our faith, shoulder to shoulder with our brothers and sisters in Christ. Because we do not suffer alone – Christians around the world face the same adversary as we do. Thankfully, we do not do this by our own power. It is God himself who restores us when we are weak and strengthens our faith.

The week ahead may be daunting if we rely on our own strength, but with God to strengthen us and fellow Christians surrounding us, we are equipped to stand firm when we face the spiritual battles that the week may bring.

- *Pray that God will strengthen you in your faith this week as you face spiritual dangers.*
- *Pray that Christians around the world facing persecution will stand firm in their faith.*

– Owen Vanstone-Hallam (2019)

18 NOV — The judge who was different

For Christ also suffered once for sins, the just for the unjust, that He might bring us to God, being put to death in the flesh but made alive by the Spirit, **1 Peter 3:18 (NKJV)**

… who Himself bore our sins in His own body on the tree, that we, having died to sins, might live for righteousness. **1 Peter 2:24 (NKJV)**

The chapel of the old Victorian London prison was packed with prisoners.

The men listened intently as the gospel was preached. Some nodded as they heard that just as their crimes must be punished at the instigation of the state, so their sins must be punished at the instigation of our holy, righteous and eternal Judge.

They heard that Jesus, our 'God with us' (Emmanuel) in human flesh, bore our sins and punishment on the cross to forgive and cleanse all who turn from their sins and receive Christ as Lord and Saviour. Some men seemed visibly moved.

'What can a human judge do other than pass sentence on a guilty offender?' They already knew the answer to that question, for even if he wanted to, no judge could leave the bench and stand in the dock to be sentenced for a guilty man.

'But our Judge left the 'bench' of Heaven, took on flesh, lived a sinless life, and bore our sins in His own body on the cross. Christ also suffered once for sins, the just for the unjust, that He might bring us to God. Each of us needs to admit and turn from our sins and trust Jesus as our Saviour.'

Those words, so well received by the prisoners, are as much for us as they are for those behind bars. What a wonderful Saviour we have!

- May we trust and rejoice in the Saviour who bore our sins.
- May we live as redeemed men and women and do our walk as spiritually renewed lawyers.
- May we pray for colleagues and clients to do the same, by God's grace.

– Gerard Chrispin (2016)

19 NOV — Instructing the perfect advocate

My dear children, I write this to you so that you will not sin. But if anybody does sin, we have an advocate with the Father – Jesus Christ, the Righteous One. He is the atoning sacrifice for our sins, and not only for ours but also for the sins of the whole world. **1 John 2:1-2 (NIV)**

Our clients, perhaps charged with a serious crime or facing a potentially devastating damages claim, can never be sure that they will prevail in court. No doubt their confidence will in some part be dependent on the skill and quality of their advocate but, as that advocate will surely tell them, you can never be sure which way the judge or jury will go.

In the same way, we are prone to doubt and trepidation when we approach the ultimate Judge burdened with the grief of our latest sin. No human advocate, however gifted, could ever extricate us from the divine penalty which we rightly deserve.

However, the glorious news, this week and forever more, is that we have the ultimate advocate in Jesus Christ the Righteous One. His defence of us is not based on clever arguments or devastating cross examination, but on His own blood shed for us on the cross – the atoning sacrifice for our sins. In other words, He tells the Father: "don't condemn them because you have already condemned me".

As John says, those of us who are in Christ will still sin. Whilst we should strive to follow John's exhortation not to do so, we must also make sure that we never let our sin come between us and God, whose love for us is greater than our frail human hearts will ever comprehend.

- *Thank God for the atoning sacrifice of Jesus, which is even now working to protect us from the judgment which we rightly deserve.*

- *Bring your sin to Him in confidence, relying on The Advocate and His sacrifice; embrace his overwhelming love.*

– Ben Fullbrook (2021)

20 NOV Wake up!

To the angel of the church in Sardis write: 'These are the words of him who holds the seven spirits of God and the seven stars. I know your deeds; you have a reputation of being alive, but you are dead. Wake up!'
Revelation 3:1-2a (NIV)

There are some passages in the Bible that can make uncomfortable reading. This passage, though about a church, may also apply to us as individuals. To the outsider we may look like a thriving committed Christian, but a closer examination of our busy lives as lawyers may reveal that the reality is different. Would the evidence show that our quiet times have slipped, Sunday has stopped being set aside for God and our Bible remains on a shelf between outings to a midweek church group?

The passage contains a warning, "But if you do not wake up, I will come like a thief, and you will not know at what time I will come to you" (v 3b). The passage also offers help, "Remember, therefore, what you have received and heard; hold it fast, and repent" (v 3a).

And finally, the passage contains a promise: "The one who is victorious will, like them, be dressed in white. I will never blot out the name of that person from the book of life, but will acknowledge that name before my Father and his angels" (v 5).

Whatever happens this week, let's take seriously the charge to "Wake up!"

- Ask God to reveal where you have let your walk with Him drift. Repent and by the Holy Spirit endeavour to make the necessary change.
- Give thanks for the opportunity to read God's word and meet with others in fellowship freely. Pray for those who are unable to do so but still hold fast to the Lord Jesus Christ.

– Ben Fullbrook (2015)

21 NOV   True riches

You say, "I am rich; I have acquired wealth and do not need a thing.' But you do not realize that you are wretched, pitiful, poor, blind and naked. I counsel you to buy from me gold refined in the fire, so you can become rich; and white clothes to wear, so you can cover your shameful nakedness; and salve to put on your eyes, so you can see. Revelation 3:17-18 (NIV)

When we look at our colleagues or peers, many seem to have life sorted. The razor-sharp mind, the sharp suits, the enormous house, hanging out in all the right circles. Whilst there is nothing wrong with these things in themselves, like the church in Laodicea to whom John was writing, they may say that they have no need for God; they have all the worldly riches they could ever need.

But God makes clear that these riches are a mirage. The Lord will see these people for who they are – wretched and poor, sinners who are blind to who Jesus really is.

We should equally look at our own hearts and lives. How easy it is for Christian lawyers to get sucked into going after worldly riches. Often not through any conscious step, but just drip by drip, as we absorb the culture around us.

But God holds out an offer to those caught up with the materialism of this world: by trusting in Jesus, and through his grace alone, they can 'buy' his riches and be made pure before God.

How ought we to look to Jesus as the one who offers the riches of a relationship with him. And, how might we tell those around us, particularly those whose lives seem 'sorted', of Jesus' grace to them. After all, we know how utterly valuable Jesus' grace is – true riches of the purest sort.

- Thank God for the true riches of his grace.
- Pray for members for strength in the battle against worldliness.
- Pray for members for bold witness to colleagues and peers, in speaking of Jesus' grace.

– Peter Thompson (2021)

22 NOV The eternal Word

*The grass withers, the flower fades,
But the word of our God stands forever.*
Isaiah 40:8 (NKJV)

In an age where religion may be seen as personal preference or cultural inheritance, our faith stands on firmer ground. While Christianity explains the human condition (why humankind is capable of both grandeur and degradation) and our subjective experiences are formative, our faith stands on the objective truth of God's word.

As lawyers we understand that words, and how they point to the truth, are crucially important. Jesus perfectly provides us with both. Jesus said He is the way, the truth and the life, and He is the way and the life because He is the truth. That must give us confidence in the flux of changing opinions, both within and outside the church.

Let's pray
- For ourselves, that our convictions about the word of God will give us the confidence and courage that we need to live for Jesus in the legal profession.
- Thanking God that The Lawyers' Christian Fellowship has, over generations, been faithful to God's word.
- For our nation's Christian leaders, that they hold fast to biblical truth.

– John Scriven (2016)

23 NOV Neighbourhood watch

He asked Jesus, 'And who is my neighbour?'
Luke 10:29 (NIV)

It might just be because I'm a litigator, but the word 'neighbour' barely features in my vocabulary at work. 'Opponent', 'other side', 'client', 'Counsel' and 'expert' are all common, but the only context in which we talk of 'neighbours' is in disputes between them over land and/or rights.

In this passage, an expert of the law is 'testing' Jesus as to how he can 'inherit eternal life' (v 25). They quickly establish that the 'lawyer' should obey the fundamental precepts of the Old Testament law to love God and neighbour (vs 26-28). Like any good litigator, the lawyer can't leave it there as he wants to justify his question (v 29). He therefore asks Jesus who his 'neighbour' is, and in response Jesus tells what has become known as the parable of the Good Samaritan (vs 30-37).

One important point that Jesus makes (among many) is to explain that our 'neighbour' particularly includes those with whom we may fundamentally disagree, and with whom there may even be outright hostility (as there was between Jews like the victim in the parable, and the Samaritan who saved him). I need to be constantly reminded not only to love my clients and colleagues, but to love everyone else that I litigate with – or against – just as much (if in different ways). How will you love your neighbours at work this week?

- *Give thanks to God that, even whilst we were his enemies, He loved us so much that He sent His Son to die for us, and reconcile us to Him.*
- *Ask God to help you to be mindful this week of who your 'neighbours' are at and through work, and for His grace to love them well, and to work out what that looks like in practice.*

– Jon Hyde (2016)

24 NOV Held on trust

'Whoever can be trusted with very little can also be trusted with much, and whoever is dishonest with very little will also be dishonest with much …' Luke 16:10 (NIV)

This is a passage in which Jesus speaks to the disciples about money, and challenges them – and the listening Pharisees – that they cannot serve both God and money. He points out that being trustworthy in handling worldly wealth is indicative of whether a person is to be trusted with real treasure.

We may have been given responsibility in our professional and personal lives for money, property, liberty, homes and businesses – belonging to ourselves and others. We have the opportunity to be trustworthy in those things, both given the expectation of our role but also as followers of Jesus. We have more than a responsibility to our client, the court, our employer. We have a responsibility before God. Whether we feel we have a little or a lot, we are called to be faithful with it. As we are faithful, we will see fruitfulness in our lives for God's glory.

- *Do you have a little responsibility or a lot? How can you strive to be faithful in what you have been given? Ask God for his help to remain faithful and resist temptation.*

– Naomi Cooke (2020)

25 NOV Abide in me

'Abide in me, and I in you. As the branch cannot bear fruit by itself, unless it abides in the vine, neither can you, unless you abide in me. I am the vine; you are the branches. Whoever abides in me and I in him, he it is that bears much fruit, for apart from me you can do nothing.' **John 15: 4-5 (ESV)**

Rejoice in the Lord always; again I will say, rejoice. Let your reasonableness be known to everyone. The Lord is at hand; do not be anxious about anything, but in everything by prayer and supplication with thanksgiving let your requests be made known to God. And the peace of God, which surpasses all understanding, will guard your hearts and your minds in Christ Jesus. **Philippians 4:4-7 (ESV)**

During the pandemic, one of the bright lights was witnessing the Church play a prominent role in helping to meet both spiritual and physical needs of believers and non-believers alike. Additionally, Christian lawyers were able to reclaim the time that would otherwise have been allocated to commuting and hurrying from one work meeting to another, and use it to seek God and to serve those around us.

Now that workplaces have re-opened their doors and various return to work policies are in place, though some of us may have days working at home, today's passage is a wonderful reminder that those in Christ must stay in Christ. Fruitfulness is a direct consequence of abiding in Christ. Apart from Him, we can do nothing. As the days get shorter and the demands on our time increase, how do we ensure that we are abiding in Christ?

For me, Philippians 4:4-7 provides the watertight blueprint: rejoice in the Lord always; do not be anxious about anything; pray about everything with thanksgiving and the peace of God will guard your heart and mind in Christ Jesus.

In the busyness of the office, may we continue to intentionally carve out time to seek God and abide in Christ.

- *Thank God that as we abide in Him, He abides in us.*
- *Pray that we would be disciplined in allocating time to seek Him and His will for our lives.*
- *Pray that we would be salt and light in our offices, chambers and places of study, diligent to proclaim the Gospel and to serve our colleagues and clients.*

– Kiki Alo (2021)

26 NOV Gracious living for Christian lawyers

Let not sin therefore reign in your mortal body, to make you obey its passions. Do not present your members to sin as instruments for unrighteousness, but present yourselves to God as those who have been brought from

death to life, and your members to God as instruments for righteousness. For sin will have no dominion over you, since you are not under law but under grace.
Romans 6:12-14 (ESV)

Another week of legal challenge, with all that can go right and all that can go wrong. And another week of challenge in living the Christian life.

Paul reminds us: Remember who you are. You have been brought from death to life. You are bought with a price. That means you are a child of God, a member of His household and precious in God's eyes.

Remember what Christ has done for you. It is He who laid down his life for you, to set you free from the dominion of sin. Sin does not control you. There is no need to give way to the passions of anger, frustration, defeat or despair, any more than you are to be controlled by pride, jealousy or avarice. The slavery of sin is over and done with.

Remember whom you belong to. You have been called into the kingdom of the living Lord. You live your day, your week, your life, under His grace, in his loving purposes, as an instrument of His righteousness. You are an exponent of His gracious rule.

Enjoy your day.

- *Present yourself to God this morning as a saved sinner*
- *Give thanks to God for the Lord Jesus Christ whose sacrifice has brought you from death to life.*
- *Pray to fulfil His purposes for you this week, as a freed instrument of His righteousness.*

– Janys Scott KC (2019)

27 NOV The competence paradox

But we have this treasure in jars of clay to show that this all-surpassing power is from God and not from us.
2 Corinthians 4:7 (NIV)

Do you feel competent for your work? The answer for you may be yes – you have done the right training, you have the qualifications, you may have years of experience, you know what is expected of you. Or it may be no – you feel out of your depth, overwhelmed, poorly prepared, inexperienced.

Competence is highly prized in the legal profession. As lawyers, we have a regulatory obligation to ensure we are competent for our roles. None of us would want to give incorrect advice, or to do a poor job for our clients or colleagues. For us as Christians, that is a matter of integrity – we are working for the Lord, as well as serving others' needs.

But Paul reminds us that none of us is fully competent to do the work that God has given us to do, that of being His ambassadors in the world. Even aside from our moral failure and sinfulness, we are all weak in other ways – physically fragile, mentally finite, emotionally easily swayed. God has designed us this way so that He might be glorified in us. He desires dependency in us, not just to prove the self-confident person wrong, nor to condemn us to perpetual self-doubt, but so that we turn away from ourselves completely and instead look to Him.

- *This week let's acknowledge and embrace the God-given way of weakness and ask Him to show His power through it. Perhaps some of the following might be helpful steps for you:*
- *Bring to God in prayer the matters you are working on, whether or not you feel capable of doing them, and ask for His help to carry them out in a way that honours Him.*
- *Expressly thank God for things that go well, rather than attributing them to your own skill or expertise (and you can thank God for the skill and expertise He has given you, too!).*
- *Rejoice in your weakness, and even in the things that you find difficult and painful, as Paul does in 2 Corinthians 12:10, precisely because they enable God to demonstrate His all-sufficiency for you.*
- *Tell another person about a time when God worked through your weakness to bring Himself glory.*

– Caroline Eade (2022)

28 NOV We're on a mission from God

Therefore, we are ambassadors for Christ, God making his appeal through us. We implore you on behalf of Christ, be reconciled to God. **2 Corinthians 5:20 (ESV)**

You meet 'experts' everywhere: in big crises like the pandemic or the war in Ukraine as well as in everyday life. When it comes to healthy eating or the last football match, many have a strong opinion on how things should be. According to Paul, however, we are not experts, but ambassadors, ambassadors of Christ. What makes an ambassador?

Firstly, we tend to give our opinion on everything; we lawyers are especially known for this. An ambassador, though, does not spread his own opinion, but the message of the government he represents.

Secondly, an ambassador should not just proclaim messages that the other person wants to hear. God admonishes through us, so we are to speak His truth. The goal is and always will be reconciliation, especially reconciliation with God. So, our mission as lawyers can be to show a client God's perspective of reconciliation in a dispute.

Thirdly, an ambassador is skilled in diplomacy. He does not clumsily barge in but brings the message at the right moment and in such a way that it is received. As ambassadors of Christ, we do not just throw God's word around, but may ask the Holy Spirit to work through us and give us diplomatic words.

As lawyers, we are exposed to much argument and conflict. As Christians, it is good to know that we are sent into this very professional life as ambassadors of Christ.

- *In the next conflict situation, ask God what His perspective of reconciliation is on the problem and ask Him to give through His Holy Spirit the right words at the right moment.*

– Patrick Menges (2022)

29 NOV Tempted to give up?

Let us not become weary in doing good, for at the proper time we will reap a harvest if we do not give up. Therefore, as we have opportunity, let us do good to all people, especially to those who belong to the family of believers. **Galatians 6: 9-10 (NIV)**

There is much in the life of the lawyer that can cause weariness: short deadlines, demanding clients and stretching billing targets. Throw in other common pressures such as busy family lives and church responsibilities, and we can often feel overwhelmed.

Paul encourages us in these verses not to "give up" when we are feeling weary. Amidst the busyness are so many chances to do real tangible good: to solve a client's problem, love our friends and families, and encourage brothers and sisters in our faith.

So where do we find the inner resources of strength to fight the weariness? Paul encourages us that if we keep going "we will reap a harvest". The good we do can – and will – make a difference for eternity.

- *Pray that God would refresh our souls so that we do not give up serving Him.*
- *Pray that He would give us a renewed vision of the good we can do for others in all areas of our lives.*

– Adam McRae-Taylor (2019)

30 NOV Practical fellowship

Devote yourselves to prayer, being watchful and thankful. And pray for us, too, that God may open a door for our message, so that we may proclaim the mystery of Christ, for which I am in chains. Pray that I may proclaim it clearly, as I should. Be wise in the way you act toward outsiders; make the most of every opportunity. Let your conversation be always full of grace, seasoned with salt, so that you may know how to answer everyone. **Colossians 4:2-6 (NIV)**

From time to time I meet up with one or two members of The Lawyers' Christian Fellowship whom I see infrequently – we live and work in different parts of the country. Although our time is short, for me the reconnections are rich and deep. We talk of important future plans and initiatives that, God willing, we may share in. All of this was important but coming away, it seems to me that what I treasured most was that as lawyers we were praying together and encouraging each other.

These verses from Colossians remind me of the encouragement I draw from the LCF – people spurring me on to be prayerful, watchful and thankful; people reminding me to think purposefully about every conversation.

- *In what ways can you be more deliberate about staying connected with lawyers in our fellowship – and are there lawyers who you can encourage, whether members or not?*
- *Are you praying for fellow members – asking that God may open a door for the message?*
- *Are you, like Paul, boldly asking for people to pray that you would be clearly proclaiming 'the mystery of Christ'?*

– Brent Haywood (2016)

1 DEC Advent

'It will be good for those servants whose master finds them ready, even if he comes in the middle of the night or toward daybreak. But understand this: If the owner of the house had known at what hour the thief was coming, he would not have let his house be broken into. You also must be ready, because the Son of Man will come at an hour when you do not expect him.' Luke 12:35-40 (NIV)

This time marks the beginning of the season of Advent from the Latin word adventus meaning 'coming'. It is a time of expectant waiting and preparation for both the celebration of the Nativity of Jesus at Christmas and the return of Jesus at the Second Coming.

Practices associated with celebrating Advent can include keeping an Advent calendar, lighting an Advent wreath, praying an Advent daily devotional, erecting a Christmas tree or lighting a Christingle. Even for those Christians who do not celebrate Advent itself, there are other ways of preparing for Christmas, such as carol services and setting up Christmas decorations.

Preparing for Christmas for most will involve working out a budget, deciding who is hosting Christmas Day and who is coming and present shopping.

In this passage Jesus tells us that it is imperative not to forget that it is more important to be ready for Christ this Christmas than it is to be ready for the time off work and spent with our nearest and dearest because, as Jesus reminds us, he will come at an hour when we do not expect him.

- Pray that, despite the busyness of business in the run up to the holiday season, we will remember the reason for the season.
- Pray that we, those with whom we will be spending Christmas and everyone else celebrating the incarnation will be ready for the Second Coming.

– Peter Brown (2019)

2 DEC Are we ready?

Be patient, then, brothers, until the Lord's coming. See how the farmer waits for the land to yield its valuable crop and how patient he is for the autumn and spring rains. You too, be patient and stand firm, because the Lord's coming is near … The Judge is standing at the door!
James 5:7-9 (NIV 1984)

At this time of year thoughts are beginning to turn towards plans for Christmas but, although the Church will be preparing to celebrate our Lord's first coming as a helpless baby, prior to that is the reminder that we need to prepare to be ready for his return in glory as Judge.

In those far-off days when I sat as a District Judge I recall all too well standing at the door into the courtroom as the usher called "All rise!" James reminds us that even now our Lord waits to return with power to reign and to judge. Are we ready?

Jesus warned that his return will be unexpected, and that we need to stay alert and be watchful. The fact of our Lord's return should spur us to greater effort to reach those who are without Christ and without hope in this world, especially those in the legal profession, whilst there is still time.

- Pray that we may be ready for our Lord's return with expectant hearts.
- Pray for a sense of urgency in reaching others for our Lord.
- Many of our Judges, advocates, and court staff are under tremendous pressure. Pray for them to be enabled to cope with the strain and particularly for those suffering as a result of delayed hearings.

– Michael Hawthorne (2020)

3 DEC Christmas is for the children

But when the set time had fully come, God sent his Son, born of a woman, born under the law, to redeem those under the law, that we might receive adoption to sonship.
Galatians 4:4-5 (NIV)

Do burdened lawyers sometimes need children to really bring our Christmas to life? The text says Christmas is not only about a child being born – it is about making us enjoy being God's children.

This is more (but not less) than recovering a childlike wonder that the Creator could be made flesh. Yes, he was born into a manger, but what was he born under? Here is a baby born under the very legal system which was designed centuries earlier for that climactic moment: to strap the weight of our destiny onto his soft little back.

Jesus was burdened from birth by the Mosaic law so that by taking it through his life, through the cross and out of the empty tomb, he would turn it upside down. Jesus satisfied all its demands for us so now we stand on it and not under it. Now its weight becomes the foundation for our legal right to enjoy being God's children and heirs.

So let's not reverse Christmas this year – as if we should sacrifice our enjoyment of being God's children for the sake of thinking only about our work in the law. Is there a way this advent that we can each diarise space amid the pressures to deliberately enjoy what God gave us Christmas for? How can we set this example to the lawyers around us – and to the children we know before they set the example for us?

- *Take time to delight in the wonder of the Incarnation, and to be filled again with His joy and peace.*
- *Ask for courage to speak to a colleague about the true meaning of Christmas and invite them to a Carol service.*

– Tim Laurence (2016)

4 DEC — What strikes you the most as you read this?

Do not be deceived: God cannot be mocked. A man reaps what he sows. Whoever sows to please their flesh, from the flesh will reap destruction; whoever sows to please the Spirit, from the Spirit will reap eternal life. Let us not become weary in doing good, for at the proper time we will reap a harvest if we do not give up. Therefore, as we have opportunity, let us do good to all people, especially to those who belong to the family of believers.
Galatians 6:7-10 (NIV)

Take a moment to pray that God will speak to you from this passage in the context of your role in the legal profession. Now re-read the scripture. Which section(s) hit home?

1. God cannot be mocked;
2. If we sow to please the flesh we will reap destruction;
3. If we sow to please the Spirit of God we will reap eternal life;
4. We must not become weary of doing good;
5. If we do not give up we will reap a harvest;
6. We should do good to all people;
7. We should especially do good to brothers and sisters in Christ.

For my part it is number 5 that strikes me in relation to my work. A couple of years ago, Christians in my diocese were encouraged to choose seven non-Christians to pray for: that God would use us to lead them to Christ. On my list of seven was one person I knew through work. After adding that person to my list, but before I had got around to praying for them, I had a phone call from them – the first time we had spoken for a year and a half. With no prompting, they asked if I would pray for them. Perhaps we should all have at least one colleague or contact from the legal profession for whom we pray regularly.

- *Start to make a list of people you want to introduce to the gospel, and then pray for them.*

– Thomas Cordrey (2017)

5 DEC Being the best decision maker

And this is my prayer: that your love may abound more and more in knowledge and depth of insight, so that you may be able to discern what is best and may be pure and blameless for the day of Christ, filled with the fruit of righteousness that comes through Jesus Christ – to the glory and praise of God. **Philippians 1:9-11 (NIV)**

Paul writes to the church in Philippi which holds a special place in his heart. And his prayer for them is that as their love for Jesus and love for each other increases, and they get to know God's will better, they are able to make decisions that are more and more in line with his will.

Let us not become weary in doing good, for at the proper time we will reap a harvest if we do not give up.

Galatians 6:9 (NIV)

This will mean that their love, by leading them to have godly insights, ultimately shapes their choices, so that they make the best decisions.

Take decisions that lawyers make every day, like how we use our time. There are lots of good things we could use our time for today – glorifying God through our work, spending time with our non-Christian colleagues, sharing something we learnt at church on Sunday, or taking some time to mentor a more junior colleague. But Paul's prayer is that as we love Jesus more and love others more, we will choose to do what is the best, the most excellent thing to do, at any one time. We will know what we should prioritise – to the glory and praise of God.

- *Pray that members would have a deeper love for the Lord that would give them a greater knowledge of his will and lead them to make the best decisions.*
- *Pray that we would continue to make Paul's prayer our own, for other members and Christians we know.*

– Peter Thompson (2020)

6 DEC Do not be anxious

Do not be anxious about anything, but in everything by prayer and supplication with thanksgiving let your requests be made known to God. And the peace of God, which surpasses all understanding, will guard your hearts and your minds in Christ Jesus. **Philippians 4:6-7 (ESV)**

A career in law often features in lists of professions whose members are vulnerable to experiencing above average stress, depression and anxiety. Particularly in the month before Christmas and the end of the year, the competing demands of family, Church life and academic or professional responsibilities can leave us feeling anxious and overwhelmed. Thankfully, there are many channels through which we can receive support and assistance in managing such pressures.

In today's passage, Paul reminds us of God's presence amidst difficult times. We are not to be anxious about anything, but instead in prayer and with thanksgiving take our requests to God. We can approach Him with thanksgiving because we know that He is sovereign in all of our circumstances and all things work together for good for those who love Him (Romans 8:28).

Importantly, laying our requests before God doesn't necessarily mean that He will remove us from the situation causing anxiety. Rather, His peace will guard our hearts and minds in Jesus Christ as He helps us to navigate those circumstances. This offers great encouragement and reassurance to the Christian lawyer given that we are often required to work with clients and colleagues in challenging circumstances.

What a blessing that our Heavenly Father who sees all things and knows all things is always with us.

- *Thank God for the gift of prayer and ask that He would help us to make prayer a priority.*
- *Thank God for Christian colleagues and ask that He would help us to seek opportunities to pray with, and for, them.*
- *Thank God that He is with us always, and ask for His perfect peace as He helps us to navigate difficult times.*

– Kiki Alo (2018)

7 DEC Learning contentment

I have learned the secret of being content in any and every situation, whether well fed or hungry, whether living in plenty or in want. I can do all this through him who gives me strength. **Philippians 4:12b-13 (NIV 1984)**

I recall a tutor at university saying that a career in the law would, at any given time, be a feast or a famine and never a happy medium. Both conditions bring their stresses (and, with proper reflection, their benefits). They also have their temptations. Times of plenty or success can lead to pride, and leaner times to envy. They can also lead to an unhealthy focus on our work and the identity it brings, especially at work and (not to be overlooked) in our church life, rather than to a focus on our true identity as children of God.

Paul teaches us that his contentment, in both plenty and want, did not come naturally. It was something that he had learned through the different circumstances of his life, and was then able to teach even when he was imprisoned. Jesus tells us that apart from Him, we can do nothing (John 15:5). We cannot do the work that He wants us to do and bear good fruit for the sake of the kingdom, unless we embrace our identity in Christ through success and failure and through good times and bad

When we are secure in our identity in Jesus in this way, we can then be assured that God will meet our needs (Philippians 4:19), both when we are aware of those needs, and at other times when we take that provision so easily for granted. Let us keep that provision firmly in mind as we go about our work this week.

Pray that each of us may find lasting contentment in resting on God's strength, whatever our present circumstances and concerns, and that we may be aware of a desire to do so this week.

– James Brightwell (2021)

8 DEC Prompted by love

We always thank God for all of you and continually mention you in our prayers. We remember before our God and Father your work produced by faith, your labour prompted by love, and your endurance inspired by hope in our Lord Jesus Christ. **1 Thessalonians 1:2-3 (NIV)**

During our time in Rwanda and Uganda on a mission trip [2018], the team had cause to echo Paul, Silas and Timothy in their thanksgiving for another group of believers. Between delivering training and visiting the work of the Lawyers of Hope and the Ugandan Christian Lawyers' Fraternity, we had the opportunity and privilege of meeting with brothers and sisters working as paralegals, lawyers and judges across East Africa.

We witnessed the way in which their faith is the root of their efforts to enable greater access to justice and pursue the rule of law in the expectation of bringing about positive change. We saw their love for each other, within and across nations, for us, and for God. We also saw examples of steadfast endurance in the face of opposition, tiredness and lack of funding. I was inspired by our friends and colleagues whose lives and work are rooted in our gospel of hope, reconciliation and restoration.

As those who work in the law, we deal with brokenness, bring order and peace out of chaos, and try to prevent things going awry in the first place. What is our inspiration to keep on going when things are tough? We may have many different motivations for doing the work we do, but what is at the root of our day to day?

- Thank God for the faithful work of our East African Partners and ask that they would continue to be inspired by the hope found in the Lord Jesus.
- *Pray that Jesus would be the centre of all you do, the source of your inspiration and hope, within and outside of work.*

– Naomi Cooke (2018)

9 DEC Even the seemingly unimportant matters

Pray without ceasing. **1 Thessalonians 5:17 (ESV)**

Formal prayer times are important, but praying all the time seems like an impossible task.

As we go about our daily work and other activities, we are usually thinking to ourselves, often about seemingly unimportant things. We can share these thoughts, and all our experiences and challenges, with the Lord. He is interested in every detail of our lives, both great and small. No other person is, or can be – the phenomenon of conversations being steered 'back to me' may be something we are familiar with.

As we talk to our heavenly Father about our lives, our relationship with him will strengthen, and he can give us insight and wisdom (at times unexpected) for the work He has given us.

- *Let us bring all our lives before Him.*
- *May His truth guide us and His mercy sustain us in all things.*

– John Scriven (2015)

10 DEC — Speaking up for others

Speak up for those who cannot speak for themselves, for the rights of all who are destitute. Speak up and judge fairly; defend the rights of the poor and needy. **Proverbs 31:8-9 (NIV)**

Today marks the anniversary of the United Nations officially adopting the Universal Declaration of Human Rights (UDHR) in 1948, drafted in the aftermath of World War II.

Seen by many as the 'constitution' of international human rights law, the UDHR sets out many fundamental rights and freedoms that recognise the importance of upholding the inherent dignity of all. Sadly, in the 70 years since the UDHR was adopted, it is apparent that many important aspects of the UDHR are being ignored, distorted or even abused.

As Christians, our understanding of human rights is best informed by our belief in God, who endowed us with dignity, who loves us, cares for us and even laid down His own 'rights' to became one of us. This passage in Proverbs urges us to consider the rights of others, and to stand up and speak up for the vulnerable.

While the UDHR is aspirational on many levels, we are ultimately called to a higher standard as believers in Christ. However, as lawyers, we can appeal to much of the foundational language and intention of the UDHR which seeks to uphold basic human rights for everyone.

As you reflect on the passage, ask the Lord how you can respond to the charge of speaking up for the rights and freedoms of those who cannot speak for themselves.

- *Praise God for His sacrificial love, which paid the debt of sin that we could never pay ourselves.*
- *Pray for opportunities to speak up for the rights of others – particularly the poor, the oppressed and the vulnerable.*

– Laurence Wilkinson (2018)

11 DEC — Building spiritual fitness

'Physical training is good, but training for godliness is much better, promising benefits in this life and in the life to come' … This is why we work hard and continue to struggle, for our hope is in the living God, who is the Saviour of all people and particularly of all believers. **1 Timothy 4:8, 10 (NLT)**

As an adult in my 30s, someone invited me to a Zumba class, exercise disguised as dancing. As an introvert who avoided regular exercise, I found myself shocked by the realization that it was a lot of fun, and both the activity and interaction with others were good for me. As time went on, I started trying different, more challenging forms of exercise. I even found myself enjoying burpees as I gained strength and capability (disgusting, I know). It wasn't always enjoyable, but what helped was the company of like-minded people and the benefits of reaching personal goals and moving ahead to new ones. Just as we train our bodies to improve our physical abilities, time spent in God's word builds strength in our spiritual resilience.

Fellowship together as Christian lawyers helps us cultivate habits of studying God's word and training our minds, souls, and spirits and to help us apply the Bible and our love for God and others to the practice of law.

The writer of Hebrews says, "for the joy set before Him [Jesus] endured the cross" (Heb.12:2 NASB) and took his place at the right hand of God [Victory! Goal achieved!].

- *How is God calling you to the "next level" in your spiritual fitness? What goal might He ask you to set? What habits can you develop to achieve that goal?*
- *Ask God to bring to mind colleagues and friends who would benefit from attending a Lawyers' Christian Fellowship event and invite them to reserve that time on their calendars.*

– Vonda Westmorland (2020)

12 DEC Rejoice...the Lord is near

Rejoice in the Lord always. I will say it again: Rejoice! Let your gentleness be evident to all. The Lord is near.
Philippians 4:4-5 (NIV)

We are now in the season of Advent leading up to Christmas which celebrates the joy of Christ's coming to earth.

This has been a(nother) year when it has sometimes been difficult to be filled with joy, a feeling of immense pleasure and happiness. Although we seem to be emerging from the long, dark tunnel of the pandemic, after a fleeting period in the light, we now face another period of darkness with a global recession caused at least in part by the ongoing war in Ukraine.

There is still joy, especially at this season – joy is one of the defining aspects of Advent. This particular joy comes from God and God alone and consequently cannot be completely counteracted by our circumstances. Particularly at this time of year, like the joy experienced by the shepherds as they rushed to Bethlehem, we should remember that the good news of Jesus' birth has the power to bring us and everyone else boundless joy this Christmas season irrespective of what is going on in our life or our world.

Lawyers in the Bible and in the modern world are not generally associated with joy and it is our duty to change this. We cannot generate our own joy – it is a gift, one that God gave us that first Christmas in the form of his Son Jesus Christ and the gift of salvation He would bring us and the rest of the world.

- *Amidst all the other gifts this Christmas let us thank God for his priceless gift of his Son.*
- *Let's also remember to pray for all those colleagues and clients who have and especially those who have not experienced the salvation that God's gift brought us who are finding it difficult to be joyful despite the time of year.*

– Peter Brown (2022)

13 DEC Outspoken fools? Perhaps…

Because of my chains, most of the brothers in the Lord have been encouraged to speak the word of God more courageously and fearlessly. **Philippians 1:14 (NIV 1984)**

What makes you confident as a lawyer? Knowing you have the answer to every counter-argument that might arise – despite your opponent's efforts to undermine you? Or maybe it is because justice will only be served by you promoting your client's cause?

And the gospel, what makes you confident in speaking about Jesus?

One might have thought that's Paul's imprisonment would undermine his confidence and that of his fellow Christians. But, on the contrary, it made the early believers bolder in proclaiming what they knew to be true – well, most of them. And the challenge to us is to follow the example of those who were fearless.

Around the world there are brothers and sisters in the law who are in prison or face this possibility because of their faith in Christ. Do we take courage and speak the word of God as a result of their witness? Do we get passionate for the gospel because of what they endure and the injustice of their situation?

It is unlikely that we will confidently have all the answers for those to whom we witness. But what is the worst that could happen – we appear a fool? Perhaps, but you are unlikely to be imprisoned and you might be surprised with a more positive outcome than you expected. That would be a cause for rejoicing and encouragement for our fellow Christian lawyers who are in far more difficult situations than us.

- *Pray for courage in taking up the opportunities to speak about Jesus.*
- *Consider asking your colleagues to come to the LCF Carol services and evangelistic events.*
- *Pray for your brothers and sisters who are in prison or who have fled their countries.*

– Mark Barrell (2015)

14 DEC Shedding true light on the law

To the law and to the testimony: if they speak not according to this word, it is because there is no light in them. **Isaiah 8:20 (KJV)**

Over recent years we have seen a bewildering erosion of laws based on biblical values brought about by successive governments.

As lawyers, we see the results at first hand with broken families, increasing confusion about sexual identity, the ever-present pressure to bring in assisted suicide, not to mention the rise of lawlessness and violence in the land. While those responsible for this erosion are regarded as liberal and enlightened by the media, this verse reminds us that they have no light. They have forgotten that godly laws exalt a nation.

Let us pray for all those who are in authority both in the executive and judiciary that they might appreciate that "the entrance of thy words giveth light" (Psalm 119:130). That light shows us that every human being is on the broad way and that leads to eternal destruction (conscious torment forever) but that by repentance and faith in the Lord Jesus Christ for the forgiveness of our sins, we might turn off that road to the narrow way that leads to eternal life.

As we approach Christmas, let us pray for all Christians in Parliament and the law to be bold in proclaiming the "… true Light which lighteth every man that cometh into the world" (John 1:9) and that as a result we might see a return to godly laws and the profession of the Gospel.

- Pray specifically for your own Member of Parliament – that they may be guided by biblical principles in their approach to the work they have been given.
- Pray for the judiciary, that they would uphold Christian principles within the law.
- Ask God for opportunities to speak with others about the need for faith in Christ. Consider who you might be able to invite to a Carol Service near you.

– Mark Mullins (2015)

15 DEC Counter-cultural expectations

Have this mind among yourselves, which is yours in Christ Jesus, who, though he was in the form of God, did not count equality with God a thing to be grasped, but emptied himself, by taking the form of a servant, being born in the likeness of men. **Philippians 2:5-7 (ESV)**

Christianity is counter-cultural.

As lawyers, we are now steeped in equality legislation. Our work involves asserting rights and grasping objectives. In contrast, Paul tells us, Christ Jesus did not count equality with God a thing to be grasped. He laid aside the glories of heaven, to be born a baby in a stable. He came not to be served but to serve. And as Christians we must have the mind of Christ. His mindset is our mindset.

So how radical are we prepared to be? Will we be swept along by the culture of ambition, accepting and holding onto the world's objectives? Or will we allow Christ to rule our attitudes and actions? As He humbled himself for us, so we are called to set aside worldly values for him.

This is, in many churches, seen as the season of Advent, when we turn towards Christmas, but in doing so prepare to meet Jesus at his second coming. Will we be ashamed of our values when we see him face to face?

Paul's message in Philippians is counter-cultural, but it is the Gospel, the good news of God blessing us in Jesus. Have a truly happy Christmas, when it comes.

- Praise God for Jesus, who, for us, laid aside the glory of heaven and was born in the likeness of men, to serve and to sacrifice Himself for us.
- Pray against being conformed to the culture and values of this world, but instead to embrace a truly radical humility and life of Christian service.
- Pray to have the mind of Christ as you prepare to welcome him as Lord and Saviour.

– Janys Scott KC (2021)

16 DEC Four words change everything!

**The Word became flesh and made his dwelling among us. We have seen his glory, the glory of the one and only Son, who came from the Father, full of grace and truth.
John 1:14 (NIV)**

You have just read probably the most outrageous sentences in history! Four words that changed the universe. "The Word became flesh". No truth ever revealed matters more, comforts more, unsettles more. Yes, Christmas is supernatural.

We know it has a strange magnetism, even in a society which has tried to empty it of its significance in the birth of Jesus. The pandemic focussed the minds of politicians and medics on 'saving Christmas'. But it was in fact part of God's plan to save us.

Unlike every other human birth, Christmas is not a beginning but a becoming. John stretches our minds to breaking point and takes us into the very heart of God's purposes. Here, in Jesus, is the 'logos', that very principle of order and purpose in the world which has preoccupied philosophers – and lawyers – down the millennia.

We need no reminding of the darkness and dysfunctionality all around us – and in our own hearts. They keep us in business! But we also know something of God's answer, and of the extraordinary privilege of being part of His story.

Don't let the familiarity of John's words, or what is so often the triviality of the Christmas 'holiday', blunt you to the scandalous particularity, the historical incontrovertibility, the glorious reality that in Jesus the eternal enters time, the all-powerful becomes knowable, the invisible becomes visible, the unreachable becomes embraceable.

Thanks be to Him for His unspeakable gift!

- *Reflect slowly on John 1: 1-18; ask God to strengthen your confidence in the Lord who, in these strange times, is the One in whom 'all things hold together' (Col. 1:17)*
- *Pray for court staff and leadership judges working under pressure to deal with a backlog of criminal and family cases, and for some of the parties and witnesses who are badly affected by delay and uncertainty.*
- *Pray for Christmas and carol events of all kinds, that through such events Jesus may be seen, known and encountered.*

– HHJ David Turner KC (2020)

17 DEC True citizenship

For, as I have often told you before and now tell you again even with tears, many live as enemies of the cross of Christ ... But our citizenship is in heaven. And we eagerly await our saviour from there, the Lord Jesus Christ, who, by the power that enables him to bring everything under his control, will transform our lowly bodies so that they will be like his glorious body. **Philippians 3:18-21 (NIV)**

As Billy Graham once famously said, "This world is not our own. We are strangers in a foreign land; our citizenship is in heaven". And Paul, much earlier, used similar thinking as he wrote to the Philippians. We are already citizens of heaven, meaning that we should expect some rejection in this world, because we are fundamentally different from those around us. So, as we seek to live for Jesus amongst our fellow trainees or associates or partners, we should expect them to question us, and even oppose us.

These verses also challenge our view of our non-believing colleagues. Look how Paul describes their status as enemies of the cross "with tears". Do we have that same heart for the lost that Paul talks of? It can be so easy for us to just focus on our own lives, but the challenge here is to love our friends deeply, and to be regularly stirred by how they need Jesus.

Notice also Paul's excitement at Jesus' return, as he "eagerly" awaits our saviour. We can amazingly share in this hope, of Jesus returning to save us from our sin, and to transform our weak bodies into perfect bodies like his!

- *Pray for members to be prepared to count the cost of following Jesus, remembering where their citizenship is.*
- *Pray for members to have a real heart for the lost, particularly with colleagues, and so to be bold in inviting to carol services and speaking of Jesus this Christmas.*

– Peter Thompson (2016)

18 DEC — Lessons in carol service failure

But you are a chosen people, a royal priesthood, a holy nation, a people belonging to God, that you may declare the praises of Him who called you out of darkness into His wonderful light. **1 Peter 2:9 (NIV 1984)**

I recently realised that I've been getting this whole carol service thing wrong. And wrong on at least two fronts …

First, I've often taken my eye off the ball as to the 'missional' nature of being a Christian lawyer. Let me illustrate what I mean. In his book 'The Heavenly Good of Earthly Work', Darrell Cosden points out that we need to practise consciously 'naming' ourselves as missionaries. Go on – do it! Say to yourself "I [insert your name] am a missionary to the legal world." When we "name" ourselves this way, it will help order our priorities and our prayers. And that will help our focus on declaring God's praises to the world around (2:9, 3:15).

Secondly, in previous years, when there was a carol service or a guest event coming up, my internal approach would be something like "I suppose I should invite someone to come with me". But that is a really impoverished approach to mission.

How much better is it to look, instead, with a different set of spectacles: "I'm part of a wonderful community – a chosen people, a royal priesthood. And this carol service that my fellow believers have organised is a wonderful opportunity for us to do mission together."

May the Lord forgive our impoverished approaches to mission. And may He help us to see the opportunities around us at Christmas with new eyes.

- *Pray that we would be better at 'getting' the missional nature of our life as Christian lawyers.*
- *Pray that we would take opportunities to do mission together with fellow believers this Christmas.*

– Dominic Hughes (2017)

19 DEC — Expect the unexpected…

And there were shepherds living out in the fields nearby, keeping watch over their flocks at night. An angel of the Lord appeared to them, and the glory of the Lord shone around them, and they were terrified. But the angel said to them, 'Do not be afraid. I bring you good news that will cause great joy for all the people. Today in the town of David a Saviour has been born to you; he is the Messiah, the Lord.' **Luke 2:8-11 (NIV)**

There are times when our work feels very ordinary. Days can go by feeling like much of a muchness as we continue with the same old routine. The French have an expression 'Metro, boulot, dodo' meaning 'travel, work, sleep'. As many of us finish up work before a break over Christmas, it may seem that this routine (with a few

Christmas parties and carol services thrown in for good measure!) is our normal.

Over 2,000 years ago, shepherds on a seemingly insignificant hillside in Judea probably felt very similar. They expected a night shift like any other. But it was not. They encountered the glory of the living God and the news that His Son was to be born.

Be encouraged as you work today – we have an extraordinary God of power who not only sent his Son to earth to save us, but who in ways big and small is filling our ordinary days with His glorious presence and purpose. Let us work expectantly today and let us take every opportunity, particularly as we move towards Christmas, to share with those around us the greatest of all news – that Jesus Christ was born to offer salvation to ALL people.

- *Pray for those who are tired and weary in this busy lead up to Christmas. Pray that they would know the presence of God in the seemingly ordinary working day.*
- *Pray that we would take seriously the proclamation of the angel – the good news was not just news for the shepherds to keep to themselves. This was news which was to cause great joy for ALL people. Let's pray that we would be bold in sharing the incredible news that the Messiah has been born with our friends and colleagues.*

– Beki Muinde (2018)

20 DEC Wait – you mean the law teaches us more than just the rules?

... select some towns to be your cities of refuge, to which a person who has killed someone accidentally may flee. ... But if the accused ever goes outside the limits of the city of refuge ... the avenger of blood may kill the accused ...

The accused must stay in his city of refuge until the death of the high priest; only after the death of the high priest may he return to his own property.
Extracts from Numbers 35 (NIV 1984 edition)

The laws governing the cities of refuge are set out in a few different passages in the Bible. To use the language of law school – if A killed B accidentally, A could flee to a city of refuge so that he was safe from a person, C, who sought to avenge B's death. But there was one problem – after fleeing there, A was effectively trapped. He would have to remain in the city until the high priest died. Only then could he leave and return home.

But did you spot that it's the death of the high priest that releases someone from the captivity of living in a city of refuge? There's a resonance here with something much, much bigger ... The book of Hebrews repeatedly demonstrates that Jesus is our great high priest. And His death – the death of the True High Priest – is what gives us true freedom from captivity.

This Christmas, as we dwell on his birth, remember this: the True High Priest who would one day liberate all who trust in Him was on His way – light was dawning on those living in captivity.

A very Merry Christmas to you all.

- Give thanks to God, and pray for, all those who, often unsung and sacrificially, enable LCF and Church events to happen.
- As the year draws to a close, why not pray through the words of Hebrews 13:20-21 (NIV) and ask "… the God of peace, who through the blood of the eternal covenant brought back from the dead our Lord Jesus, that great Shepherd of the sheep, [to] equip you with everything good for doing his will, and [that he may] work in us what is pleasing to him, through Jesus Christ, to whom be glory for ever and ever. Amen."

– Dominic Hughes (2015)

21 DEC 'GET ME A MEDIATOR!'

For there is one God, and there is one MEDIATOR between God and men, the man Christ Jesus, who gave himself as a RANSOM for all, which is the testimony given at the proper time. **1 Timothy 2:5-6 (ESV (emphasis added))**

My heart sank when I read the solicitor's text: "Can you please advise on a suitable mediator for this dispute?"

Alternative Dispute Resolution is fashionable. Like me, you will want to distance yourself from the cynical suggestion that ADR appeals to the bench merely to reduce workload. It's surely better that disputing parties work together to agree a solution instead of having one imposed on them.

So, what's on your checklist when selecting a Mediator among so many potential candidates? You'll want independence, technical competence, and good soft skills to win the respect and confidence of all sides. And then? What about a willingness (determination, even) by the Mediator to invest his own private resources to get the dispute sorted? Would you trust such a Mediator or doubt his sanity?

Far from the world of modern ADR with its many rival candidates, the original Christmas story opens in first century Judea with a unique baby who was born to die three decades later outside Jerusalem, before ascending to Heaven, where he intercedes for His people.

Still, the New Testament claims He is the world's sole mediator to restore us to God and that He spent Himself to bridge the gap … could it be true? And if it were true, would you tell?

Lord Jesus, help me to tell others about you as the unique and exclusive Mediator between God and lost people. Amen!

– Stephen Shaw KC (2021)

22 DEC — A Christmas message from a litigator

For you know the grace of our Lord Jesus Christ, that though he was rich, yet for your sake he became poor, so that you through his poverty might become rich. **2 Corinthians 8:9 (NIV)**

For some, the days just before the Christmas holiday present the opportunity for some last-minute Christmas shopping, or to start the Christmas festivities. For some litigators who are less full of Christmas cheer, it presents a quite different opportunity: the chance to get a hard-hitting letter off to one's opponent just before he or she starts their Christmas break. As a fellow Christian litigator once put it to me one Christmas – in jest, I should emphasize – "It is more blessed to give than to receive" (Acts 20:35).

The proper context for that verse in Acts 20 is, of course, wildly different. It was Jesus who originally said that it is more blessed to give than to receive. Christmas shows Him doing just that. In the words of Frank Houghton's famous hymn, "He who was rich beyond all splendour, all for love's sake became poor". He surrendered thrones for a manger, and sapphire-paved courts for a stable floor.

Our legal work is often about creating, asserting and enforcing rights. That might be totally legitimate but, in contrast, Jesus' birth is about surrendering rights, of choosing to become poor so others might become rich. You work out which is more blessed. Merry Christmas.

- *May we this Christmas learn the blessing of sacrificial giving to make others rich.*
- *May all Christian lawyers be able to rest this Christmas, and take time to reflect on He who for love's sake became poor.*

– Andrew M (2018)

23 DEC — All I want for Christmas is …?

*One thing have I asked of the LORD,
that will I seek after:
that I may dwell in the house of the LORD
all the days of my life,
to gaze upon the beauty of the LORD
and to inquire in his temple.*
Psalm 27:4 (ESV)

"What would you like for Christmas?" I've asked and been asked that question many times. When I ask that question (with the exception of my children), I don't anticipate a list. I anticipate a choice – one thing. But it can be difficult to choose. As a lawyer, advising clients in typically dire situations, I asked clients about their objectives, "What do you seek?" Typically they choose one thing, "I want my case to be heard." They seek an audience with a person; someone who can put wrong right.

David, in this psalm, contemplates death (v 2), war (v 3) and the "day of trouble" (v 5), but his confidence in the Lord, his light and salvation, remained steadfast. How so? David had chosen one thing. He longed for the best thing. And that one thing he was resolved to pursue above all things in life.

To dwell. To gaze. To enquire. David chose to centre his life in his Saviour, the one who would – by his own redeeming love on the Cross – die to make those who have done wrong, right.

What one thing would you ask of the Lord? What is the best gift that He could give to you this Christmas? The Lord Jesus Christ is the only Saviour. This Christmas, above all this life's gifts, let us choose to centre our lives upon Him

Draw near to God this Christmas, and resolve to centre your lives upon Christ, to esteem God's best gift above all things.

– Mark Bainbridge (2020)

24 DEC The centre-peace this Christmas

For to us a child is born, to us a son is given; … and his name shall be called Wonderful Counsellor, Mighty God, Everlasting Father, Prince of Peace. Isaiah 9:6 (ESV)

Every year I think this Christmas will be different from my first 'working' Christmas. Nearing deadlock in a claim with a sub-contractor, heading towards arbitration, we joined the Directors for the Christmas Eve speeches, mince pies and an early afternoon finish: finally, time to reflect on Jesus. Fast-forward to Christmas Day, our US-based General Counsel started sending emails relating to the claim. To reply or not to reply was not the question!

Rather: What is the source of peace?

The Prince of Peace spent most of His earthly life surrounded by people who were often quarrelsome, demanding or downright hostile. Jesus was constantly busy and pressured, yet was full of peace. He carried it about with Him in His heart and never let the outside world steal it away. Wonderful Lawyer, He truly is.

Yet to us, again He says this Christmas "Peace I leave with you; my peace I give to you" (John 14:27). His kind of peace does not depend on the absence of strife. Jesus wants us to inherit His internal and eternal peace, but first we must choose to accept His gift.

Whether it's the family coming, the roast potatoes burning, that one piece of work that missed the Christmas deadline, or the case/exam that awaits your attention after Christmas … may you enjoy the gift of His peace as you remember that He alone remains the centrepiece of Christmas.

- *Give thanks for the gift of Jesus and His peace. Through Him we have eternal life! May we remember to put Him alone at the centre of our Christmas.*
- *Christmas without Jesus is no Christmas at all – pray for opportunities and boldness to share this most wonderful gift, even today.*

– Fiona Mahendran-Gilliland (2016)

25 DEC Glory to the new-born King

While they were there [Bethlehem], the time came for the baby to be born, and she gave birth to her firstborn, a son. She wrapped him in cloths and placed him in a manger, because there was no guest room available for them. Luke 2:6-7 (NIV)

What are the big events in your life which determine who you are and the way you live? Getting a place to study law? A training contract or pupillage? Qualifying or being taken on? Perhaps it is the hope of a future event: partnership, taking silk or an appointment by the Lord Chancellor?

In the year 731 the Anglo-Saxon scholar Bede dated all events in his Ecclesiastical History to Jesus' date of birth and the BC/AD system we still use today became dominant in the western world. Every time you or I date anything in our lives, we date it relative to the birth of Jesus.

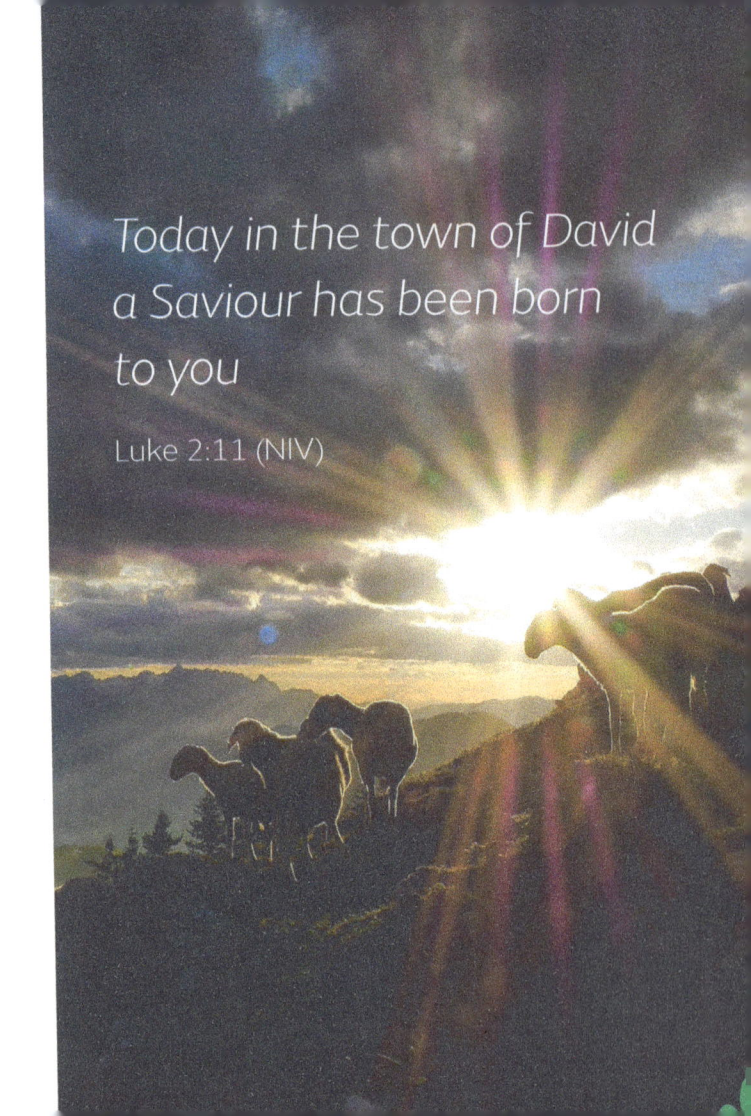

Today in the town of David a Saviour has been born to you

Luke 2:11 (NIV)

This was the moment to which the whole of the Old Testament looked forward: God the Son leaving his place in glory to be conceived and born into poverty, living a sinless life, paying the price for our sin on the cross, rising from the dead and ascending to sit at the right hand of God. Are these the events that determine the way we live? Is the prospect of Jesus' return the future event which governs our lives? May we find time this Christmas to ponder afresh its implications.

- Pray that God will help us grasp the full implications of Jesus' birth for our lives.
- Pray that we will find time this Christmas to think through and delight in what he has done.
- Pray for those who do not yet have the joy of knowing Jesus as Lord and Saviour.

– Rev. Ian Miller (2017)

26 DEC Huge problem: even more massive solution

For whoever shall keep the whole law, and yet stumble in one point, he is guilty of all. For He who said, 'Do not commit adultery', also said, 'Do not murder'. Now if you do not commit adultery, but you do murder, you have become a transgressor of the law. So speak and so do as those who will be judged by the law of liberty. For judgment is without mercy to the one who has shown no mercy. Mercy triumphs over judgment. James 2:10-13 (NKJV)

If we say that we have no sin, we deceive ourselves, and the truth is not in us. If we confess our sins, He is faithful and just to forgive us our sins and to cleanse us from all unrighteousness. 1 John 1:8-9 (NKJV)

Breaking God's moral law is like breaking a pane of glass. If we break any part of it, the whole pane goes. That is easily seen if we compare murder (thought by many to be the greatest crime and sin) with adultery (not even a crime in our legal system, though a sin against others before God). But we also 'break the pane' if we tell a so-called 'white lie'. All sin is sin. It all will be punished – unless …? Unless what?

Unless we find that for us 'Mercy triumphs over judgment'. All must face God's judgment on sin after death (Hebrews 9:27), but not if we have confessed our sins to God and found Him 'faithful and just to forgive us our sins'. We are then cleansed from 'all unrighteousness' through faith alone in Christ alone.

What a huge problem is eternal judgment for the sinner who will not turn from their sin in repentance and trust in Jesus Christ. But what a merciful and eternal blessing to trust in Jesus, who "Himself bore our sins in His own body on the tree" (the cross) – and therefore to say, as per an old chorus*, that our sins are "gone, gone, gone" and are "buried in the … sea" of God's forgetfulness through faith in the One who was punished in our place at Calvary, and who rose again to live forevermore!

What a massive and eternally applicable solution by God's mercy and grace for those trusting Jesus!

*From 'Gone, gone, gone' by Helen Griggs

- *Why not share this good news with someone else you meet today?*
- *Let's reflect with thankfulness that, when we trust in Jesus, God's mercy triumphs over judgment.*

– Gerard Chrispin (2021)

27 DEC Marvelling at the manger

Today in the town of David a Saviour has been born to you; he is the Messiah, the Lord. This will be a sign to you: you will find a baby wrapped in cloths and lying in a manger. Luke 2:11-12 (NIV)

This is what the shepherds were told by an angel. The saviour of the world is coming, and you will find him lying in an animals' feeding trough.

For those of us who have given our lives to the Lord, our belief must be that he is all mighty and all knowing. He could have chosen for God veiled in flesh to be born absolutely anywhere. The manger was not poor timing or a coincidence, it was a choice and a sign of the radically different kingdom Jesus represented.

If Jesus was this humble, are we? I sometimes come across a perception of lawyers as pompous. Do we challenge that by always choosing humility in the way we interact with everyone, whatever their status in work or where we study? Do we struggle with feeling like we're not being recognised enough or being treated as we deserve? Jesus deserved a king's throne, but he chose a manger and ultimately the cross.

Perhaps, as we come to Christmas and the end of the year, we had expected things to go differently. We had thought we'd get that holiday, we would be working in the office every day, we would have finally found that job. Let's be encouraged by and marvel at the manger. In the least promising looking situations, God always has a plan.

- *Pray for true humility and servant heartedness to be the hallmarks of our working lives. That as Christian lawyers we would be known by all as those who "walk humbly with God" (Micah 6:8)*
- *Pray that we would be encouraged by the fact that God's ways are not our ways. Pray particularly for those who are feeling discouraged by their situation.*

– Beki Muinde (2021)

28 DEC — There are no shortcuts to the top of the palm tree

For as the days of a tree, so will be the days of my people; my chosen ones will long enjoy the work of their hands. They will not labour in vain, nor will they bear children doomed to misfortune;
for they will be a people blessed by the LORD, they and their descendants with them.
Isaiah 65:22b-23 (NIV)

It's that funny period in-between. You might be at your desk trying to catch up in this quieter period hoping the phone won't ring and fewer emails will arrive, or at home recuperating from the excess. But, with Christmas over and New Year looming, this is often a time for reflection on what has passed and what is to come.

These words of Isaiah are a hope-filled prophecy of what is to come and a complete reversal of the past. Having broken God's law, Adam and Eve were told those on earth would toil in vain and labour in pain (Genesis 3). But the prophet speaks of a time when God will overturn the effects of the Fall for all those who belong to Him. In the new creation we will forever enjoy our work and be blessed in His presence.

As we await this hope, we are called in this 'in-between time' to follow Him, wheresoever and to whomsoever that may lead, taking every opportunity to speak about the hope in Jesus Christ and live out the gospel. At times the journey will be challenging, as an African proverb says, "there are no shortcuts to the top of the palm tree", but the end reward and promise we have in Christ is more than enough to compensate.

- As you look back, give thanks to God for all He has done for you in this past year and for the hope he has given to us in the saving work of the Lord Jesus Christ.
- As you look forward ask for a renewed sense of our eternal hope praying that this may encourage you even more to pass on the message of the Good News next year.

– Mark Barrell (2017)

29 DEC — A trustworthy saying for the year ahead

Here is a trustworthy saying: Whoever aspires to be an overseer desires a noble task. Now the overseer is to be above reproach, faithful to his wife, temperate, self-controlled, respectable, hospitable, able to teach, not given to drunkenness, not violent but gentle, not quarrelsome, not a lover of money. He must manage his own family well and see that his children obey him, and he must do so in a manner worthy of full respect. (If anyone does not know how to manage his own family, how can he take care of God's church?) 1 Timothy 3:1-5 (NIV)

The precious Christmas break is often one of the times where a Christian lawyer gets to spend most time away from the workplace and with their family.

Now might be a good moment to check whether our time at home over Christmas has demonstrated the qualities Paul refers to in the passage: avoiding drunkenness, showing hospitality, exuding gentleness, resisting the love of money, eschewing quarrels? What about managing our families well – Paul places a great emphasis on this.

These qualities should be characteristics of any Christian lawyer, but all the more so of those who are "overseers" (defined in verse 5 as people who "take care of God's church") locally.

Is a renewed commitment in order for the coming year: that we will manage our families well by prioritising them over our work? Or perhaps it is one of the other qualities Paul refers to which has slipped during the last year. Ask for God's help to honour him in the year ahead.

- *As you read the qualities above ask God to show you what he wants you to prioritise in the year ahead.*
- *Give thanks for the worldwide family of Christ, for the fellowship we have together in Christ and that we may bring glory to His name in the coming year.*

– Thomas Cordrey (2015)

30 DEC Another year ends: every year counts

A thousand years in your sight are like a day that has just gone by, or like a watch in the night.
Our days may come to seventy years, or eighty, if our strength endures; yet the best of them are but trouble and sorrow, for they quickly pass, and we fly away.

Psalm 90:4,10 (NIV)

Another year ends.

Psalm 90 shows the sharp contrast between the Lord of Eternity (v 2: "from everlasting to everlasting you are God") and mortal man (v 10: "our days … quickly pass and we fly away"). To God an entire millennium is just like a day, or a few hours even (v 4). However, for us, the year change tomorrow evening will be one of only perhaps 70 or 80 that we will experience on this earth. They will quickly pass, and then we fly away (v 10). Mankind is mortal.

The Psalmist's reminder that we will see-in only a limited number of new years should spur us into using those new years that remain wisely. In particular, it should spur us lawyers into using our years at work well: being a beacon of integrity; working with a yearning for justice; being more interested in helping our clients than hitting our targets; using the opportunities our work affords to speak clearly of the Good News of the One who offers us all everlasting life.

Moses ended this Psalm by praying that in his few days on earth God would "establish the work of our hands for us" (v 17). May God do that for us in this forthcoming year.

- In the words of Rt. Rev. Timothy Dudley-Smith's from 'Lord for the Years': "past put behind us, for the future take us: Lord of our lives, to live for Christ alone."

– Andrew M (2020)

31 DEC PRESS ON!

But one thing I do: forgetting what lies behind and straining forward to what lies ahead, I press on toward the goal for the prize of the upward call of God in Christ Jesus. **Philippians 3:13-14 (ESV)**

How was this last year for you? Was it a year of personal and professional joy and achievement; or was it one that, quite frankly, you cannot wait to put behind you?

The cusp of a new year can be a good time to look back and evaluate what has gone before in the past 12 months, but such a process comes with two obvious dangers: basking in our successes or wallowing in our failures.

As one prone to (sometimes unhealthy and unhelpful) introspection, these well-known verses have become precious to me. The earlier part of chapter 3 lists Paul's considerable achievements, while we see his considerable failings prior to his conversion in the book of Acts. But neither are his focus. Paul kept moving forward, with that prize of the upward call of God in the Lord Jesus in his sights.

As we move into the coming year, let's not be complacent in or hamstrung by what's gone before. Let's press on confident in God and his grace into all the opportunities and challenges that the next year holds.

- *May we commit the year to the Lord, with our eyes set on Him.*
- *Pray that the new year would be abundant in opportunities to bring God glory in our work and studies.*

– Gavin Callaghan (2017)

Word for the Week Contributors

Adam McRae-Taylor (Feb 28, Apr 25, Aug 19, Aug 20, Sep 27, Nov 11, Nov 29) is a solicitor specialising in education and employment law, and a Senior Associate at a law firm in Guildford.

Adenil Pjetri (Feb 29) is a Christian lawyer based in Tirana, Albania.

His Honour Alan Taylor (Apr 13, Apr 21, Jul 8, Aug 17, Aug 26, Sep 3, Sep 8, Oct 2, Oct 11, Oct 17) is a retired circuit judge. He lives in Devon.

Alasdair Henderson (Jan 18, Mar 22, Mar 23, Nov 14) is a barrister in London, practising in public law and human rights, employment and equality, clinical negligence and environmental law. He is also a Commissioner of the Equality and Human Rights Commission.

Andrew M (Jan 3, Feb 26, Jun 13, Aug 5, Aug 7, Aug 11, Aug 15, Oct 29, Dec 22, Dec 30) is a solicitor advocate and partner specialising in property disputes, contract disputes and bringing professional negligence claims. He works in London.

Beki Muinde (Aug 23, Aug 24, Dec 19, Dec 27) is a solicitor and Director of Business Development and Regulatory Affairs in London.

Ben Fullbrook (Jun 20, Sep 4, Nov 19, Nov 20) is a barrister at a chambers in London. He practises in public, planning and environmental law.

Brent Haywood (Mar 2, Mar 27, May 28, Jun 9, Jul 29, Aug 14, Sep 21, Sep 28, Nov 10, Nov 30) is a solicitor advocate and a Partner in dispute resolution and litigation in Edinburgh.

Caroline Eade (Jan 14, Feb 11, Feb 22, Mar 18, Apr 24, May 2, Jul 11, Jul 28, Aug 3, Sep 12, Nov 27) is Deputy Managing Director, Senior Solicitor and Head of Charities. She lives in Cambridge.

Claire Thompson (Sep 7, Oct 23, Nov 12) is an in-house solicitor. She lives in Leeds.

Claire Wilkinson (Feb 17, May 6, Jun 3) is a solicitor-advocate currently working for an international human rights non-profit. She lives in Nairobi, Kenya.

Damilola Makinde (Jan 16, Sep 13) works at King's Cross Church (KXC) and the Evangelical Alliance. She is a former Student and Young Lawyers Ministry Associate at the Lawyers' Christian Fellowship. She lives in London.

Dr David McIlroy (Feb 18, Mar 1, Mar 12, Apr 4, Apr 23, May 1, May 3, Jun 19, Jul 2, Jul 27, Sep 18, Oct 4) is a barrister and Head of Chambers in London. He specialises in banking and financial services law, commercial law, and professional negligence.

His Honour Judge David Turner KC (Feb 14, Dec 16) is a Circuit Judge and Deputy High Court Judge dividing his time between criminal and family work in Chelmsford and London. He is also Chancellor of the Diocese of Chester and Deputy Chair of the Clergy Discipline Commission.

Debbie Woods (Jan 15, Jan 19, Feb 1, Mar 3, Mar 13, Apr 19, Apr 30, Oct 7) teaches law and is an Associate Professor in Manchester. She is a former solicitor.

Dominic Hughes (Jan 28, Mar 29, May 10, Jun 5, Jun 6, Jul 20, Jul 24, Sep 2, Oct 3, Dec 18, Dec 20) is a barrister practising in intellectual property law in London.

Rev. Ed Veale (May 13) is Curate at Holy Trinity, Clapham, He also works part-time as a solicitor in social housing law, and is a visiting lecturer at the University of Law Bloomsbury

Elsa Glauert (Jun 18, Jun 23, Jul 15, Sep 20, Oct 30) is a solicitor specialising in intellectual property, and Supervising Associate in London.

Esther Harrison (Feb 20, Mar 30, Apr 28, May 18, May 29, Jul 5, Jul 31, Oct 9, Oct 31) is a criminal barrister in Nottingham, and a Deputy District Judge (Magistrates' Court).

Esther Wade (Jun 22, Aug 18, Oct 13) is former Ministry Associate (International) at the Lawyers' Christian Fellowship. She lives in Switzerland.

Felipe Carvalho (Oct 14) is Director of Student and Young Lawyer Ministries at the Lawyers' Christian Fellowship and Law Network Coordinator at UCCF. He previously worked for the Brazilian Association of Christian Lawyers (ANAJURE). He is a PhD Candidate in Law at the University of Coimbra.

Fiona Mahendran-Gilliland (Jan 30, Feb 23, Feb 24, Mar 25, Dec 24) is Women's Worker at Grace Church Greenwich. She was previously Director of Student and Young Lawyers Ministries at the Lawyers' Christian Fellowship.

Gavin Callaghan (Mar 21, Mar 24, Mar 28, Apr 2, Apr 8, Apr 26, Jun 8, Sep 15, Dec 31) is a solicitor. He lives in Scotland.

Gerard Chrispin (Apr 15, May 8, Jun 30, Aug 9, Sep 5, Sep 23, Sep 29, Nov 9, Nov 16, Nov 17, Dec 26) is a solicitor and former Senior Crown Prosecutor and contracts specialist now working as a Voluntary Prison Chaplain. He lives in Farnham, Surrey.

Graham Whitworth (Feb 3, Feb 4, Feb 6, Feb 9, Jul 9, Jul 22, Aug 21, Sep 10, Sep 30, Nov 6, Nov 7) is a retired solicitor and was a trustee of LCF from 2011 to 2017.

Hilary Underwood (Jan 25, May 15) is a solicitor specialising in family law. She lives in East Kent.

Hugo Porter (Aug 6, Sep 9) is a solicitor specialising in international humanitarian law and military law. He lives in Upavon, Wiltshire.

Rev. Ian Miller (Apr 1, Apr 5, Apr 16, Aug 10, Oct 27, Dec 25) is one of the clergy at St Mary's Church, Maidenhead. He is a former barrister and Chair of the Lawyers' Christian Fellowship.

James Brightwell (Jan 20, Mar 17, May 5, May 12, May 23, Jun 11, Jun 14, Nov 15, Dec 7) is a Chancery Master. He lives in London.

James Crabtree (Mar 6, Mar 16, Mar 20, May 25, May 26, May 27) is a solicitor specialising in international insurance and reinsurance disputes. He lives in St. Albans, Hertfordshire.

Jane Sutton (Oct 18, Nov 3) is former Ministry Associate (International) at the Lawyers' Christian Fellowship. She lives in Cambridge and works as a paralegal in London.

Jane Edwards (Jun 1) is a mission worker with BMS World Mission, living and serving in Mozambique, and a non-practising solicitor.

Janet Cole (Jan 26, Sep 26) is former Director of Operations and Resources at the Lawyers' Christian Fellowship. She lives in Hungerford.

Janys Scott KC (Apr 27, Aug 1, Nov 26, Dec 15) is a Scottish advocate, specialising in family law, and part-time Sheriff. She lives in the Scottish Borders.

Jennifer McKelvin (Feb 2, Jul 21, Oct 28) is a barrister practising in criminal law. She was previously Director of Operations and Resources at the Lawyers' Christian Fellowship. She lives in Newcastle-upon-Tyne.

Sir Jeremy Cooke (Jan 23, Feb 8, Feb 21, Mar 19, Apr 9, Apr 17, Jun 15, Jun 25, Aug 13) is a former High Court Judge, was Presiding Judge on the South East Circuit from 2008-2012 and was Judge in charge of the Commercial Court from 2012 to 2014. He is now an International Arbitrator and lives for most of the time in London.

John Head (1939 – 2020) (Apr 3, Apr 20, May 17, May 20, May 22, May 30, Jun 27, Jul 26, Aug 25) was a solicitor and law firm partner, Chair of trustees of the Lawyers' Christian Fellowship, and long-term supporter of the LCF International Ministries.

John Scriven (Feb 15, Mar 8, Mar 10, Apr 29, May 4, Jul 1, Aug 12, Sep 11, Sep 19, Nov 22, Dec 9) is a retired solicitor and was chairman of the LCF from 2003 to 2011. His books include EPC Contracts and Major Projects (2011), Belief and the Nation (2013) and Beyond the Odds, Providence in Britain's Wars of the 20th Century (2021).

Jon Hyde (1980 - 2022) (Jan 29, Apr 11, Jun 12, Jun 26, Jul 12, Jul 23, Sep 25, Nov 23) was a solicitor and Partner in the City of London specialising in professional liability and insurance law, Chair of trustees of the Lawyers' Christian Fellowship, and a Word for the Week editor.

Jonathan Storey (Feb 27) is a barrister specialising in professional regulation and Director of Regional Ministries at the Lawyers' Christian Fellowship. He lives in Herefordshire.

Kiki Alo (Jan 17, Apr 7, Apr 18, Nov 25, Dec 6) is a regulatory lawyer practicing in London.

Laurence Wilkinson (Jun 16, Oct 22, Dec 10) is a solicitor and Law Clerk for Alliance Defending Freedom in the United States, where he specialises in freedom of expression and freedom of religion or belief.

Mark Bainbridge (Jan 1, Apr 6, Oct 15, Dec 23) is Executive Director of the Lawyers' Christian Fellowship, and a solicitor specialising in employment and equality law. He lives in South Wales.

Mark Barrell (Mar 5, Mar 11, Mar 26, May 24, Jun 4, Aug 2, Aug 29, Nov 4, Dec 13, Dec 28) is Head of Advocacy and Influencing. He was previously a mission worker in Mozambique and Uganda and, before that, Executive Director of the Lawyers' Christian Fellowship after a career as a solicitor in private practice. He lives in Bury St Edmunds.

His Honour Judge Mark Cawson KC (Jan 22, Feb 19, Mar 9, Apr 12, May 7, May 14, Jul 3, Jul 6, Oct 20) is a Specialist Circuit Judge, sitting in the Business and Property Courts in Manchester.

Mark Jones (Jan 4, Jan 5, Jan 6, Jan 7, Jan 8, Jan 9, Jan 10, Jan 11, Jan 12, Jan 13, May 16) is a solicitor and Head of Employment. He is a former Chair of the Lawyers' Christian Fellowship and lives in Surrey.

Mark Mullins (Jan 21, Jan 31, Mar 31, Apr 22, Jun 17, Jun 24, Jul 16, Sep 6, Dec 14) is a criminal barrister in London.

Martin Franke (Mar 14, Jul 10) is a German lawyer. A Partner at a firm in Frankfurt, he is a specialist in the non-profit sector and sits on the board of Christ und Jurist.

Rev. Matthew Price (Aug 31) is Vicar of St Mary Magdalene, Gorleston. He was previously a solicitor in the City of London, a mission worker with BMS World Mission, and successively International Director and Student and Young Lawyers' Director at the Lawyers' Christian Fellowship.

Mhairi Hamilton (Feb 16, Jun 2, Jun 10, Jun 21, Jul 4, Sep 16, Oct 10, Oct 12, Oct 25) is Director of International Ministries at the Lawyers' Christian Fellowship. She lives in Ashford.

Michael Hawthorne (Jan 27, Mar 7, May 11, May 19, May 21, Jul 13, Aug 16, Sep 1, Oct 5, Oct 26, Nov 5, Dec 2) is a retired district judge. He lives in Broadstairs and is a Reader in his local Anglican Church.

Naomi Cooke (Apr 14, Oct 16, Nov 24, Dec 8) is a criminal barrister practising in the south east of England.

Nat Johnson (Feb 13, Jul 19, Sep 17, Oct 24) is a solicitor and Partner specialising in charity law and based in Leeds.

Nelson Ashitiva (Aug 4) is a Kenyan lawyer who works as Senior Partner and Head of Strategy at Ashitiva Advocates in Nairobi. He is chair of the Kenya Christian Lawyers Fellowship.

Niazi Fetto KC (Jan 24, Feb 10, Jun 7, Jul 14, Jul 30) is a barrister specialising in personal injury and employment in London. He lives in South West London and in Douai, France.

Owen Vanstone-Hallam (Feb 12, Jul 17, Nov 18) is a solicitor practising in commercial disputes. He lives in Canterbury.

Patrick Menges (Nov 28) is a German lawyer and Partner in Munich, where he practises in intellectual property, tax law and contract law. He is on the board of Christ und Jurist.

Peter Brown (Apr 10, May 9, Jun 28, Aug 27, Aug 30, Oct 6, Dec 1, Dec 12) is a solicitor in Limavady, Northern Ireland.

Peter Thompson (Feb 5, Sep 24, Oct 19, Nov 1, Nov 2, Nov 13, Nov 21, Dec 5, Dec 17) is a solicitor, practising in commercial litigation. He lives in London.

Phil Roberts KC (Jan 2, Feb 25, Sep 22) is a barrister in London. He practises in the law of intellectual property and information technology.

Richard Borgonon (Aug 28) has been an international insurance executive within the Lloyd's of London insurance market for 48 years. He is the co-author of The Word One to One which, in 74 countries and growing, enables any believer to easily share the Gospel of John and book of Aacts with their non-Christian contacts. www.THEWORD121.com

Rob Horner (Mar 15, Jul 7, Oct 8) is a barrister practising in personal injury and clinical negligence. He lives in Oxford.

Robin Younghusband (Feb 7, Jul 18, Jul 25, Sep 14) is a practising barrister and Case Worker in London.

Stephen Shaw KC (Dec 21) practises in commercial, chancery and public law, and was called to the senior Bar in 2001. He lives just outside Belfast.

Thomas Cordrey (Jun 29, Nov 8, Dec 4, Dec 29) is a barrister and specialist in employment law in London.

Tim Grainger (Oct 21) is a solicitor and Partner responsible for employment and personal injury law in Warrington.

Tim Laurence (Mar 4, May 31, Aug 8, Aug 22, Oct 1, Dec 3) is a former solicitor, and works for UCCF in university ministry on the relationship between the gospel and culture.

Vonda Westmoreland (Dec 11) is Communications Coordinator for Faith and Law Around the Globe. She lives in Orlando.